FACTS
AND
LISTS

OMNIBUS EDITION

D1374681

EARTH FACTS

Lynn Bresler

CONTENTS

Designed by Teresa Foster

**Illustrated by Tony Gibson
and Ian Jackson**

With thanks to Chris Rice and Stephen Capus

Earth's vital statistics

Earth's place in the Universe

Our galaxy is one of 400 million galaxies in the Universe. The small part of our galaxy which you can see in the sky is called the Milky Way. It contains over 3,000 million stars. If each star was a full stop, like this, . . . they would make a line stretching from London to Moscow.

Earth statistics

Diameter:	
at the Poles	12,718 km
at the Equator	12,756 km
Circumference:	
round the Poles	40,000 km
round the Equator	40,075 km
Density:	5.518g/cm^3
Volume:	1.08 x 10^{12} km^3
Total surface area:	510,066,000 sq km
Weight:	6,000 million million million tonnes

The solar system

The Sun is one of the stars in the Milky Way. Nine planets revolve around it. Scientists think the Sun and planets were all formed about 4,600 million years ago.

The Earth's Moon

The Earth is the third nearest planet to the Sun. It has one natural satellite orbiting it, the Moon, which is 384,365 km (238,840 miles) from the Earth. The Moon is a quarter the size of the Earth.

The short way round

The Earth is not a true sphere. It is slightly flattened at the top and bottom. The diameter through the Poles is 43 km (26 miles) less than it is at the Equator.

Watery Earth

About 70 per cent of the Earth's surface is covered in water. The southern hemisphere is more watery than the northern hemisphere. Over 80 per cent of the people on Earth live north of the Equator.

The Continents

Continent	Area in sq km
Asia	44,391,200
Africa	30,244,000
North America	24,247,000
South America	17,821,000
Antarctica	13,338,500
Europe	10,354,600
Oceania	8,547,000

Faraway

The 299 people on Tristan da Cunha, in the Atlantic Ocean, live on the most isolated inhabited island on Earth. Their nearest neighbours are on the island of St Helena, 2,120 km (1,320 miles) away.

Bouvey Oya, in the South Atlantic Ocean, is the most isolated uninhabited island on Earth. It is 1,700 km (1,050 miles) from the east coast of Antarctica.

New land

New islands are still being formed by volcanoes erupting under the sea. Surtsey emerged from the sea off the coast of Iceland in 1963. The newest island is Lateiki, off the east coast of Australia, which was first spotted in 1979.

Surtsey

Largest islands	
Island	Area in sq km
Greenland	2,175,000
New Guinea	789,900
Borneo	751,000
Madagascar	587,000
Baffin	507,400
Sumatra	422,200
Honshu	230,000
Great Britain	229,800
Victoria	217,300
Ellesmere	196,200

DID YOU KNOW?

The Pacific Ocean, the largest ocean, is three times bigger than Asia, the largest continent.

Inside the Earth

The surface of the Earth is a thin crust of rock. Under this, scientists believe, is a layer of liquid rock, the mantle, which surrounds an outer core of liquid iron and nickel. The inner core at the centre of the Earth is probably a solid ball of iron and nickel.

Inside the Earth statistics

Layer	Depth in km	Layer	Temperature
Crust under sea	8	Crust	21°C average
Crust under land	40	Mantle	1500-3000°C
Mantle	2,870	Outer core	3900°C
Outer core	2,100	Inner core	4000°C
Inner core	1,370 (radius)		

The Earth's history

In the beginning

Scientists think that the Earth was formed, about 4,600 million years ago, from a spinning cloud of dust and gases, which shrank to a hot, molten globe. As this cooled, a crust of rock formed on the surface. The oldest of the Earth's rocks are in west Greenland, and are 3,820 million years old.

Jigsaw

The crust of the Earth is not one solid piece. It is cracked into a jigsaw of 7 huge pieces, and several smaller ones. The pieces, called plates, are about 64 km (40 miles) thick. The plates float on the hot, liquid rock of the mantle, the deep layer beneath the crust.

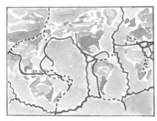

Bump! Crunch!

The cracked, jigsaw pieces of the crust have drifted on the surface of the Earth for millions of years. Where the plates bumped and collided, the crust crumpled – forming deep trenches in the sea floor, and forcing the rocks up to form mountains on the land. Some of the land is still rising – Tibet has risen over 3 km (2 miles) in the last 2 million years.

Slip sliding away

The plates can slip past each other on land, as well as under the sea. The San Andreas Fault, in the USA, a boundary between 2 plates, is a great crack, stretching for 1,126 km (700 miles) from the Gulf of California. Over 15 million years, California has moved about 300 km (186 miles) north-westwards, and in 50 million years' time, might have split away.

The changing crust

New crust is being made all the time on the sea floor. Hot, liquid rock bubbles up through the huge cracks between the plates, such as the ridge in the middle of the Atlantic Ocean. As much as 10 cm (4 in) of new rock a year can be formed, on either side of the crack.

The ridge is close to the surface underneath Iceland. The island is expanding very slowly, where liquid rock spills out from great cracks which run across the island.

In other places on the sea floor, the plates slide over each other. This forces some of the crust down deep sea trenches, such as the Peru-Chile Trench in the Pacific Ocean, back into the hot mantle.

Continental drift

The drifting of the Earth's crust means the continents have not always been in the same place. North Africa was once covered in a sheet of ice and was where the South Pole is today. And the South Pole was once covered with rain forests.

Yesterday

About 200 million years ago, most of the land was probably joined up into a large continent, called Pangaea. This split into two – Laurasia, now mainly in the northern hemisphere, and Gondwanaland, now mainly in the southern.

Today

The continents are still moving today. In 50 million years' time, Alaska and the USSR may have joined together.

Tomorrow?

Wearing away

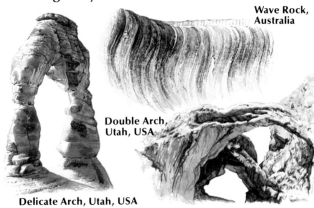

Wave Rock, Australia

Double Arch, Utah, USA

Delicate Arch, Utah, USA

The landscape has changed over millions of years. Erosion by ice, wind and water has worn away the surface of the Earth. Glaciers have carved valleys, fjords and jagged mountain peaks. Rivers have carved great canyons, such as the Grand Canyon in Arizona, USA, which is 349 km (217 miles) long. Rain and wind have sculpted cliffs, such as Wave Rock in Australia, and natural arches, such as Delicate Arch, in Utah, USA.

All change!

The people on Earth have changed the landscape too. They have cleared forests, straightened rivers, and terraced steep hillsides for farming. They have quarried rocks, metals and minerals out of the ground. The Bingham Canyon copper mine in Utah, USA, has created a hole 3.7 km (2.3 miles) across and 789 m (2,590 ft) deep. People have also created new land, by reclaiming land from the sea, such as one-third of the farm land in The Netherlands.

The Earth's atmosphere

Outside the Earth

The Earth is surrounded by a blanket of air, called the atmosphere, which is divided into different layers. The highest reaches up into Space, 8,000 km (5,000 miles) above the Earth.

In the beginning

The Earth's atmosphere was originally a hot, steamy mixture of gases. Scientists think that it was made up of gases such as methane, nitrogen, hydrogen and carbon dioxide, as well as water vapour.

DID YOU KNOW?

There is enough water in the atmosphere, that if it all fell as rain at the same time, it would cover the entire surface of the Earth with 2.5 cm (1 in) of water.

Oxygen – the air that we breathe

Oxygen was first formed only about 2,000 million years ago, when plants, called algae, started to appear on the Earth. Plants produce oxygen in sunlight, which animals, including people, breathe in. All animals breathe out carbon dioxide, which plants breathe in.

Gasping for air

The higher you go, the thinner the air, which is why mountaineers need extra oxygen. The density of air at the top of Everest is only about one-third that at sea level.

Atmospheric heights

Layer	Height above Earth
Exosphere	500-8,000 km
Thermosphere	80-500 km
Mesosphere	50-80 km
Stratosphere	8-50 km
Troposphere	
(over Equator)	16 km
(over Poles)	8 km

What is the atmosphere made of?

The highest layer, the exosphere, is probably made mostly of helium, hydrogen and oxygen.

The lower layers are made of:

Gas	Per cent
Nitrogen	75.51
Oxygen	23.15
Argon	1.28
Carbon dioxide	
Neon	
Helium	
Krypton	.06
Hydrogen	
Xenon	
Ozone	

Plus water vapour, and microscopic dust particles, plant spores and pollen grain

Atmospheric temperatures

Layer	Temperature
Exosphere	2200°C minimum
Thermosphere	−80°C to 2,200°C
Mesosphere	10°C to −80°C
Stratosphere	−55°C to 10°C
Troposphere	
(at 16 km high)	−55°C
(at sea level)	15°C

Dust high

A giant volcanic eruption can throw dust and ash as high as the stratosphere. The dust and ash can travel halfway around the world, and take as long as three years to fall back to Earth.

Bouncing waves

Radio signals move at the speed of light, 300,000 km (186,420 miles) per second. The signals can travel around the curve of the Earth, by bouncing off the electrically-charged air in the mesosphere and thermosphere.

Flying high

The troposphere is the storm, wind and cloud layer. Planes fly high above the weather, in the stratosphere, where they use air currents, called jet streams, which can blow at up to 483 km (300 miles) per hour. Most of the jet streams blow from west to east.

Force of gravity

The atmosphere is held to the Earth by the force of gravity. Astronauts have to travel through the atmosphere at more than 27,360 km (17,000 miles) per hour to break free of Earth's gravity.

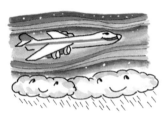

Record heights

	Height above Earth
Unmanned balloon	52 km
Mig-25 fighter plane	38 km
Manned balloon	35 km
Concorde	18 km
747 Jumbo jet	12 km
DC9 plane	8 km

In comparison, Mount Everest is 9 km high.

Sunscreen

Up in the stratosphere, 24 km (15 miles) above the Earth, is the ozone layer. This filters out the Sun's harmful ultra-violet rays – without the ozone, life would not survive on Earth.

Mountains

High ground

About 25 per cent of the Earth's land surface is 914 m (3,000 ft) or more above sea level. Of this, most of the continent of Antarctica is about 1,829 m (6,000 ft) high and the country of Tibet averages 4,572 m (15,000 ft) high.

Capital fact

The highest capital city in the world is La Paz, in Bolivia. It is 3,625 m (11,893 ft) up in the Andes.

Avalanche!

The slam of a car door, a falling branch or the movement of a skier can start an avalanche. The snow can slide down at a speed of 322 km (200 miles) an hour.

High living

There is less oxygen the higher up you go. Mountain people and animals can live at great heights because they have bigger hearts and lungs, which carry more blood, and therefore more oxygen.

Quechua Indians live 3,650 m (12,000 ft) up in the Andes, where they grow potatoes and corn, and herd sheep.

Mountain heights

People and wildlife can survive at different heights up a mountain. This shows some of the life of the Himalayas.

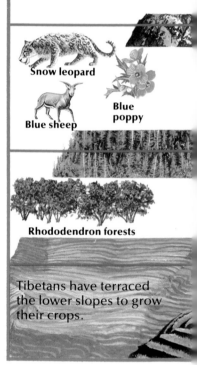

Snow leopard

Blue sheep

Blue poppy

Rhododendron forests

Tibetans have terraced the lower slopes to grow their crops.

Cliff climbers

Rocky Mountain goats can climb up cliffs which are almost vertical. Tough pads on their hooves act as suction cups, and stop them from slipping on the steep rocks.

Highest mountain by continent

Continent	Location	Mountain	Height
Asia	Nepal/Tibet	Everest	8,848 m
Africa	Tanzania	Kilimanjaro	5,895 m
North America	Alaska	McKinley	6,194 m
South America	Argentina	Aconcagua	6,960 m
Antarctica	Ellsworth Land	Vinson Massif	5,140 m
Western Europe	France	Mont Blanc	4,810 m
Eastern Europe	USSR	Elbrus	5,633 m
Oceania	New Zealand	Cook	3,764 m

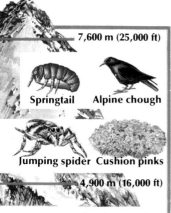

7,600 m (25,000 ft)

Springtail   **Alpine chough**

Jumping spider   **Cushion pinks**

4,900 m (16,000 ft)

Tibetans take their yaks up as high as 4,600 m (15,000 ft) to graze during the summer.

3,000 m (10,000 ft)

Red panda   **Asian black bear**

1,200 m (4,000 ft)

Longest mountain ranges

Range	Location	Length
Andes	South America	7,240 km
Rockies	North America	6,030 km
Himalaya/Karakoram/ HinduKush	Asia	3,860 km
Great Dividing Range	Australia	3,620 km
Trans-Antarctic	Antarctica	3,540 km

The Andes are over twice as long as North America is wide.

Mountain climate

The higher you go up a mountain, the colder it gets. The temperature drops by 2°C (3.6°F) for every 300 m (984 ft) of height. The temperature is as low as −20°C (−4°F) at the top of the Himalayas, where fierce winds can reach over 300 km (186 miles) an hour.

DID YOU KNOW?

Seashells can be found in rocks high up on some mountains, such as the Apennines in Italy. The rocks were once at the bottom of the sea. They were pushed upwards over millions of years, as the crust of the Earth crumpled.

Changing shape

As they get older, mountains gradually change shape. Frost and ice split and wear away the rock. Scientists think mountains lose about 8.6 cm (3½ in) every 1,000 years.

Mountain ages

Mountain ranges are millions of years old, but they are not all the same age.

Scientists have worked out the approximate age of mountain ranges. Here are some examples.

Million years old	Location	Mountain range
400	Scotland	Highlands
250	USA	Appalachians
	USSR	Urals
80	South America	Andes
70	North America	Rockies
40	Asia	Himalayas
15	Europe	Alps

Tundra

Frozen prairie

The frozen prairie, the flat tundra, stretches between the tree line (the northern edge of forest lands) and the Arctic polar region. It is almost 1½ times the size of Brazil, covering nearly one-tenth of the Earth's land surface, including northern Canada, Norway, Sweden, Finland and Greenland, Siberia, Alaska and Iceland.

Soggy landscape

The tundra has only about 20 cm (8 in) of rain a year. The permafrost stops the water from draining away, so about half the area of tundra is dotted with marshes and shallow lakes. Only the top few cms of tundra thaw each summer.

Northern dawn

The ghostly lights of the Aurora borealis shimmer and glow high in the atmosphere in the far north. Curtains and streamers of light move across the winter skies.

Tundra people

About 90,000 Eskimos live in the tundra area. Most of them now live in wooden houses, but in Greenland and Canada, a few still live in igloos. Other tundra dwellers include 300,000 Yakuts in Siberia and 30,000 Lapps in Scandinavia.

Commuter caribou

Herds of caribou, as many as 100,000 in each herd, trek 600 km (373 miles) north to the tundra every spring, where the young caribou are born. As summer ends, they return south, following routes they have used for centuries.

Amazing But True

Scientists were able to make a 10,000-year-old seed germinate and sprout. The Arctic lupin seed was found in Yukon, in Canada.

Tundra statistics

Area of tundra	13,000,000 sq km
Depth of permafrost	305-610 m
Temperature	
Winter	−29 to −34°C
Summer	3 to 12°C

Winter white

Many of the birds and animals which live on the tundra all year round change colour according to the season. In autumn they turn white to match the snow; in spring, they change back to their summer colours.

Arctic fox

Snowy owl

Snowshoe rabbit

Stoat

Arctic hare

Ptarmigan

DID YOU KNOW?

The Trans-Alaskan oil pipeline stretches 1,300 km (800 miles) from the Arctic Ocean to southern Alaska. The oil is heated to at least 45°C (130°F), to stop it freezing in the pipe.

Buzz off!

In calm weather, during the short summer, plagues of mosquitoes and other flies infest the tundra. Warble flies are so ferocious, they can cause madness in some of the caribou herds.

Deep freeze

The permafrost can act as a deep freeze. Ice Age mammoths have been found in Siberia. And the body of John Torrington, a British naval officer who died in 1845, on an expedition to the Bering Strait, was found in 1983.

Colder than ice

In the winter, under its blanket of ice and snow, the tundra in north-east Siberia is colder, at −70°C (−94°F), than it is at the North Pole.

Permafrost

The permafrost, the deep layer of ground beneath the tundra, is frozen all the year round. A layer as much as 1,500 m (4,921 ft) deep has been recorded in Siberia.

Low life

You can walk on top of the tundra forests. Near to the tree line, the trees are so blasted by the cold, dry winds, they grow close to the ground. Branches of ground willow can be up to 5 m (16 ft) in length, but they only rise above the surface by about 10 cm (4 in).

11

Forests . . . 1

Coniferous trees

Coniferous trees have cones and needle-like leaves. Most conifers are evergreen, but some, such as larches, lose their needles in the autumn. Coniferous forests grow in colder climates in the far north, and high up on mountains – even those in the Tropics.

Broad-leaved trees

Broad-leaved trees have flowers and wide, flat leaves. Some broad-leaved trees are deciduous, they lose their leaves in autumn; others are evergreen. Deciduous broad-leaved forests grow in warm, temperate climates. Evergreen broad-leaved forests grow where it is hot and wet all the time.

Forest statistics

Coniferous forests stretch across northern Europe, Asia and North America, and are found in mountain regions, such as the Rockies, Alps and Urals. Mixed and deciduous broad-leaved forests are found mostly in west and central Europe, eastern USA, and parts of Japan, China and New Zealand.

Type of forest	Type of trees
Coniferous	Conifers
Mixed	Deciduous broad-leaved/conifers
Deciduous	Deciduous broad-leaved
Tropical rain	Evergreen broad-leaved

The tropical rain forests equal all the other forest types added together.

Timber merchant

Coniferous trees supply almost three-quarters of the world's timber, as well as nearly all the paper used. It takes one tree to produce 270 copies of a 190-page paperback book.

Rooted deep

Hickory trees grow to 37 m (120 ft) tall. The main root, the taproot, could be as long as 30 m (100 ft) – the root may be nearly as deep as the tree is high.

Coniferous forest trees

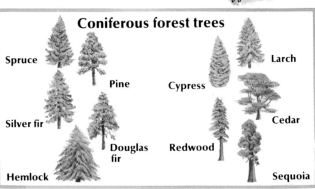

Spruce
Pine
Silver fir
Douglas fir
Hemlock
Cypress
Redwood
Larch
Cedar
Sequoia

Deciduous broad-leaved forest trees

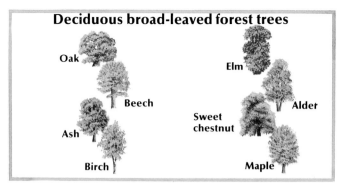

Oak

Elm

Beech

Alder

Sweet chestnut

Ash

Birch

Maple

Oldest, largest, tallest

The mountain forests of north-west America have the oldest and the largest and the tallest trees on Earth.

Bristlecone pines nearly 5,000 years old, about the same age as the Pyramids in Egypt. Giant sequoias up to 7.6 m (26 ft) across - wide enough to drive a car through. Redwoods up to 107 m (350 ft) tall. Four balanced on top of each other would be nearly as high as the Sears Roebuck Tower, the world's tallest building.

Fire-proof trees

Fires can burn forests at a rate of up to 15 km (10 miles) an hour, and the roar of the fire can be heard 1.6 km (1 mile) away. Trees protected by very thick bark, for example pine and sequoia, are only scarred by the fire, the wood is undamaged.

Woodlands

Woodland flowers bloom in the spring, before the trees come into leaf and block most of the sunlight. When the leaves fall in autumn they rot, forming humus, which makes the soil more fertile.

Crops from coniferous trees

Part of tree	Some examples of use
Timber	Furniture
	Matches
	Tannic acid
Pulp	Paper
	Plastics
	Rayon
Cellulose	Cellophane
	Turpentine
Needles	Pine-leaf oil (used in soap)
	Vitamins A and E

Amazing But True

Each year, every person in the USA uses up enough items made from wood to equal a tree 30 m (100 ft) tall and 41 cm (16 in) in diameter. That adds up to over 230 million trees a year.

Giant cone

The largest pine cones grow on the sugar pine trees of the USA. They reach 66 cm (26 in) long, nearly two-thirds the length of a baseball bat.

Forests . . . 2

Tropical rain forests

Rain forests cover about 6 per cent of the Earth's land surface. A hundred million years ago, rain forests grew in Norway. Today, they are mostly on or south of the Equator, for example in New Guinea, Malaysia and parts of Africa, Burma, Indonesia and South America.

Treeless forests

Great forests of bamboo, over 18 m (60 ft) high, grow in the south-western mountains of China, where giant pandas live. Bamboo is not a tree, it is a type of grass. Field grass grows to an average of only 100 cm (39 in).

Flying frogs

Asian tree frogs (10 cm, 4 in long) can "fly" from one tree to another, as much as 12 m (40 ft) away. The webs of skin between their toes act as parachutes.

DID YOU KNOW?

About 2,500 million people, half the world's population, use wood for cooking and heating.

Daily rain

It rains nearly every day in the tropical rain forests. At least 203 cm (80 in) and as much as 381 cm (150 in) can fall each year. The temperature rarely drops below 26.6°C (80°F) and the air is 80 per cent moisture.

Rain forest layers

The plants and trees in the tropical rain forests grow up to different heights. The forest can be divided into five "layers".

Layer	Height
Attic	up to 91 m
Canopy	46-76 m
Understorey	6-12 m
Shrub	0.6-6 m
Herb	up to 0.6 m

Slowcoach

In the forests of South America is the slowest moving land mammal. The sloth spends much of its time hanging upside-down from trees. When it does move, it creeps along at 2 m (7 ft) a minute.

Bush ropes

Bush ropes, or lianas, hang down from the rain forest canopy. They can be 60 cm (2 ft) thick and as much as 152 m (500 ft) long, and are strong enough to swing on.

Perching plants

Perching plants grow on trees high up in the canopy, where they absorb food and moisture from the air. Plants, such as bromeliads, can provide a home for insects and frogs, 70 m (230 ft) above the forest floor.

HOME, SWEET HOME

Life in the rain forest

Only 1 per cent of sunlight reaches the rain forest floor. So most of the insects, birds and animals have to live up in the canopy, where there is more sunlight and food.

Amazing But True

Tree kangaroos live in the New Guinea forests. They mostly live up in the trees, but can jump down to the forest floor from a height of 18 m (59 ft). Their tails are longer than their bodies.

Rain forest crops

The Earth's rain forests supply many of our crops. Rubber, lacquer, gum, waxes and dyes can all be made from rain forest trees. Here are some other examples.

Timber	Mahogany
	Teak
Fruit	Bananas
	Pineapples
Spices	Paprika
	Pepper
Oils	Palm
	Patchouli
Fibres	Jute
	Rattan
Beans	Coffee
	Cocoa

Cloud forest giants

Giant plants grow 3,000 m (9,842 ft) up in the cloud forests on Mount Kenya, where the trees are blanketed in fog and mist. Groundsel, over 6 m (20 ft) high, look like giant cabbages on trunks. Lobelias, up to 8 m (26 ft) tall, look like furry columns because of their hairy leaves.

Medicine cabinet

Some of our medicines are made from rain forest trees. Quinine and aspirin are made from tree bark; cough mixture is made from tree resin.

Lakes and rivers

Drop of water

Only 3 per cent of all the water on Earth is fresh; the rest is salty. Of that 3 per cent, over 2 per cent is frozen in ice sheets and glaciers; so less than 1 per cent is in lakes, rivers and under the ground.

Longest rivers by continent

Continent	Country	River	Length
Asia	China	Yangtze	5,520 km
Africa	Egypt	Nile	6,670 km
North America	USA	Mississippi/ Missouri	6,020 km
South America	Brazil	Amazon	6,437 km
Eastern Europe	USSR	Volga	3,688 km
Western Europe	Germany	Rhine	1,320 km
Oceania	Australia	Murray/Darling	3,720 km

Some of the rivers flow through more than one country. Most of each river is in the country listed.

DID YOU KNOW?

Not all rivers end up in an ocean. The rivers flowing south from the Tassili Mountains in north Africa, slow down to a trickle and disappear into the dry Sahara sands.

Deepest lake

Lake Baikal, in the USSR, is 644 km (400 miles) long and 48 km (30 miles) wide. It is so deep, ranging from 1,620-1,940 m (5,315-6,365 ft), that all five of the Great Lakes in North America could be emptied into it.

Amazing But True

Piranhas are ferocious, flesh-eating fish. Their triangular teeth are so sharp, the Amazonian Indians use them as scissors.

Living afloat

One of the highest lakes is Titicaca, 3,810 m (12,500 ft) up in the Peruvian Andes. There are "floating" islands on the lake, some as big as football fields, made from thickly matted totora reeds. People live on the islands, and build their houses, boats and baskets from the reeds – and they eat the roots of the reeds too.

Highest waterfalls

Waterfall	Location	Height
Angel	Venezuela	979 m
Tugela	South Africa	948 m
Yosemite	USA	739 m
Southern Mardalsfossen	Norway	655 m
Cuquenan	Venezuela	610 m

The mighty Amazon

The Amazon is the greatest river on Earth. It starts 5,200 m (17,000 ft) up in the snows of the Andes, and ends 6,437 km (4,000 miles) later on the Atlantic coast, in a maze of islands and channels, 300 km (186 miles) wide.

The Amazon's flow of water is so great, one-fifth of all river water, that the freshwater stretches 180 km (112 miles) out to sea, colouring the sea with yellow-brown silt.

Niagara on the move

Niagara Falls are midway along the Niagara River, which flows between Lakes Ontario and Erie. The Falls date back 10,000 years, to the end of the last Ice Age.

At that time they were 11 km (7 miles) further downriver; the pounding water has gradually worn away the rocks at the edge of the Falls. In about 25,000 years' time, Niagara will disappear when the Falls reach Lake Erie – and the Lake may drain away.

Busy waterfall

The Iguazu Falls in Brazil are 4 km (2½ miles) wide and 80 m (260 ft) high. During the rainy season, November to March, the amount of water pouring over the Falls every second would fill about 6 Olympic-size swimming pools.

Largest lakes and inland seas

Most lakes contain freshwater, but two of the largest – the Aral and the Caspian – are really inland seas, as they contain saltwater.

Lake/inland sea	Location	Size
Caspian Sea	Iran/USSR	372,000 sq km
Superior	Canada/USA	82,414 sq km
Victoria	East Africa	69,485 sq km
Aral Sea	USSR	66,500 sq km
Huron	Canada/USA	59,596 sq km
Michigan	USA	58,016 sq km
Tanganyika	East Africa	32,893 sq km

Grasslands and savannahs

Grassy places

Grasslands and savannahs cover about one-quarter of the land on Earth. Savannahs have patches of grass, up to 4.5 m (15 ft) tall, and scrub, bushes and a few small trees. Grasslands can be used for growing crops, such as wheat, or as pasture, for grazing animals. The grass height ranges from 30-215 cm (1-7 ft).

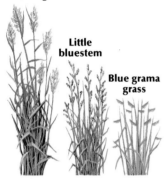

Indian grass

Little bluestem

Blue grama grass

Grassy names

Grasslands and savannahs are called different names in different parts of the world. These are some examples.

Grasslands

Country	Name
Argentina	Pampas
North America	Prairie
South Africa	Veldt
Central Asia	Steppes
Australia	Scrub

Savannahs

Country	Name
East Africa	Savannah
Brazil	Campo
Venezuela	Llanos

Grasslands

There are grasslands in Europe, Asia, North America, South America, South Africa and Australia in areas where there is too little rain for forests to grow, but enough rain to stop the land turning to desert.

Grasslands have hot summers and cold winters. In the North American prairies, the temperature in winter can drop to freezing (0°C, 32°F) and climb to 38°C (100°F) in summer. Rainfall can vary between 50-100 cm (20-40 in) a year.

All about grasses

There are about 10,000 different kinds of grass on Earth. Most grasses have hollow stems, although some have solid stems, such as maize and sugar cane.

Grasses are flowering plants, but are pollinated by the wind carrying pollen from flower to flower. So grasses do not need brightly coloured flowers to attract insects to carry the pollen.

New grass

Grass fires, which can be sparked off by lightning, can destroy grass stems, but the grass soon grows back again. The growing point of grass is so close to the ground, at the base of the leaves, that it does not get burnt – or even eaten by animals as they graze the grass.

Crops

Cereal crops have been developed by people from wild grasses. They are used as food for people and for animals. Here are some examples.

Wheat

Rice

Oats

Millet

Maize

Rye

Barley

Sorghum

Savannah choice

Different animals on the savannah eat different plants. Giraffes feed on branches high in trees; antelopes feed on lower branches. Zebras eat the tops of grasses; wildebeest eat the rest of the stem; and gazelles eat the young shoots.

Rice

Rice is the only grass which can grow in water, and is the main food of more than half the world's population. Almost all of the rice – about 90 per cent – is grown in Asia.

Upside-down trees

The baobab trees of Africa have enormous, swollen trunks, in which water is stored, topped by short, stumpy branches which look more like tree roots. Old trees are sometimes hollow, and have been used as bus shelters – or even as houses.

Savannahs

Savannahs are mostly near the Equator, in Africa, South-East Asia and India, and in Australia, in areas where it is warm all the year round. Some savannahs are dry for as much as 10 months of the year, with only 20 cm (8 in) of rain. Others are dry for only 3 months, with as much as 120 cm (47 in) of rain.

Staying alive

The colours of animals living in savannahs help to protect them from predators, but also hides the predators themselves. Striped or spotted animals, such as cheetahs and leopards, are difficult to see from a distance, especially when they move through sunlight and shadow. The tawny colour of a lion hides it in the long, dry grass.

Deserts

What is a desert?

A desert is an area which has less than 25 cm (10 in) of rain a year, and very little plant life. In some deserts, the total rain for the year might fall in only two or three storms. But that is enough for plant seeds to sprout and bloom, turning parts of the desert into carpets of flowers for a few days.

Largest deserts		
Desert	Location	Size in sq km
Sahara	North Africa	8,400,000
Australian	Australia	1,550,000
Arabian	South-West Asia	1,300,000
Gobi	Central Asia	1,040,000
Patagonia	South America	670,000
Kalahari	Southern Africa	520,000
Turkestan	Central Asia	450,000
Takla Makan	China	320,000
Sonoran	USA/Mexico	310,000
Namib	South-West Africa	310,000

Deserted places

Deserts cover about 20 per cent of the Earth's land surface. Many desert areas are bare rock, or are covered with pebbles and gravel. Sand accounts for only about 15 per cent of the Earth's desert regions.

Colossal cacti

Cacti are found only in American deserts. The tallest are saguaros which can reach 15 m (50 ft) tall, weigh 7 tons and live for 200 years. Water is stored in the stem and used in times of drought.

The driest land

The Atacama in northern Chile is the driest desert on Earth. Parts of the desert had no rain for 400 years, from 1570-1971, and in other parts, rain has never been recorded.

Death Valley

WATER 100KM

At 57°C (134°F), Death Valley is the driest, hottest place in North America. Gold prospectors died there, in 1849, when they ran out of food and water on their way to the Californian goldfields – which is how the Valley got its name.

Sandstorm

One of the sandiest deserts is the Takla Makan. Sandstorms can whip up the sand as high as 3,048 m (10,000 ft). Wind-blown sand in the Sahara can be so fierce, it will sandblast the paint off a car or aeroplane.

Hot and cold deserts

There are 10 major desert regions. "Cold" deserts have hot summers and relatively cold winters. "Hot" deserts are hot during the day, all the year round.

Cold deserts
West/south-west North
  America
Patagonia
Turkestan
Gobi

Hot deserts
Sahara
Namib/Kalahari
Arabian
Iranian
Atacama
Australian

Sahara

The Sahara is almost one-third the size of Africa, and is nearly as big as the USA, the fourth largest country. It was not always a desert. Over millions of years it has been covered in ice, sea, forests and grasslands.

Moving dunes

Sand dunes move. The wind blows the sand up one side of the dune, and some of the sand trickles over the top and slips down the other side. Dunes creep forward between 10 and 50 m (33 to 164 ft) a year, and can engulf villages and oases.

Temperature

The temperature at night in a hot desert can drop below freezing, to −4°C (24°F). During the day, the sand can be as hot as 79°C (175°F).

Desert snow

Each year, a thin layer of snow (5 cm, 2 in) blankets the cacti in many North American deserts. And snow sometimes falls on the Ahaggar Mountains in the Sahara Desert.

Desert dinosaurs

Dinosaurs once lived in the Gobi Desert in Asia. Fossilized eggs and bones have been found there, and the skeleton of *Tarbosaurus bataar,* a giant tyrannosaur.

The seashore

The coastline of the world

If all the coastlines were straightened out, they would stretch nearly 13 times around the Equator. The total amount of coastline in the world, not counting small bays and inlets, is 504,000 km (313,186 miles).

Stormy weather

On the shores of the northern Pacific Ocean, the force of the waves in winter is equivalent to the impact of a car crashing into a wall at 145 km (90 miles) an hour. Storm waves on the east coast of North America tossed a 61 kg (135 lb) rock 28 m (91 ft) high – on to the roof of a lighthouse.

Rising tide

On the shore, the sea rises and falls twice a day, at high and low tides. The difference between high and low tide levels ranges from 12 m (40 ft) on some British and Alaskan coasts, to only 30 cm (1 ft) on the Gulf of Mexico coast. The greatest tide is in the Bay of Fundy, eastern Canada, which rises an enormous 16 m (53 ft). The Mediterranean Sea barely has a tide at all.

Beach dunes

Sand dunes on the Atlantic coast of France reach an amazing 91 m (300 ft) high, although beach sand dunes are usually no more than 15 m (50 ft) high. The dunes, blown along by the wind, creep slowly inland, by about 6 m (20 ft) a year, and may bury buildings – and even whole forests.

Skeletons galore!

Corals, which grow in warm, tropical waters, are the skeletons of billions of tiny animals. The Great Barrier Reef is made of coral, and stretches in a series of islands and reefs for 2,028 km (1,260 miles) along the north-east coast of Australia. The Reef has taken at least 12 million years to grow.

DID YOU KNOW?

The highest sea cliffs are on the north coast of Moloka'i, Hawaii – a towering 1,005 m (3,300 ft) high. That is about the same height as a 275-storey building.

Sand between the toes

Sand is worn down rock, washed down to the sea by rivers, or made by waves battering and grinding down rocky cliffs. A few beaches have some desert sand, such as those on the Mediterranean Sea, where sand has been blown by the wind across from the Sahara Desert. Some beaches have sand of all one colour, such as the beaches of black lava on Tahiti. Other beaches are a mixture of colours, made from different types of rock, or from worn down coral or seashells. These are some of the sand colours.

Colour	Made of
Black	Lava
Grey	Granite, feldspar
Light brown/tan	Granite, quartz
Yellow	Quartz
Gold	Mica
Red	Garnet
Pink	Feldspar
White	Coral, seashells, quartz

Rock carving

Coastlines are always changing. On rocky shores, the waves pound against the cliffs, flinging up boulders, pebbles and sand. These grind away the rock, forming bays, caves and arches. The top of an arch may collapse, leaving a sea stack, such as the 137 m (450 ft) tall Old Man of Hoy, off the Orkney Islands.

The waves can act as a huge saw, cutting away the softer rock at the foot of a cliff, so that part of the cliff collapses. The lighthouse on the coast at Martha's Vineyard, Massachusetts, USA, has had to be moved 3 times. The waves wear away about 1.7 m (5.5 ft) of the cliff every year.

Mangrove swamps

Enormous mangrove swamps grow in shallow waters on some shores in tropical regions, such as around the mouth of the Ganges River in India. Some mangrove swamps can stretch for 97 km (60 miles) or more inland. The mangrove trees can reach 25 m (82 ft) tall, and have curious stilt-like roots, which prop up the trees.

The changing shore

The level of the sea on the seashore can change over long periods of time. Many of the Ancient Roman ports around the Mediterranean Sea, such as Caesarea on the coast of Israel, are now drowned. In contrast, on Romney Marshes, in Kent, England, the old port of Rye is now over 3 km (2 miles) inland.

The sea

The blue planet

Saltwater covers nearly 70 per cent of the surface of the Earth. The continents and islands divide all that water into the Pacific, Atlantic, Indian and Arctic Oceans – but the four oceans form one continuous expanse of water.

The oceans		
Name	Size, excluding major seas	Average depth
Pacific Ocean	165,384,000 sq km	4,000 m
Atlantic Ocean	82,217,000 sq km	3,300 m
Indian Ocean	73,481,000 sq km	3,800 m
Arctic Ocean	13,986,000 sq km	1,500 m

The largest ocean, the Pacific, covers nearly one-third of the Earth's surface. At its widest point, between Panama and Malaysia, the Pacific stretches 1,770 km (11,000 miles) – nearly halfway around the world.

DID YOU KNOW?

Sound can travel through water at 1,507 m (4,954 ft) a second. That is about 3 times faster than sound travelling through air – 331 m (1,087 ft) a second.

Saltwater

Saltwater contains over 96 per cent pure water and nearly 3 per cent common salt. More than 80 other elements, including gold, make up the rest. These nine elements are found in the greatest quantity.

Sulphate	Bromide
Magnesium	Boron
Calcium	Strontium
Potassium	Fluoride
Bicarbonate	

Drinking the sea

When saltwater freezes, the ice contains little or no salt. People living in polar regions, such as Eskimos, can melt the ice – and use it as fresh drinking water.

Tsunamis

Tsunamis, often wrongly called tidal waves, are huge waves caused either by an underwater volcanic explosion or by an earthquake.

One tsunami, triggered by an earthquake, took just over 4½ hours, to travel a distance of 3,220 km (2,000 miles) – from the Aleutian Trench under the north Pacific to Honolulu, in the mid Pacific. The tsunami hit the island with waves more than 15 m (50 ft) high.

24

Oceans and seas

Each ocean is divided into different areas – the main part, called by the ocean name, and various seas. The seas are mostly around the coasts of the continents and islands. These are the largest seas in each of the oceans.

Ocean	Name of sea	Size
Pacific	Coral	4,790,000 sq km
	South China	3,680,000 sq km
Atlantic	Caribbean	2,750,000 sq km
	Mediterranean	2,510,000 sq km
Indian	Red	450,000 sq km
	Persian Gulf	240,000 sq km
Arctic	Hudson Bay	1,230,000 sq km
	Baffin Bay	690,000 sq km

Hot and cold water

The surface of the sea varies in temperature. The warm, tropical currents can be as hot as 30°C (86°F), the polar currents can be as cold as −2°C (29°F). In the north Atlantic, where the warm Gulf Stream meets the cold Labrador Current, there is a 12°C (22°F) difference in temperature.

Sailing clockwise

The water in the seas is constantly moving around the Earth, flowing in great currents, like rivers in the sea. The currents may be as wide as 80 km (50 miles) and flow at up to 6 km (4 miles) an hour.

The currents in the southern hemisphere mostly swirl anti-clockwise; those in the northern hemisphere swirl in a clockwise direction. In 1492, Columbus sailed from Spain to the West Indies along two currents, the Canaries and the North Equatorial.

Amazing But True

If all the salt was taken out of the seas and spread over the land surface of the Earth, there would be a layer of salt 152 m (500 ft) thick.

Salty seas

The amount of salt in seawater varies. The Red Sea, in the Near East, has almost six times as much salt as the Baltic Sea, in Europe.

Icelandic warmth

The warm Gulf Stream flows from the Caribbean eastwards across the Atlantic Ocean and on past Iceland as far as northern Europe. The winds blowing across the Gulf Stream keep Reyjavik, in Iceland, warmer in winter than New York City, USA 3,862 km (2,400 miles) further south, where there are winds blowing from the cold Labrador Current.

Under the sea

The ocean floor

The ocean floor is not completely flat – there are volcanoes, mountains, valleys and plains, just as there are on dry land.

The ocean plains are solid rock, covered in places in a layer of sand, gravel, clay, silt, or ooze – the remains of countless billions of sea creatures. On average, the layer is 30 m (100 ft) thick; on the floor of the Mediterranean Sea, it is 2,000 m (6,500 ft) thick.

DID YOU KNOW?

The deeper under the sea you go, the greater the pressure, that is the weight of the water above you. At a depth of 9,100 m (30,000 ft), the pressure is equivalent to a 1 tonne weight balanced on a postage stamp.

Undersea mountains

There are mountains in every ocean – together, they form a chain over 60,000 km (37,284 miles) long. In the Pacific Ocean alone there are 14,000 sea mountains, their peaks 610-1,829 m (2,000-6,000 ft) below the surface. Other sea mountains are so huge, they poke through the surface as chains of islands. This map shows the underwater mountain chains.

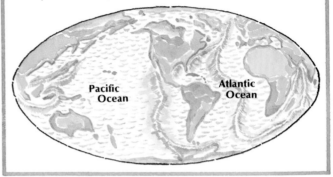

Pacific Ocean

Atlantic Ocean

Flashlight fish

Many fish living 3,000 m (9,842 ft) down in the dark ocean waters, have their own lights, which are made by bacteria inside the fish. The bacteria glow all the time, but the fish can "switch" the lights off and on.

The angler fish has a bulb of bacteria light at the end of a long spine, which hangs over the fish's mouth. The light attracts other fish – which are gobbled up by the angler.

Light and dark

In the muddy waters off the shores, the water is clear for only about 15 m (50 ft) down. Out in the open ocean, it is clear down to about 110 m (360 ft), and some sunlight can reach 244 m (800 ft) deep. Below that level, it is dark, still – and cold. Deep water is about 3.8°C (39°F), which is close to freezing all the year round.

Diving records

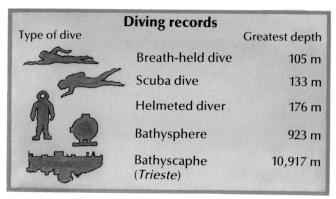

Type of dive		Greatest depth
Breath-held dive		105 m
Scuba dive		133 m
Helmeted diver		176 m
Bathysphere		923 m
Bathyscaphe (*Trieste*)		10,917 m

Deepest dive

Explorers, inside the bathyscaphe *Trieste*, have dived almost to the bottom of the Mariana Trench, the deepest point on Earth. The Trench, south-west of Guam in the Pacific Ocean, plunges to a depth of 11,033 m (36,198 ft) below sea level.

Fishy depths

Different plants and animals live at different depths in the oceans. Floating on the surface, mostly around the coasts and in tropical seas, are billions of tiny plants and animals, called plankton.

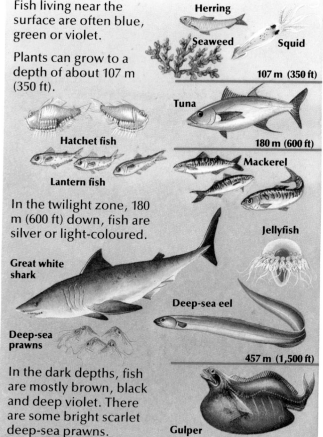

Fish living near the surface are often blue, green or violet.

Plants can grow to a depth of about 107 m (350 ft).

Herring

Seaweed **Squid**

107 m (350 ft)

Hatchet fish

Tuna

180 m (600 ft)

Lantern fish

Mackerel

In the twilight zone, 180 m (600 ft) down, fish are silver or light-coloured.

Jellyfish

Great white shark

Deep-sea eel

Deep-sea prawns

457 m (1,500 ft)

In the dark depths, fish are mostly brown, black and deep violet. There are some bright scarlet deep-sea prawns.

Gulper

Amazing But True

Huge worms, 3 m (10 ft) long, blind crabs and giant white clams survive 2,400 m (8,000 ft) down in the darkness of the Pacific Ocean, off the coast of South America. They live near a crack in the ocean floor, where hot mineral-rich water gushes out, providing them with food.

Poles apart

The Arctic Ocean

The Arctic is the smallest of the four oceans, and is less than one-tenth the size of the Pacific, the largest ocean.

Arctic Circle
Arctic Ocean
North Pole
Greenland

Greenland ice sheet statistics

Area of ice sheet	1,479,000 sq km
Volume of ice	2,800,000 cu km
Thickness of ice	1.6-3 km
Temperature	
July	over 10°C
December	−50°C
Average	−20°C

Arctic Ocean statistics

Total area	13,986,000 sq km
Area of floating ice	12,000,000 sq km
Average depth of water	1,500 m
Thickness of pack ice	0.6-7.43 m
Coldest water temperature	−51°C

Greenland

About 85 per cent of Greenland is covered by an ice sheet, stretching 2,400 km (1,491 miles) from north to south and up to 1,100 km (683 miles) east to west. The ice sheet is 7½ times the size of Britain. The 50,000 people on the island can only live on the coasts.

Slow-growing plants

Some Arctic lichens may be over 4,500 years old, and have taken hundreds of years to grow 2.5 cm (1 in).

All that ice

The polar ice sheets hold just over 2 per cent of all the Earth's water. If all the ice melted, the sea level around the world would rise by about 60 m (200 ft). Many coastal areas would be drowned, including major cities such as London, Tokyo and New York.

Hunt the seal

In the Arctic, seals spend much of their time under water, but need to come up for air about every 20 minutes. When the seas are frozen, the seals chew several big breathing holes in the ice.

Polar bears hunt seals, and wait on the ice by a breathing hole. When the seal comes up, the polar bear grabs it.

Midnight Sun

As the Earth travels around the Sun, one of the Poles is always facing towards it. The North Pole has continuous daylight from mid-March to mid-September. From mid-September to mid-March, it is the South Pole's turn for continuous daylight.

Antarctica

Nearly one-tenth of the Earth's surface is permanently covered in ice. About 90 per cent of all that ice is in the ice sheets of Antarctica and Greenland. The other 10 per cent is in mountain glaciers.

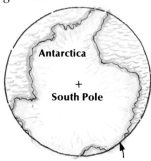

The Antarctic ice sheet is 1½ times the size of the USA, and has nine times more ice than the Greenland ice sheet.

Antarctic wildlife

Insects, 13 mm (0.5 in) long, are the only creatures living all the time on Antarctica itself. The wildlife lives in the seas and islands around the coast, including the blue whale, the largest creature on Earth, 30 m (98 ft) long and 136 tonnes in weight.

Penguins live on the islands. Scientists think that Adelie penguins might use the Sun to navigate back to their nests from up to 3,058 km (1,900 miles) away. Penguins can "fly" underwater at 40 km (25 miles) an hour.

There is no land at the North Pole – it is a floating raft of ice. In 1958, *Nautilus*, the US submarine, was the first to cross the Arctic Ocean – a distance of 2,945 km (1,830 miles) – by travelling underneath the North Pole.

Volcano

There is still one active volcano in Antarctica. Mount Erebus, in the Transantarctic Range, reaches up 4,900 m (16,075 ft) above the ice. Erebus steams and spouts ash, even though it is covered in snow.

Antarctica statistics	
Area of ice sheet	13,000,000 sq km
Volume of ice sheet	29,000,000 cu km
Thickness of ice	3-4 km
Area of sea ice	
March	3,000,000 sq km
September	22,000,000 sq km
Average thickness of sea ice	4 m
Temperature	
Interior average	−50°C
Coastal average	−20°C

Icebergs and glaciers

Icing

Glaciers cover 10½ per cent of the Earth's land surface, an area equal to the size of South America. Glaciers contain enough ice to cover the entire Earth with a layer of ice, 30 m (98 ft) thick.

Glacier lengths

Name	Location	Length
Lambert/Fisher Ice Passage	Antarctica	515 km
Novaya Zemlya Glacier	USSR	418 km
Arctic Institute Ice Passage	Antarctica	362 km
Nimrod/Lennox/King Ice Passage	Antarctica	289 km
Denman Glacier	Antarctica	241 km
Beardmore Glacier	Antarctica	225 km
Recovery Glacier	Antarctica	225 km
Petermanns Gletscher Glacier	Greenland	200 km
Unnamed Glacier	Antarctica	193 km

Glaciers on the move

Glaciers creep down mountains at a rate of between 2.5-60 cm (1-24 in) a day. A few glaciers move much faster, such as two on Greenland: up to 24 m (79 ft) a day for the Quarayag Glacier and 28 m (92 ft) for the Rinks Isbrae Glacier.

Busy glacier

The Jakobshavn Isbrae Glacier in Greenland moves at about 7 km (4 miles) a year. Every day, over 142 million tonnes of ice break off and float away as 1,500 or so icebergs each year.

DID YOU KNOW?

At least 75 per cent of all the freshwater on Earth is deep frozen inside glaciers. That amount of water would equal non-stop rain all over the Earth for as much as 60 years.

Tropical glaciers

Glaciers and snowfields are found near the Equator, on mountains which are over 6,000 m (20,000 ft) high. There is glacier ice 61 m (200 ft) deep in the Kibo Peak crater on Mount Kilimanjaro in Tanzania.

Deep ice

A depth of glacier ice as thick as 4,330 m (14,206 ft) has been recorded on Byrd Station in Antarctica. Most glaciers are between 91-3,000 m (299-9,842 ft) deep.

Crevasse

Crevasses, cracks in glaciers, can be 40 m (131 ft) deep. The bodies of climbers who fell into a crevasse in the Bossons Glacier on Mont Blanc in the Alps in 1820, were not found until 1861, when they reached the melting "snout", the end of the glacier.

Amazing But True

An Arctic iceberg drifted about 4,000 km (2,486 miles), nearly as far south as the island of Bermuda. An Antarctic iceberg drifted about 5,500 km (3,418 miles), nearly as far north as Rio de Janeiro, in Brazil.

Biggest berg

The largest iceberg ever recorded, off the coast of Antarctica, was 335 km (208 miles) long and 97 km (60 miles) wide. It covered an area of 31,000 sq km (12,000 sq miles), about the same size as Belgium.

Hidden depth

Only about one-tenth of an iceberg floats above the surface. If there is 122 m (400 ft) above the water, then there must be as much as 1,098 m (3,600 ft) below the water.

Icy heights

The tallest iceberg ever recorded, off west Greenland, was 167 m (550 ft) high. That is more than half as tall as the Eiffel Tower in Paris, France.

Iceberg ahoy!

The International Ice Patrol keeps track of all icebergs, and warns ships of any possible danger. The Patrol was set up after the giant liner, the *Titanic,* sank after hitting an iceberg on the night of 14 April 1912: 1,490 people drowned out of a total of 2,201 passengers and crew.

Watering the desert

Icebergs are made of freshwater and could be used to supply water in desert areas. Scientists think that tugs could be built, which could tow large icebergs at a rate of 400 km (250 miles) a day.

The journey from Antarctica to western Australia might take 107-150 days, and to the Atacama Desert in Chile 145-200 days. Only about half of each iceberg would melt on the way.

Long-life bergs

Satellites can track the lives of icebergs. The Trolltunga iceberg in Antarctica was tracked for 11 years, until it broke up into several smaller bergs. At up to 25 km (15½ miles) a day, icebergs can travel a total distance of as much as 2,500 km (1,550 miles).

Earthquakes

Earthquake areas

Earthquakes happen under the sea as well as on land. Ninety per cent occur in the "ring of fire", which circles the Pacific Ocean. Many others occur along the Alpine Belt, which stretches from Spain to Turkey, and on through the Himalayas as far as South-East Asia.

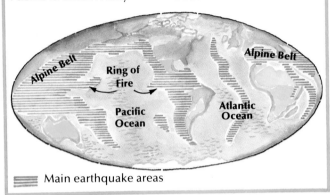

Main earthquake areas

Disaster area

China, on the Alpine Belt of earthquakes, has the worst record for earthquake deaths. In 1556, an earthquake killed 830,000 people in Shanxi province. In 1976, the earthquake in Tangshan province – 8.2 on the Richter Scale – killed 750,000 people.

Danger!

Animals, such as dogs and chickens, some people believe, can sense faint vibrations or smells and warn people that an earthquake might happen. In 1975, in Haicheng, China, thousands of people escaped an earthquake because they were warned of the danger.

Magnitude

The magnitude, that is the power, of an earthquake is measured on the Richter Scale. Starting at 1, each number on the Scale is ten times more powerful than the number below. An earthquake of magnitude 7 is about as powerful as a one megaton nuclear bomb; the worst earthquake so far recorded was 8.9.

A million earthquakes

There are about a million earthquakes every year – any vibration of the Earth's crust is an earthquake. Most are so tiny, they only register on a seismograph, which measures the slightest movement in the crust. A large earthquake occurs about every two weeks – mostly under the sea, where it does little harm.

DID YOU KNOW?

Earthquakes under the sea can trigger off great avalanches of mud and sand. These can cause undersea currents strong enough to snap underwater cables. Telephone cables broke under the Atlantic Ocean, after the earthquake off Newfoundland in 1929.

Splash!

The shock of an earthquake can sometimes be felt hundreds of kilometres away. Water splashed in swimming pools in Houston, USA, after the earthquake in Mexico in 1985 – 1,609 km (1,000 miles) away.

Shocking

An earthquake usually lasts for less than 1 minute. The earthquake in Lisbon, Portugal, in 1755 lasted for 10 minutes, and the shock waves were felt as far away as North Africa.

Rock avalanches

The 1970 earthquake off the coast of Peru caused an avalanche of snow and rock on land – high on the Nevados Huascaran mountain. The avalanche fell 4,000 m (13,123 ft), and buried the town of Yungay under 10 m (33 ft) of rock, killing at least 18,000 people.

Fire! fire!

Huge fires can break out after an earthquake. In 1906, after the earthquake in San Francisco, USA, fire destroyed the wooden buildings of the city. The water pipes had burst, and the fire raged for 3½ days. But within 9 years, the city had been rebuilt.

Amazing But True

The ground can roll like waves on the ocean in a very bad earthquake. The 1964 earthquake in Alaska lasted for 7 minutes. The shaking opened up huge cracks in the ground, up to 90 cm (3 ft) wide and 12 m (40 ft) deep. Many buildings tilted and slid down into the cracks.

Twentieth-century earthquakes

These are some of the most serious earthquakes this century, measured on the Richter Scale.

Date	Location	Richter Scale
1906	Coast of Colombia	8.9
1906	Jammu and Kashmir, India	8.6
1906	Valparaiso, Chile	8.6
1920	Kansu province, China	8.5
1929	Fox Islands, Alaska	8.6
1933	North Honshu, Japan	8.9
1941	Coast of Portugal	8.4
1950	Assam, India	8.3
1960	Lebu, Chile	8.5
1964	Prince William Sound, Alaska	8.5

Volcanoes

Hot spots

There are more than 600 active volcanoes on Earth. About half of these are in the "ring of fire" – on land and under the sea – which circles the Pacific Ocean; Indonesia alone has about 160 active volcanoes. Many islands are volcanic, such as the Hawaiian islands – and Iceland, which has about 200 active volcanoes.

Iceland

Hawaii

Indonesia

Ring of Fire

Pacific Ocean

Atlantic Ocean

∷ Main volcanic areas

Living dangerously

A blanket of ash can cover the countryside when a volcano explodes. But the ash helps make the soil very fertile, and many people risk the danger of living near an active volcano. Three crops of rice a year can be grown on the slopes of Gunung Agung, in Bali, a volcano which exploded in 1963, killing 2,000 people.

Eruptions

On average, between 20-30 volcanoes erupt each year. A few volcanoes erupt more or less all the time, such as the island of Stromboli, Italy, which shoots a shower of glowing ash into the sky every 20 minutes or so. Other volcanoes are dormant; sometimes they do not erupt for tens or hundreds of years. Mount Etna, in Sicily, has erupted about 150 times in the last 3,500 years.

Rivers of fire

Lava is fiery hot molten rock – up to 1200°C (2190°F). On Mount Tolbachik, in the Kamchatka Peninsula, USSR, in 1975, the lava flow gushed out at 168 m (550 ft) a second. And when Laki, in Iceland, exploded in 1782, the hot lava flowed a distance of about 65 km (40 miles).

Hot water

Underground water is heated by the hot rocks in volcanic areas. The water can bubble to the surface as a hot spring, or can spout high in the air as a geyser – a jet of steam and scalding water. Yellowstone Park in the USA has hot springs and 10,000 geysers; Old Faithful Geyser erupts 40 m (130 ft) high every 30-90 minutes.

Glowing clouds

Volcanoes can release clouds of ash, as well as cinders, gases and lava. Ash clouds can flow downhill at 200 km (124 miles) an hour, or can billow upwards. When Mayon, in the Philippines, erupted in 1968, ash and blocks of lava were hurled 600 m (1,968 ft) into the air, and the ash clouds rose to a height of 10 km (6 miles).

Mud avalanches

Some volcanic explosions trigger off a lethal avalanche of mud. When the Nevado del Ruiz, in Colombia, erupted in 1985, the heat melted the ice and snow on the peak. This caused a torrent of mud and water, which destroyed the town of Armero in five minutes, killing 20,000 people.

Major active volcanoes by continent			
Continent	Country	Volcano	Height
Asia	USSR	Kluchevskaya	4,750 m
Africa	Zaire	Nyiragongo	3,520 m
North America	Alaska	My Wrangell	4,270 m
South America	Argentina	Antofalla	6,127 m
Antarctica	Ross Island	Erebus	3,720 m
Europe	Sicily	Etna	3,340 m
Oceania	New Zealand	Ruapehu	2,797 m

DID YOU KNOW?

The largest active volcano on Earth is Mauna Loa, in Hawaii. It is 4,168 m (13,677 ft) high, and one eruption lasted for 1½ years.

Lava tubes

Lava flows can be 20 m (66 ft) thick, and can take several years to cool. Inside some flows are huge tunnels – lava tubes, as much as 10 m (33 ft) high. Hot lava hangs down from the tube roof as lava stalactites, and drips on to the tube floor, forming lava stalagmites.

Krakatoa

The loudest sound ever recorded was the eruption which blew up the island of Krakatoa, near Java, in 1883. The noise was heard in Australia, 4,800 km (3,000 miles) away, and the shock was felt in California, USA, 14,500 km (9,000 miles) away.

Rock and fire blasted 80 km (50 miles) up into the air. The wind carried volcanic dust around the Earth, causing vivid sunsets as far away as London, England. Tsunamis, huge waves 30 m (100 ft) high, crashed 16 km (10 miles) inland on Java and Sumatra, killing 36,000 people.

Natural resources

What are natural resources?

Many resources from the Earth provide light and heat, such as oil, coal and gas from under the ground, and firewood and charcoal from trees. And hot water and steam can be piped up from under the ground.

The power of the water in rivers, and the speed of the wind, are used to generate electricity. And sunlight is collected in solar panels and cells, to heat water and supply electricity.

Will natural resources last forever?

The supply of fossil fuels, that is oil, coal and gas, which were formed millions of years ago, will run out one day. At the rate we are burning them at present, scientists think that oil and gas may be used up in 70 years' time, and coal in 300 years' time. But there may be more supplies in the ground and under the sea which have not yet been found.

Oil rig

Twenty per cent of the world's oil comes from wells beneath the sea. One North Sea oil rig can produce up to 320,000 litres (70,400 gallons) of oil a day. At an average of 55 litres (12 gallons) each, that would fill the petrol tanks of 5,800 cars.

Coal supply

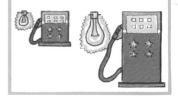

Coal was mined by the Romans as long ago as the 1st century AD. But there is still a huge amount of coal in the ground. These countries have the biggest reserves of coal.

USSR	UK
USA	Poland
China	Australia
West Germany	

DID YOU KNOW?

Only 5.5 per cent of the world's population live in the USA. But they use nearly 29 per cent of the world's petrol and nearly 33 per cent of the world's electricity.

Sources of energy

These are the major natural resources that are used for energy on Earth today.

Source of energy		Per cent
🝗🝗🝗🝗🝗	Oil	39
🪨🪨🪨🪨🪨	Coal	27
💧💧💧💧💧💧	Gas	17
🌳🌳🌳🌳	Fuelwood/charcoal	12
🌊🌊	Hydro (water) power	2
⛲⛲⛲⛲⛲	Other, such as underground heat and hot water springs	2
🏭🏭🏭🏭🏭	Nuclear power	1

River power

The force of flowing water in rivers and over waterfalls is used to generate nearly one-quarter of the world's electricity. These are some of the countries using water power to make their electricity.

Country	Per cent
Norway	100
Brazil	93
Switzerland	79
Canada	70
France	50
Italy	50
Japan	30
West Germany	20
USA	20
USSR	20

Boiling water

Hot water is piped from under the ground in Iceland, and used to heat homes, factories – and outdoor swimming pools. The capital city, Reykjavik, is supplied with 250 litres (55 gallons) of boiling water every second.

Products from fossil fuels

Many products are made from coal and oil. These are just a few examples.

Products from coal

Plastics
Heavy chemicals
Perfumes
Insectides
Antiseptics
Road surfaces
Coal gas

Products from oil

Petrol (gasoline)
Kerosene (jet fuel)
Diesel fuel
Paraffin wax
Pharmaceuticals
Explosives
Pesticides
Detergents
Cosmetics
Adhesives
Polishes
Paints
Nylon
Plastics

Using the Sun

Solar panels in the roofs of houses trap the heat from the Sun. Many homes in Israel, Canada, Australia and Japan have solar panels. Panels covering as little as 3 sq m (32 sq ft) can heat as much as 226 litres (50 gallons) of water a day – enough for 2 baths and all the washing up.

Rocks, minerals and metals

The rocks of the Earth's crust

The Earth's crust is made up of different kinds of rocks. They all belong to one of the 3 rock families, which are called igneous, sedimentary and metamorphic. These are some examples of the different families.

Igneous rocks

Igneous rocks are made from hot, molten rock, deep inside the Earth's mantle.

Granite
Hard, coarse-grained rock

Basalt
Hard, fine-grained rock

Obsidian
Black or greenish volcanic glass

Sedimentary rocks

Sedimentary rocks are layers made from worn fragments of rock, and may contain the remains of plants and animals.

Limestone
Hard rock; often contains lots of shells

Chalk
Soft rock; contains remains of small animals and shells

Sandstone
Formed from beach, river or desert sands

Metamorphic rocks

Metamorphic rocks are made from rocks which are pushed back down in the mantle, where they change under heat and pressure into different rocks.

Slate
Formed under high pressure from shale

Marble
Formed under heat from different limestones

Quartzite
Formed under heat and high pressure from sandstone

Minerals

The rocks of the Earth's crust contain a mixture of over 2,000 minerals. But about 90 per cent of the crust is made up of just 20 minerals, such as mica, quartz and feldspar. These are the uses of some minerals.

Mineral	Use
Graphite	Lead pencil
Gypsum	School chalk
Silica	Glass, mirrors
Potassium Sodium	Fertilizers
Fluorite	Toothpaste
Cobalt	Blue colouring
Sodium chloride	Household salt

Elementary!

Rocks are a mixture of one or more minerals. Minerals are made up of chemical elements. These are the chemical elements found in the greatest quantity in the Earth's crust.

Name of element	Per cent
Oxygen	46.60
Silicon	27.72
Aluminium	8.13
Iron	5.00
Calcium	3.63
Sodium	2.82
Potassium	2.59
Magnesium	2.09 = 98.6%
Titanium	0.44
Hydrogen	0.14
Phosphorus	0.12
Manganese	0.10
Fluorine	0.08
Sulphur	0.05
Chlorine	0.04
Carbon	0.03 = 1.0%
Others, including gold and silver	0.41 = 0.4%

Sparklers

About 100 minerals, because of their beauty and rarity, are known as gemstones, such as diamonds and sapphires. Emeralds and rubies are the most valuable gems; they are the rarest.

DID YOU KNOW?

Minerals are graded according to their hardness, on a scale from 1 to 10. Talc, used as talcum powder, is the softest mineral, rated 1; quartz rates 7. Diamond is rated 10 – the hardest mineral on Earth. Only a diamond can be used to cut and polish another diamond.

Diamond bright

Diamonds are found in a rainbow of colours – white, yellow, pink, green, blue, brown, red and black. In the ground, they usually look like dull, rounded pebbles – they only glitter and shine once they have been cut and polished. The small and badly-coloured diamonds are used in cutting tools.

Metalwork

Many of the metals in the rocks of the Earth's crust, such as silver, tin, mercury, iron and lead, have been mined for thousands of years. In the Middle East, 8,000 years ago, copper and gold were used for making jewellery. The gold mask of the Pharaoh Tutankhamun was made over 3,000 years ago.

Gold diggers

Miners today have to dig as much as 2 tonnes (2 tons) of rock to find only 28 grams (1 oz) of gold. If the 50 million tonnes of waste rock from just one South African gold mine were spread out, the rock would bury Manhattan island, New York, USA, under a layer 2.4 m (8 ft) deep.

Changing the world

The people on Earth

The Earth has a limited amount of oil and coal, wood and soil. People are using up these natural resources at an alarming rate, as well as spoiling the landscape and polluting the water and air – and may be changing the future of the Earth.

Croplands

Trees and hedges have been dug up to make enormous fields. One cornfield in the American Midwest can be 810 hectares (2,000 acres) in size. This makes harvesting the crops easier. But growing the same crop every year makes the soil less fertile and the harvest becomes smaller each year. And pests can destroy whole fields of crops.

Deserts

The deserts of the world are growing bigger, taking over the farmland at the edges, because of creeping sand dunes. The Sahara Desert alone is expanding southwards at an average of 0.8 km (½ mile) a month.

Water pollution

Chemical waste from factories is dumped or washed into seas, lakes and rivers, where it kills fish and plants. The Mediterranean Sea is one of the most polluted areas of water on Earth. In some places, the surface is now covered with a thin film of oil spilled from ships, and it is not safe to swim.

The changing climate

Some scientists think that burning coal and oil, and burning tropical forests, might lead to a change in the weather – the Earth might grow warmer, by as much as 7°C (12.5°F) at the Poles. This would melt some of the ice, and sea levels could rise by up to 7 m (23 ft), drowning all the ports.

Other scientists think that the dust produced by burning coal, oil and wood could block out some of the Sun's rays. The Earth might become colder – great sheets of ice could cover the northern hemisphere at least as far south as London, England.

Farmland

Only 11 per cent of the Earth's land is used for farming. But each year, less and less land can be used for growing crops and grazing cattle because the soil is washed away by the rain or blown away by the wind.

In the 1930s, farmers in the American Southwest ploughed up the plains to grow wheat. But as much as 25 cm (10 in) of soil was blown away by the wind – creating the Dust Bowl, where no plants could grow.

DID YOU KNOW?

Every year, the amount of trees cut down could cover a city the size of Birmingham, England, with a pile of wood, ten storeys high.

Vanishing forest

Forests cover just over a quarter of the Earth. But every year, forests the size of England, Scotland and Wales are cut down or spoilt. By the year 2000, one-third of all the tropical forests may have been destroyed.

Too much traffic

The exhaust fumes from cars, buses and trucks can poison the air. More than one-third of West Germany's Black Forest is dying, probably from the effect of these fumes. Cities, such as Los Angeles, USA and Tokyo, Japan, are often covered with a thick, choking smog. This is caused by the reaction of exhaust fumes and sunlight.

Acid rain

Factories and power stations burning oil and coal put huge amounts of poisonous gases and chemicals into the air. These combine with rain and snow and can fall hundreds of kilometres away, destroying forests and killing all the life in lakes.

Carried by the wind, pollution from British factories has killed many of the fish and plants in 18,000 lakes in Sweden. And more than half the pollution which falls on Canada comes from the USA.

Mining

Mining for minerals, such as bauxite, can destroy vast areas of land, and can cause pollution. Waste from copper mining in Malaysia has been washed into rivers, poisoning the fish.

The Earth's future

The people on Earth

Over the centuries, people have made great changes to the Earth – many of them bad. But people are now trying to do something to look after the soil, recycle rubbish and help stop some of the air and water pollution.

Cleaning up

Polluted lakes and rivers can be cleaned up. Filters fitted to power stations can remove some of the gases pouring into the air, or some of the gases can be treated and turned into fertilizer. Fish now swim in the River Thames, once one of the most polluted rivers in Europe, because factory wastes are treated and not dumped in the river.

Terracing

Heavy rain can wash the soil away on steep mountain slopes. Building terraces holds back the soil, and crops can be grown. There are terraces in Bali, where three crops of rice can be grown each year.

Pest control

In parts of China, ducks are used instead of pesticides to control insect pests in rice fields. In the Big Sand commune, thousands of ducks eat about 200 insects each an hour. This system has another advantage, because rain can wash the pesticide off the fields into lakes and rivers, where it pollutes the water.

Saving water

Spraying crops with water in dry areas is very wasteful because so much is lost in evaporation. Huge amounts of water can be saved by giving plants small measured amounts of water, through holes in thin plastic tubes. In Israel, computers control when to turn the water off and on and when to give the plants fertilizer.

Looking after the soil

The soil can be made more fertile by growing different crops together, rather than growing only one crop. In Java, pineapples and winged beans are grown in alternate rows, which keeps the soil fertile.

Tree planting

More trees are being planted, to supply wood for industry, and fuel for heating and cooking. In South Korea, where most of the wood is used for fuel, 70 per cent of the country has now been planted with young trees. And in Gujarat, India, school children are planting tree seedlings, to provide wood for heating and cooking.

Recycling rubbish

Rubbish can be sorted and recycled. Over half the aluminium drinks cans in the USA are melted down and recycled. In Britain, glass bottles are sorted into different colours, melted and reused.

Planting the desert

Expanding deserts can be stopped by planting bushes at the edges to hold back the sand dunes. And the bushes can be used for crops too – jojoba produces liquid wax, and guayule and a type of dandelion can produce latex, which is used as rubber.

Farming the wind

Electricity can be generated by windmills – rather than by power stations which burn oil or coal. Fields full of windmills could supply 8 per cent of electricity in California, USA by the year 2000. A wind "farm", with about 4,600 windmills, can supply as many as 30,000 homes with electricity.

Saving coal and oil

Using rubbish for fuel saves oil or coal. In Edmonton, England, electricity is generated by burning about 2 per cent of Britain's total rubbish, saving about 100,000 tonnes of coal each year.

Saving trees

About 35 million trees could be saved each year, if 75 per cent of waste paper and cardboard was recycled into pulp and used to make new paper.

DID YOU KNOW?

A quarter of all the cars in Brazil run on fuel made from sugar cane, and half the cars in South Africa use fuel made from liquid coal.

Earth map

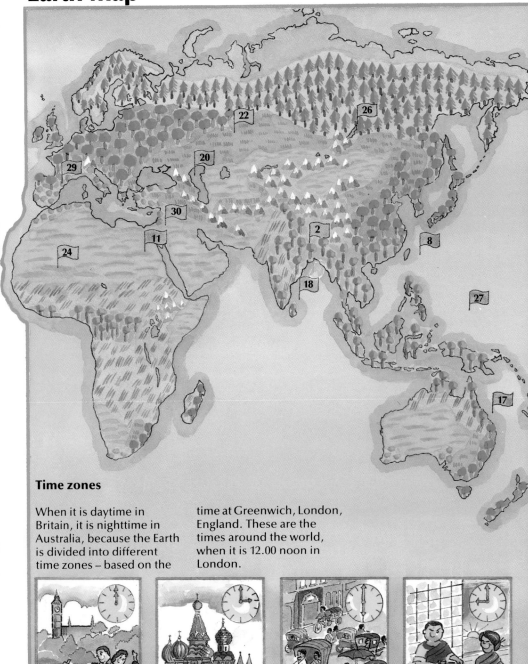

Time zones

When it is daytime in Britain, it is nighttime in Australia, because the Earth is divided into different time zones – based on the time at Greenwich, London, England. These are the times around the world, when it is 12.00 noon in London.

London, England

Moscow, USSR

Dacca, Bangladesh

Tokyo, Japan

44

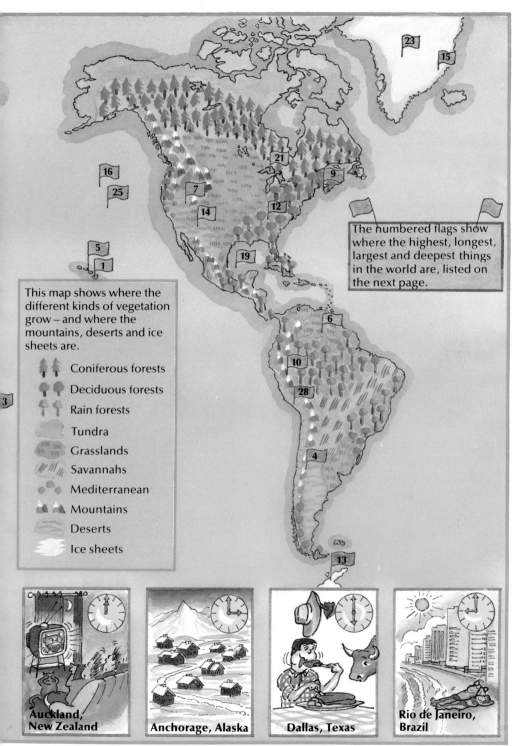

The numbered flags show where the highest, longest, largest and deepest things in the world are, listed on the next page.

This map shows where the different kinds of vegetation grow – and where the mountains, deserts and ice sheets are.

Coniferous forests
Deciduous forests
Rain forests
Tundra
Grasslands
Savannahs
Mediterranean
Mountains
Deserts
Ice sheets

Auckland, New Zealand

Anchorage, Alaska

Dallas, Texas

Rio de Janeiro, Brazil

The Earth in a nutshell

The highest . . .

1 Mountain on Earth
Mauna Kea, Hawaii
10,023 m measured from
the sea floor

2 Mountain on land
Mount Everest, Nepal/Tibet
8,843 m

3 Mountain under the sea
Near Tonga Trench, Tonga
Islands, Pacific Ocean
8,690 m

4 Active volcano
Antofalla, Argentina
6,127 m

5 Sea cliffs
Umilehi Point, Moloka'i,
Hawaii
1,005 m

6 Waterfall
Angel Falls, Venezuela
979 m

7 Active geyser
Service Steamboat Geyser,
Yellowstone, USA
Maximum 115 m

8 Tsunami
Ishigaki Island, Japan
85 m

9 Tide
Bay of Fundy, Nova Scotia,
Canada
Range of 14.5 m

The longest . . .

10 Mountain range
Andes, South America
7,240 km

11 River
River Nile, Egypt
6,670 km

12 Cave system
Mammoth Cave National
Park, Kentucky, USA
484 km

13 Glacier
Lambert/Mellor, Antarctica
402 km

14 Canyon
Grand Canyon on Colorado
River, Arizona, USA
349 km

15 Fjord
Nordvest Fjord, Greenland
313 km

The largest . . .

16 Ocean
Pacific Ocean
165,384,000 sq km

17 Sea
Coral Sea (part of Pacific
Ocean)
4,790,000 sq km

18 Bay
Bay of Bengal
2,172,000 sq km

19 Gulf
Gulf of Mexico
1,544,000 sq km

20 Inland sea
Caspian Sea, Iran/USSR
372,000 sq km

21 Lake
Lake Superior, Canada/USA
82,414 sq km

22 Continent
Asia
44,391,200 sq km

23 Island
Greenland
2,175,000 sq km

24 Desert
Sahara Desert, North Africa
8,400,000 sq km

The deepest . . .

25 Ocean
Pacific Ocean
Average depth 4,000 m

26 Lake
Lake Baikal, USSR
Maximum 1,940 m

27 Sea trench
Mariana Trench, Pacific
Ocean
11,033 m

28 Canyon
Colca Canyon, Peru
3,223 m

29 Cave
Gouffre Jean Bernard,
France
1,535 m

30 Land below sea level
Dead Sea, Israel/Jordan
395 m

Index

COUNTRIES
OF THE WORLD
FACTS

Neil Champion

CONTENTS

Designed by Stephen Meir, Joe Coonan,
Anil Dumasia and Tony Gibson

Illustrated by Tony Gibson
Additional illustrations by Mario Saporito,
Ian Jackson and Chris Lyon

Researched by Margaret Harvey and Karen Medd

Country facts

The 5 largest countries
(square km)

Russian Federation	17,100,000
Canada	9,976,000
China	9,597,000
USA	9,363,000
Brazil	8,512,000

The 5 smallest countries
(square km)

Vatican City	0.4
Monaco	2
Nauru	21
Tuvalu	26
San Marino	61

The largest island

Greenland is the largest island. It is almost 10 times larger than Britain but only 57,000 people live there. This means that if all the people were spread out evenly, each person would have 10,000 times as much room as each person living in Britain.

Longest coastline

Canada has a very jagged coastline 250,000 km (155,000 miles) long. If straightened out it would stretch around the world over 6 times.

Record reigns

A six year-old boy who became Pharaoh of Egypt in 2,281 BC reigned for a record 94 years. The shortest reign was in 1908 when the King of Portugal was shot dead and his son was mortally wounded at the same time. The son survived his father as King for only 20 minutes. Japan has the longest ruling house. Present Emperor Akihito is 125th in line from Emperor Zinmu (40 to 10 BC).

The biggest desert

The world's largest desert is the Sahara. It covers part or all of 10 northern and west African countries, including Chad, Niger, Libya, Algeria, Egypt, Mali and Mauritania. It is larger than Australia, the world's sixth largest country. A person left in the desert with no water or shade would die in a day. The temperature can reach 50°C (122°F).

DID YOU KNOW?

The Vatican City, the smallest country in the world, has a population the size of a small village – 1,000 people. One hundred of these are Swiss Guards; their uniforms were designed by Michelangelo in the 15th century.

Amazing But True

Antarctica contains 70 per cent of the world's fresh water in the form of ice. In 1958, one iceberg was spotted that was thought to be the size of Belgium. Antarctica has large deposits of minerals, oil and natural gas, but it is not officially owned by any country.

The largest lake

Lake Superior in Canada is the largest lake in the world. If it were drained of all its water, the land reclaimed would cover an area twice the size of the Netherlands.

Years of education

Most countries have laws about the number of years children must spend at school. In Belgium, children attend for at least 12 years, whereas in Bangladesh and Vietnam it is 5 years.

Without a coast

There are over 30 countries without a coastline. Switzerland is one, but it still maintains its own merchant navy.

Busy frontier

More than 120 million people cross the border between Mexico and the USA every year, making it the busiest frontier. The least busy frontier used to be between East and West Germany, where the Berlin Wall once stood. The wall was pulled down in 1990.

How many countries?

There are now about 200 countries whereas in 1900 there were only 53. It is not possible to say exactly what today's figure is as there are many changes taking place world-wide.

DID YOU KNOW?

China shares its frontiers with 16 other countries:

North Korea	1.	Bhutan	11.
Russia	2.	Burma	12.
Mongolia	3.	Laos	13.
Kazakhstan	4.	Vietnam	14.
Kyrgyzstan	5.	Macau	15.
Tajikistan	6.	Hong Kong	16.
Afghanistan	7.		
Pakistan	8.		
India	9. 9a. 9b.		
Nepal	10.		

Country of islands

Indonesia is made up of over 13,000 islands, together covering about 2 million sq km (770,000 sq miles). This is equal to the area of Mexico.

51

Populations

Largest populations

China	1,155,800,000
India	849,640,000
USA	249,920,000
Indonesia	187,760,000
Brazil	153,320,000

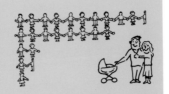

Age distribution

In Africa almost half the population is under 15 years old and only 3 out of 100 can expect to live to 65. The situation in Europe is very different. Only one fifth of the population is under 15 and 12 in every 100 live to be 65.

Population density

Although Australia has a population 3 times larger than Hong Kong, it is 8,000 times larger in area. If the people were spread out evenly over the land each Australian would have 500,000 sq m (5,382,000 sq ft) compared with only 200 sq m (2,153 sq ft) for each person in Hong Kong.

DID YOU KNOW?

The population of New York, the USA's largest city, is only 3 per cent of the entire population. The population of Mexico City, Mexico's largest city, is 20 per cent of the population.

Life expectations

Men and women live to an average age of 77 years in Iceland and to an average age of 76 in both Sweden and Japan. In Yemen and Ethiopia people can expect to live about 40 years.

AGE

(bar chart showing ages: Iceland, Sweden, Japan, Yemen, Ethiopia)

Crowded countries
(people per sq km)

Macao	25,882
Monaco	15,789
Hong Kong	5,308
Singapore	4,228
Vatican City	2,500
Bermuda	1,132
Malta	1,076
Bangladesh	824
Bahrain	772
Maldives	762

More men or women?

For every agricultural worker in Belgium there are at least 10 industrial workers. In Portugal there are almost as many people working on the land as there are in industry.

There are about 20 million more women than men living in Russia. This works out to a ratio of 7 women for every 6 men. But world-wide there are slightly more men than women.

Amazing But True

The world population in 1991 was over 5 billion. It is increasing daily, which means that 200 babies are born a minute. At this rate, the world's population will be over 6 billion by AD 2000.

The emptiest countries
(people per sq km)

Western Sahara	0.5
Mongolia	1.3
Botswana	1.9
Mauritania	1.9
Australia	2.1
Namibia	2.1
Iceland	2.4
Libya	2.4
Surinam	2.5
Canada	2.8

Where no-one is born

In the Vatican City no one is born. This is because married people do not live there. It has a population that remains around 1,000. Kenya, on the other hand, has one of the highest recorded birth rates, with a 5 per cent annual increase in population. This is over twice the world-wide average.

Religions of the world

Christianity is the largest religion, with one third of the world belonging to it. Islam (Muslim) is the second largest, with 900 million worshippers (just over half the number of Christians).

Amazing But True

At its present rate of increase, Honduras will double its population by the year AD 2005.

Rich and poor countries

World incomes

Half the population of the world earns a mere 5 per cent of the world's total wealth. A very rich 15 per cent takes two thirds of this wealth.

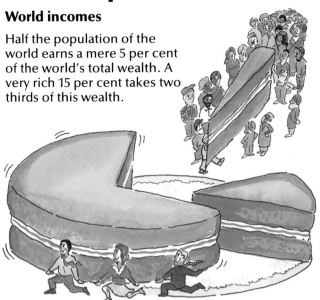

The poorest people?

By Western standards the Tasaday tribe, who live in the Philippines, are one of the poorest people in the world. They live in caves and do not keep any animals, do not grow crops, make pots or clothes or even use wheels.

How many doctors? (people per doctor)

Top 5 countries		Bottom 5 countries	
Former USSR*	235	Ethiopia	100,000
Italy	236	Burkina	42,128
Austria	256	Malawi	41,108
United Arab		Niger	40,209
Emirates	666	Burundi	20,942
UK	668		

How many people can read and write?

(per 100 people)

Top 5 countries

France	99
Italy	99
Barbados	98
USA	96
Israel	92

Bottom 5 countries

Ethiopia	9
Somalia	12
Niger	14
Afghanistan	33
Haiti	35

DID YOU KNOW?

In Iceland there are 61 people on average for each hospital bed. In Bangladesh there are 4,586 people per bed, 75 times as many people for each bed as there are in Iceland.

*Figures are not yet available for the Russian Federation.

Electricity at home

In developed countries most homes have electricity. In poorer countries many families do not. Only 3 per cent of the homes in Haiti, 18 per cent in Paraguay and Pakistan and 25 per cent in Thailand have electricity.

Pakistan

Thailand

Paraguay

Haiti

Water in our homes

In many parts of the world only a few people are lucky enough to have piped water in their homes. In countries like Afghanistan, Ethiopia and Nepal less than one in 10 homes do.

Countries in debt

Many countries have to borrow money from world banks. These countries have the biggest debts:

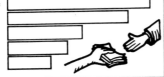

Brazil	$116 billion*
Mexico	$97 billion
Argentina	$61 billion
Poland	$49 billion
Nigeria	$36 billion

Amazing But True

The 400 richest citizens in the USA have a combined wealth of $288 billion*. One saw his fortune increase by $1 billion in a year. This is 12½ million times the average annual wage of a person in Bhutan.

Privately owned cars (people per car)

Top 5 countries		Bottom 5 countries	
Guam	1.1	Bangladesh	2,950
USA	1.5	Burma	1,460
Australia	2.2	Ethiopia	1,200
New Zealand	2.2	Uganda	1,425
Brunei	2.4	Somalia	950

Rich and poor countries

(To find out the average annual income for people in different countries, we have taken the wealth a country makes in a year and divided it by the number of people who live there.)

Switzerland	$37,361*
Sweden	$22,448
Luxembourg	$21,281
USA	$20,702
Bhutan	$150
Chad	$130
Ethiopia	$120
Mozambique	$95

Natural products

Top 5 wool producers
(tonnes per year)

Australia	1,100,000
Former USSR	471,000
New Zealand	304,000
China	240,000
Argentina	146,000

Most important fibre

Cotton is the world's most important fibre. It was made into cloth over 3,000 years ago in India and Central America. Today it is used to make lace, clothes, sheets, carpets, and industrial products such as thread, film, plastics and special paper.

Top 5 cotton producers
(tonnes per year)

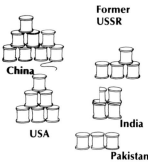

China	5,100,000
USA	3,819,000
Former USSR	2,420,000
India	2,193,000
Pakistan	1,785,000

Amazing But True

The Dutch grow and sell about 3,000 million flowers a year. This is 80,000 flowers for every sq km in the country.

Top 5 tobacco producers
(tonnes per year)

China	2,501,000
USA	732,000
India	510,000
Brazil	431,000
Former USSR	240,000

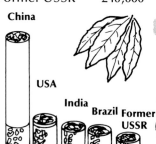

Most expensive oil

The most expensive oil used in perfumes is Musk oil. It sells at $633* for 28 gms or 1 oz. It comes from glands of the male Musk deer, which are found in the mountains of Korea and Mongolia.

Fastest growing plant

Bamboo, used for making window blinds, furniture, floor mats and poles, is one of the fastest growing plants. It can shoot up 90 cms (36 ins) in a day and reaches a height of around 30 m (100 ft). It grows in India, the Far East and China.

*See page 96

Expensive spice

One of the most expensive spices is saffron. It comes from a crocus flower and is used to colour and give an aroma to rice dishes. Grown in China, France, Spain and Iran, over 200,000 stamens are needed to make ½ kilo (1 lb).

The secret of silk

Silk comes from the cocoon of the silkworm. One cocoon contains about a kilometre of thread. It came originally from China, where for hundreds of years its source was kept a secret. One story tells us that in 140 BC a Chinese princess hid some eggs of the silkworm in her hair and took them to Turkestan. From there silk was brought to Europe.

Top 5 rubber producers (tonnes per year)	
Malaysia	1,300,000
Indonesia	1,200,000
Thailand	1,165,000
India	315,000
China	258,000

Amazing But True

Wild ginseng roots, found in China and Korea, sell for £10,000* for 28 gms (1 oz).

DID YOU KNOW?

Tobacco was first smoked by the American Indians. It was brought to Europe in the 16th century as an ornamental plant. The habit of smoking the dried leaves did not catch on until some years later.

Where rubber comes from

Rubber comes from the sap (called latex) of the rubber tree. To drain it out, the bark has to be cut. Long before Europeans explored the jungles of Central and South America (the original home of the rubber tree) Indians were using latex to waterproof their clothes and footwear.

Best quality wool

Merino wool comes from a breed of sheep that was originally found in Spain. It is considered the best quality wool.

*See page 96

57

Fuel and energy

Top 10 coal producers
(millions of tonnes per year)

China	1,086	Australia	168
USA	823	Poland	141
Former USSR	409	UK	96
India	222	Germany	73
South Africa	177	North Korea	41

DID YOU KNOW?

More than one third of the world's population still depends on wood for fuel. In some areas of Africa and Asia, timber provides 80 per cent of energy needs. This is equivalent to the use developed nations make of gas and nuclear power.

Fuel consumption

An average American uses about 1,000 times as much fuel in his or her life as does an average Nepalese citizen and about twice as much as a European.

World's largest oil platform

The largest oil platform is the Statfjord B, built at Stavanger in Norway. It weighs 816,000 tonnes, cost £1.1 billion*to construct and needed 8 tugs to tow it into position. It is the heaviest object ever moved in one piece.

Nuclear submarines

The first nuclear-powered submarine *(The Nautilus)* was built in the USA in 1955. It travelled 530,000 km (330,000 miles) using only 5 kg (12 lb) of nuclear fuel. A car covering the same distance at an average speed would use 38,000 litres of petrol (8,250 gallons).

Amazing But True

If we could make use of all solar, wind, water and wave power that exists on the earth's surface, we would have 20 billion times as much energy as we need at present.

Top 10 producers of petroleum
(millions of tonnes per year)

Former USSR	584,900
USA	417,600
Saudi Arabia	327,100
Iran	155,300
Mexico	145,300
China	139,000
Venezuela	119,400
Iraq	98,200
Canada	93,300
UK	91,600

*See page 96

Longest oil pipeline

The longest oil pipeline stretches from Edmonton, Canada, to Buffalo in New York State, USA. This is a distance of 2,856 km (1,775 miles). If it were laid out like a road, it would take a car 2 days to drive along it doing an average speed of 60 km (38 miles) an hour.

Fuels used in industry since 1850

	1850	1900	1950	2000
Wood	65%	37%	—	—
Coal	10%	55%	59%	—
Oil	—	8%	32%	15%
Gas	—	—	9%	48%
Nuclear	—	—	—	37%

Cause for alarm

By the year AD 2100 some scientists believe that the world could have run out of oil, coal and gas. This may cause some problems as it has also been estimated that we will be using 5½ times as much energy as today.

Top 10 consumers of petroleum

(millions of tonnes per year)

USA	778,900
Former USSR	402,600
Japan	245,000
Germany	126,200
Italy	92,300
France	88,700
UK	82,400
Canada	74,800
Mexico	73,845
Brazil	57,931

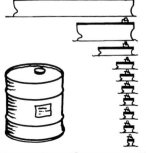

Top 5 producers of uranium (nuclear fuel)

(tonnes per year)

Canada	7,813
Australia	3,776
USA	3,000
Niger	2,964
Namibia	2,450

Amazing But True

One tonne of nuclear fuel can produce as much energy as 20,000 tonnes of coal. The first nuclear power station to produce electricity was opened in 1951 in the USA.

Metals and precious gems

World's deepest mine

The Western Deep gold mine in South Africa is 3,480 m (12,720 ft) deep. This makes it almost 9 times deeper than the tallest building is high and about 2½ times deeper than the deepest cave. It has a temperature up to 55°C (131°F) at the bottom and is cooled by special refrigerators for people working there.

Top 5 copper producers
(tonnes per year)

Chile	1,814,400
USA	1,635,400
Former USSR	900,000
Canada	777,000
Zambia	412,200

Lighter than steel

Aluminium is used to make beer and soft drink cans. A very light metal, it is replacing steel in such things as aircraft, cars, cameras, window-frames and bicycles.

Top 5 tin producers
(tonnes per year)

China	35,800
Brazil	31,000
Indonesia	29,700
Malaysia	20,700
Former USSR	13,000

Commonest precious metal

Silver is the commonest precious metal. It is lighter than gold. About half the silver mined is used as a coating for photographic film.

Largest underground mine

The San Manuel Mine in Arizona, USA, is the largest underground mine. This copper mine has over 573 km (350 miles) of tunnels. If laid out in a straight line, the tunnels would reach Los Angeles, California.

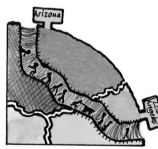

Top 10 iron ore miners
(tonnes per year)

Former USSR	251,000,000
Brazil	131,600,000
China	100,000,000
Australia	100,000,000
India	52,000,000
USA	47,600,000
Canada	37,600,000
South Africa	22,000,000
Sweden	19,600,000
Venezuela	17,800,000

Worth its weight

Platinum is the most expensive metal in the world. Unlike silver, it does not tarnish and is used in jewellery for mounting precious gems.

Amazing But True

South Africa produces more than twice as much gold per year as either of its nearest rivals, the former USSR and the USA. It mines 600 tonnes. 28 gms of pure gold can be beaten into a fine wire, 88 km (55 miles) long.

Top 5 lead producers
(tonnes per year)

USA	1,291,000
Former USSR	730,000
Germany	394,000
Japan	329,000
UK	329,000

Top 5 aluminium miners
(tonnes per year)

USA	4,048,300
Former USSR	2,200,000
Canada	1,600,000
Australia	1,200,000
Brazil	930,000

USA
Former USSR
Canada
Australia
Brazil

DID YOU KNOW?

The world's most valuable gem stone is not the diamond but the ruby. The largest cut stone comes from Burma and weighs 1184 carats (one carat = 200 mgs). It is thought to be worth over $7½ million.*

*See page 96

DID YOU KNOW?

The *Cullinan*, once the largest uncut diamond, was discovered in South Africa in 1905. It was the size of a man's fist and weighed over ½ kg (1 lb). The largest gem cut from it, named the 'Star of Africa', is in the British Royal Sceptre in the Tower of London.

The oldest gems

India has records going back to 300 BC that tell us about the mining of moonstones, sapphires, diamonds, emeralds, garnets and agates.

The golden fleece

Some streams and rivers carry gold particles after running over rocks containing the precious metal. An ancient method of extracting this gold was to put a sheep's fleece in the stream, trapping the tiny pieces of metal in the wool.

A tough gem

Diamonds are 90 times harder than any other naturally occurring substance. Some are used in industry for cutting very hard substances. Dentists use them on their drills.

City of Jewels

Ratnapura, in Sri Lanka, is known as the 'City of Jewels' because of the amazing variety of gems found there. These include sapphires, diamonds and rubies.

61

Business and industry

Top 5 car producers
(cars per year)

Japan	9,753,000	
USA	5,440,000	
Germany	4,700,000	
France	3,188,000	
Spain	1,750,000	

DID YOU KNOW?

China makes three times as many bicycles as its closest rivals, the USA and Japan. If the 17½ million made in a year were ridden end to end they would stretch three quarters of the way round the world.

Giant companies

Some of the world's largest companies earn more money in a year than many countries. For example, the US car giant, General Motors, has sales of around $127 billion* – more than Belgium's national income.

Stock exchanges

In stock exchanges governments and companies sell shares to raise money. There are 138 in the world at present. The oldest is in Amsterdam and dates back to 1602. The stock exchange in Tokyo holds the record for the largest amount of trading ($1,450 billion* in 1990).

The largest tanker

The *Happy Giant*, a Japanese supertanker built in 1981, is the largest tanker in the world. It is almost ½ km (a third of a mile) long, equal to about 5 football pitches end to end. It can carry 565,000 tonnes of crude oil around the world. It would take 15 of these supertankers to supply the USA with her daily needs of imported oil, or 5,500 ordinary tankers every year.

Most expensive offices

The most expensive city to rent office space in is Tokyo, where 1 sq m (11 sq ft) costs $2,600*. Even a very small company could expect to pay over $20,000 per year for floor space.

Who makes the most?
(amount produced per year)

Typewriters	Japan	2,998,000
Refrigerators	Former USSR	5,993,000
Socks	Former USSR	976,000,000
Calculators	Japan	52,435,000
Pianos	Japan	360,338

*See page 96

The power of oil

Over 30 countries in the world make money from oil export. The countries of the Middle East are thought of as big producers of oil, but Mexico, Britain, the former USSR, Nigeria and Venezuela are often forgotten. Oil accounts for one quarter of world trade.

Largest papermill

The Union Camp Corporation at Savannah, Georgia, USA, is the largest papermill, producing almost 100,000 tonnes of paper a year. This is equal to about 28,000,000 sheets of A4 paper, or 250,000 paperback books, a day.

Top 5 radio producers	
(radios per year)	
Hong Kong	47,986,000
China	19,990,000
Singapore	15,165,000
Japan	13,338,000
USA	11,089,000

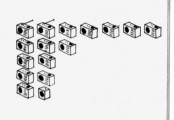

Top 5 TV producers	
(sets per year)	
Japan	13,275,000
USA	12,084,000
Former USSR	8,578,000
South Korea	7,641,000
China	6,840,000

The oldest company

The Faversham Oyster Fishery Company, Britain, has been going since before 1189. This makes it the oldest company on record.

Advertising products

The USA spends more money on advertising than all the other countries of the world put together. In 1978, during the Super Bowl football match final, the price of advertising on American TV was $325,000*a minute.

Amazing But True

Nippon Steel of Tokyo, Japan, produces about 27 million tonnes of steel a year. This is enough to cover all of Spain and Portugal if the steel was beaten out paper-thin.

Farming

Top grain and bean producers
(tonnes per year)

Soya beans	USA	54,039,000
Barley	Former USSR	42,000,000
Corn (maize)	USA	189,867,000
Wheat	China	95,000,000
Rice	China	187,450,000

Top 5 potato growers
(tonnes per year)

Former USSR	60,000,000
China	32,553,000
Poland	32,000,000
USA	18,919,000
India	15,655,000

Top 5 banana growers
(tonnes per year)

India	6,400,000
Brazil	5,410,000
Philippines	3,545,000
Ecuador	2,654,000
Indonesia	2,400,000

A field of wheat

About 750 years ago, an average sized field of wheat may have provided enough food for 5 people for a year. Today, the same field in a developed country would feed between 20 and 50 people for a year and supply enough seed to sow for the next crop.

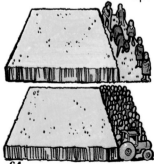

DID YOU KNOW?

The amount of protein produced from a field of soya beans is 13 times greater than the same field used to graze cattle for meat.

Largest mixed farms

Collective farming was common in the former USSR, where many people looked after their own section of a huge mixed (arable and dairy) farm. Farms could be over 25,000 hectares (62,000 acres) which is twice the size of Malta.

Top 5 beef producers
(tonnes per year)

USA	10,558,000
Former USSR	7,600,000
Brazil	2,800,000
Argentina	2,640,000
Germany	2,176,000

Top 5 cows' milk producers
(tonnes per year)

Former USSR	96,000,000
USA	67,420,000
Germany	29,800,000
India	27,000,000
France	26,600,000

A land of sheep

In Australia there are more than 3 times as many sheep as people. The largest sheep station is in South Australia. It is 1,040,000 hectares (2,560,000 acres). This is larger than Cyprus.

Top 5 grape growers
(tonnes per year)

Italy	9,300,000
France	7,020,000
Former USSR	5,400,000
Spain	5,107,000
USA	4,778,000

Top 5 sugar producers
(tonnes per year)

India	12,528,000
Former USSR	8,750,000
Brazil	8,675,000
China	7,836,000
Cuba	5,040,000

Experiments with food

What do you get when you cross the American buffalo with an ordinary cow? The beefalo of course! This animal has been bred to produce more meat to help world food production.

DID YOU KNOW?

American scientists have predicted that they will be able to breed cows weighing 4.5 tonnes. This is about the size of an elephant.

Amazing But True

A certain type of bacteria grown on petrol can be used as a source of food. The bacteria multiplies at a rate of 32,000,000 a day. It is harvested and processed into a highly nutritious food.

Top 5 butter producers
(tonnes per year)

Former USSR	1,570,000
India	1,040,000
Germany	653,000
USA	620,000
France	500,000

Forestry

Top 5 softwood log producers

(cubic metres per year)

USA	178,900,000
Former USSR	129,800,000
Canada	115,900,000
China	32,300,000
Sweden	22,400,000

Top 5 hardwood log producers

(cubic metres per year)

Brazil	34,900,000
Malaysia	31,000,000
USA	31,000,000
Indonesia	24,000,000
Former USSR	21,000,000

The tallest tree

The largest living thing on earth is the giant redwood tree, growing in the USA and Canada. The tallest is 112 m (367 ft) high. This is considerably taller than the Statue of Liberty, New York, which stands at 93 m (305 ft).

DID YOU KNOW?

The fastest growing tree in the world is the Eucalyptus. One tree in New Guinea grew 10.5 m (35 ft) in 1 year. This is almost 3 cm (over 1 in) a day. In contrast, a Sika Spruce inside the Arctic Circle takes some 98 years to grow 28 cm (11 in); some 4,000 times slower.

Forests in peril

Nearly half the world's rain forests have been cut down and are still being cut down at a rate of 24 sq km (9 sq miles) an hour or 200,000 sq km (80,000 sq miles) a year – an area almost the size of Britain.

The rubber tree

Rubber trees were originally found only in the Amazon rain forest. In 1876 Sir Henry Wickham shipped 70,000 seeds to Kew Gardens in London. Seedlings were then sent to Sri Lanka and Malaysia where rubber plantations were started.

World's largest forest

About 25 per cent of the world's forests cover an area of the Russian Federation and Scandinavia and extend as far as the Arctic Circle. It is the world's largest forest.

World of trees

There are about 40 million sq km (15 million sq miles) of forest in the world. This is more than the total area of the Russian Federation, Canada and China.

The oldest tree

Some bristlecone pines found in California, USA, are over 4,500 years old.

Top 5 producers of paper and board
(tonnes per year)

USA	71,519,000
Japan	28,086,000
Canada	16,466,000
China	13,719,000
Germany	11,873,000

A tree of gold

In 1959 a nursery in the USA bought a single Golden Delicious apple tree for $51,000 (at the time, £18,214)*, making it the most expensive tree the world has known.

The lightest wood

Wood from the Balsa tree weighs 40 kg per cubic metre (2½ lb per cubic ft). It is the world's lightest wood. The black ironwood tree is forty times heavier.

Amazing But True

In Borneo (Indonesia), a fire raged non-stop for 10 months from September 1982. It covered over 36,000 sq km (14,000 sq miles) and about 13,500 sq km (5,000 sq miles) of forest was destroyed. Several rare species of trees and wildlife were made extinct.

*See page 96

Fishing

Freezer trawlers

Fish caught at sea are often frozen on board the trawlers. They are gutted and left in piles to freeze together. Once back in port, they are defrosted, filleted and sold.

Over 95 per cent of all the fish caught in the world are caught in the northern hemisphere.

DID YOU KNOW?

A special substance found in the scales of some fish (especially herrings) is used to make a paint. This paint is coated on to glass beads to make imitation pearls.

Top fish-eating nation

The Japanese eat their way through 3,400 million kg (7,500 million lbs) of fish a year. This means that each person has an average 30 kg (65 lbs) of fish a year. They are the world's biggest fish-eating nation. Their nearest rivals, the Scandinavians, eat only half as much fish on average and the Americans only one fifth.

The most expensive fish

The Russian sturgeon fetches the highest price of any fish in the world. The eggs of the female sturgeon (caviare) are a prized delicacy. The best caviare costs over £28*for 50 gms (1¾ ozs) or £570 per kg (£258 per lb).

Top 5 most caught fish
(millions of tonnes per year)

Alaska Pollack	4.5
Japanese Pilchard	4
Chilean Pilchard	3.25
Atlantic Cod	2.25
Chilean Jack Mackerel	2

Top 3 oyster catchers
(tonnes per year)

Japan	250,288
Korea	189,204
USA	81,336

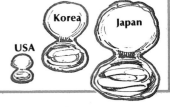

*See page 96

Greatest catch

The most fish ever caught in one haul was made by a Norwegian trawler. It is estimated that in one net it pulled on board more than 120 million fish; over 2,400 tonnes in all. This is enough to feed every man, woman and child in Norway for two weeks.

Largest fishing vessel

A whaling factory ship built in the former USSR in 1971, called *The Vostok*, weighs 26,400 tonnes, making it the largest fishing vessel in the world. It is 224.5 m (736.5 ft) long, which means that you could fit 9½ tennis courts end to end along its deck.

Fishing with birds

In Japan, cormorants are trained to catch fish and to fly back to a boat. Each bird is stopped from swallowing the fish by a tight leather collar around its neck.

Fish farming

Many countries now breed fish in special underwater farms. These are the leading countries in this sort of farming:

(in tonnes per year)

China	2,300,000
India	600,000
Former USSR	300,000
Japan	250,000
Indonesia	240,000

DID YOU KNOW?

Out of all the fish caught in the world, about three quarters are eaten as food. The other quarter is used to make such things as glue, soap, margarine, pet food and fertilizer.

Amazing But True

A prehistoric fish that was thought to have become extinct about 70 million years ago, was caught in the sea off South Africa. It is called the coelacanth and since 1938 many more of these fish have been caught.

Top 5 fishing countries
(tonnes per year)

Japan	11,841,000
Former USSR	11,159,000
China	9,346,200
USA	5,736,000
Chile	4,814,400

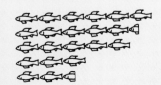

Food and drink

How many calories?

Calories measure the energy content of different foods. We all need a certain amount every day to make our bodies work properly. People in Europe and the USA eat about 3,500 calories a day. Many people in Africa and Asia have at most 1,600. Some people in these countries live on a very poor diet. This may consist of beans, vegetables and grains, and may be too low in calories and protein.

A world-wide drink

There are about 200 countries in the world and Coca-cola is sold in 185 of them. Every day 492 million servings are consumed. If all the cans sold in one month were placed on top of each other they would make three chains, each reaching the moon.

Top 5 wine producers
(tonnes per year)

France	6,200,000
Italy	6,000,000
Spain	3,107,000
Argentina	2,100,000
USA	1,580,000

Top 5 beer producers
(tonnes per year)

USA	23,655,000
Germany	11,806,000
China	6,926,000
Japan	6,232,000
UK	6,006,000

DID YOU KNOW?

The largest cake ever weighed over 58 tonnes. It was baked in the USA in 1989 to celebrate the 100th birthday of Fort Payne, Alabama.

Meals within meals

Bedouin sometimes prepare a meal of stuffed, roast camel for wedding feasts. They start by stuffing a fish with eggs, putting this inside a chicken, the chicken inside a whole roast sheep and the lot inside a cooked camel.

Most nutritious fruit

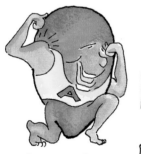

The avocado pear contains about 165 calories for every 100 gms of edible fruit. This is more than eggs or milk. It also contains twice as much protein as milk, and more vitamin A, B and C. In contrast, the cucumber has only 16 calories per 100 gms.

Most expensive food

L'Aquila white truffles from France cost £22.40* for 28 gms (1 oz), which is equivalent to £780 per kg (£358 per lb).

Top 5 honey producers
(tonnes per year)

Former USSR	240,000	
China	190,000	
USA	91,000	
Mexico	52,700	
Argentina	44,000	

Top 5 tea producers
(tonnes per year)

India	742,000
China	546,000
Sri Lanka	247,700
Kenya	203,600
Turkey	135,000

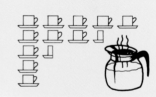

Top 5 coffee producers
(tonnes per year)

Brazil	1,286,000
Colombia	870,000
Indonesia	408,000
Mexico	299,000
Ivory Coast	240,000

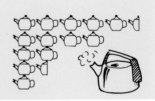

A monster melon

The largest melon weighed over 90 kg (14 stone). The size of a large human being, it would have fed 400 people.

Super sausage

A sausage-maker in Birmingham, Britain, made one specimen that was 9 km (5½ miles) long. This amounts to about 87,000 ordinary sausages.

*See page 96

Buildings and structures

The largest hotel

The world's largest hotel is the Excalibur Hotel and Casino in Nevada, USA. It has 4,032 deluxe rooms, 7 restaurants, and employs 4,000 staff. It opened in April 1990 and cost $290 million*.

DID YOU KNOW?

The most expensive hotel in the world is the Fairmont Hotel in San Francisco, USA. It costs $6,000* plus tax per night. This includes a butler and a maid, and a limousine service.

World's longest wall

The Great Wall of China stretches for 3,460 km (2,150 miles), ranges between 4½ and 12 m (15 and 40 ft) high, and is up to 10 m (32 ft) thick. Another 2,860 km (1,780 miles) can be added because of spurs and kinks. This makes it as long as the River Nile, the longest river in the world. Six Great Walls laid end to end would reach round the circumference of the Earth.

The largest palace

The Imperial Palace in the middle of Peking, China, covers an area of 72 hectares (178 acres). This is equal to 100 football pitches. It is surrounded by the largest moat in the world – 38 km (23½ miles) in length.

The tallest buildings

Sears Tower, Chicago, USA	443 metres
World Trade Centre, New York, USA	411 metres
Empire State Building, New York, USA	381 metres
Standard Oil Building, Chicago, USA	346 metres
John Hancock Center, Chicago, USA	343 metres
Chrysler Building, New York, USA	319 metres
60 Wall Tower, New York, USA	290 metres
First Canadian Place, Toronto, Canada	289 metres
40 Wall Tower, New York, USA	282 metres
Bank of Manhattan, New York, USA	274 metres

Highest homes

The highest settlement is on the Indian and Tibetan border. Basisi is 5,988 m (19,650 ft) above sea level. This is only 2,860 m (9,384 ft) lower than Mount Everest, the highest mountain in the world.

The highest dam

The highest dam is in Russia. Completed in 1990, the Rogunsky dam towers 335 m (1098 ft) high. This is higher than the Grande Dixence in Switzerland which is only 15 m (50 ft) short of the Eiffel Tower.

The oldest buildings

Twenty-one huts were discovered in 1960 in Nice, France, that have been dated to 400,000 BC. They are the oldest recognizable buildings in the world.

Smallest house

A fisherman's cottage in North Wales has only 2 tiny rooms and a staircase inside. The outside measures 1.8 m (6 ft) wide and only just over 3 m (10 ft) high.

DID YOU KNOW?

The longest bridge span in the world is the Humber Estuary Bridge, Britain. It is 1,410 m (4,626 ft) across. It was opened in 1981, having taken 9 years to build.

The tallest lighthouse

The steel tower lighthouse in Yokohama, Japan, is 106 m (348 ft) high. But almost 7 of these would be needed standing on top of each other to reach the world's tallest structure, the Warszawa Radio Mast in Poland.

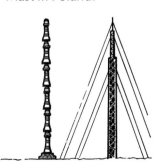

Seven Wonders

The Seven Wonders of the World were first mentioned in the 2nd century BC by a man called Antipater of Sidon. They were:

The Pyramids of Giza, Egypt
The Hanging Gardens of Babylon, Iraq
The Tomb of King Mausolus, Turkey
The Temple of Diana, Ephesus, Turkey
The Colossus of Rhodes, Greece
The Statue of Jupiter, Olympia, Greece
The Pharos of Alexandria, Egypt

Of the Seven Wonders, only the pyramids are still standing. The others have been destroyed by fire, earthquake and invading nations.

Cities

Fastest growing city

Mexico City is growing at a rate of 25 per cent every 5 years. With a population of over 19 million, it is estimated, that by the year 2000 it will be over 31 million. This is 5 times as many people as there are in Switzerland at present.

Mount Isa, Queensland, Australia, spreads over almost 41,000 sq km (15,800 sq miles). It covers an area 26 times greater than that of London and is about the same size as Switzerland.

Top 10 most crowded cities
(people per city)

Mexico City	19,400,000
New York	18,000,000
Los Angeles	13,500,000
Cairo	13,000,000
Shanghai	12,500,000
Peking	10,700,000
Seoul	9,700,000
Calcutta	9,200,000
Moscow	8,800,000
Paris	8,700,000

Traffic City

The greatest amount of vehicles in any city is to be found in Los Angeles, USA. At one interchange almost 500,000 vehicles were counted in a 24-hour period during a weekday. This is an average of 20,000 cars and trucks an hour.

The cheapest city

In 1626 a Dutchman bought an island in America from some local Indians. He gave them some cloth and beads worth about $24* for an area of land he thought covered 86 sq km (34 sq miles). In fact it was 57 sq km (22 sq miles). But it was still a bargain. He had bought Manhattan, now one of the most crowded and expensive islands in the world. He named his town New Amsterdam but it was later renamed New York.

How many people live in cities?

About one third of people in the world live in towns or cities. By the year 2000, experts believe that over half will live in urban areas. But this may vary from place to place. In the USA about 74 per cent live in towns and cities compared with 20 per cent in India.

*See page 96

The oldest city

Archaeologists believe that Jericho, in Jordan, is the oldest continuously inhabited place. There were as many as 3,000 people living there as early as 7,800 BC.

Longest underground

London has 400 km (247 miles) of underground tracks, making it the longest in the world. This includes 267 stations and about 450 trains. All the track laid end to end would stretch from London to Land's End in Cornwall.

An island city

Venice, in the north of Italy, is built on 118 islands in a lagoon. Canals serve as streets and roads and everybody uses boats instead of cars to get around. There are over 400 bridges crossing the canals.

Poles apart

The most northerly capital is Reykjavík in Iceland. The southern-most is Wellington, New Zealand. They are 20,000 km (12,500 miles) apart.

The longest name

Krung Thep is the shortened name of the capital of Thailand, known in the West as Bangkok. Its full name has 167 letters and means in English,

The City of Gods, the Great City, the Residence of the Emerald Buddha, the Impregnable City (of Ayutthaya) of God Indra, the grand capital of the world endowed with nine precious gems, the happy city, abounding in an enormous Royal Palace which resembles the heavenly abode where reigns the reincarnated god, a city given by Indra and built by Vishnukarn

So far from the sea

Urungi, capital of the Uighur Autonomous Region in China, is the furthest city from the sea. It is about 2,250 km (1,400 miles) from the nearest coast.

Communications

Telephones – top 5 countries
(per 1,000 people)

Monaco	1250	
Liechtenstein	1000	
Bermuda	909	
Sweden	909	
Switzerland	883	

Televisions – top 5 countries
(per 1,000 people)

USA	785	
Bermuda	709	
Guam	672	
Monaco	630	
Japan	562	

A black and white TV with a 3.5 cm (1⅖ in) screen was designed and made by Seiko in Japan. It fits on to a wrist watch. The smallest colour TV has a 21 cm (8 in) screen.

Amazing But True

A black and white TV with a 3.5 cm (1⅖ in) screen was designed and made by Seiko in Japan. It fits on to a wrist watch. The smallest colour TV has a 21 cm (8 in) screen.

Largest and smallest book

The smallest published book measures 1 x 1 mm (0.004 x 0.004 in) and is called *Old King Cole*. Only 85 copies were printed by Gleniffer Press of Scotland. Over 4 million copies would fit on the cover of the world's largest book (the *Super Book*) which measures 2.74 x 3.07 m (9 x 10 ft).

Secret codes

Coded messages have been used since 400 BC. Probably the best known is the Morse code, invented in the 19th century by Samuel Morse.

Newspapers – top 9 countries

(bought daily per 1,000 people)

Japan	575
Liechtenstein	558
Germany	530
Sweden	524
Finland	515
Norway	483
Britain	421
Iceland	420
Monaco	410

Dates of famous inventions

Telephone	1876
Gramophone	1877
Moving film	1885
Television	1934
Audio film	1927
Tape recorder	1935
Photocopier	1938
Computer	1946
Transistor radio	1948
Stereo recording	1958
Microcomputer	1969

Longest telephone cable

A telephone cable running beneath the Pacific Ocean links Canada and Australia via New Zealand and the Hawaiian Islands. It is 14,500 km (9,000 miles) long and cost £35 million* in 1963 to build.

Crossed wires

The Pentagon, Washington DC, is the centre of American defence. It has the largest switchboard in the world. About 25,000 telephone lines can be used at the same time.

*See page 96

Mail bag

The USA has the largest postal service in the world. In one year its citizens sent over 120 billion letters and packages. This is equal to 521 letters a year or about 1½ letters a day, for everyone living in America.

Communicating flags

Semaphore is a method of signalling with flags. With one flag in each hand, the signaller holds them in different positions to spell out the alphabet. A way of passing messages over a short distance, it was invented by the French army in 1792 during the French Revolution.

Computers for speech

The *Sprite* is a piece of computer technology that has been designed to imitate the human voice. It helps those with speech problems.

A long-distance chat

Men have talked to each other directly between the moon and the earth, a distance of 400,000 km (250,000 miles), making this the longest distance chat. A powerful radio signal sent into space is expected to take 24,000 years to reach its destination, a group of stars 10 billion times further away than the moon. It could be the longest awaited reply.

A golden pen

The ballpoint pen was invented in 1938 by a Hungarian named Biro. In its first year in the UK 53 million were sold.

Newspaper facts

When *The Times* newspaper reported Nelson's victory over the French at the Battle of Trafalgar in 1805, the news took 2½ weeks to reach London. When the same newspaper, 164 years later, showed pictures of the first men on the moon, they came out only a few hours after the landing.

DID YOU KNOW?

The world's first postage stamp was the *Penny Black*, issued in Britain in May, 1840. A one-cent British Guiana (Guyana) stamp of 1856, of which there is only one example, is thought to be worth £500,000*.

Shrinking world

Using satellites orbiting the earth, television can now reach a potential audience of about 2½ billion people. An event like the Olympic Games, can be beamed live into the homes of half the people in the world.

*See page 96

Travel

Airship travel

Hydrogen-filled airships were in regular use up until 1938, taking people across the Atlantic. They were stopped because too many caught fire.

Road building

To move their armies the Romans built over 80,000 km (50,000 miles) of road in Europe and the Middle East. After their conquest of Britain, it took only 6 days by horse to get from London to Rome. About 1,500 years later in the 19th century, it took just as long.

Most travelled person

An American, named Jesse Rosdall, went to all the countries and territories in the world except North Korea and the French Antarctic. He claimed to have travelled a total of 2,617,766 km (1,626,605 miles). This is equal to almost 7 trips to the moon or 65 journeys round the world.

Petrol consumption

In the USA, over 1,364 million litres (300 million gallons) of petrol are used each day – enough petrol in a year to fill an oil drum 36.5 km (22.7 miles) high and 26.5 km (16.5 miles) wide. This would fill Lake Baikal in Russia, the lake with the greatest volume.

Top 5 road countries
(km of road)

USA	6,365,590
Canada	3,002,000
France	1,502,000
Brazil	1,411,936
Former USSR	1,408,800

Longest and shortest flight

The shortest scheduled flight (from the island of Westray to Papa Westray off Scotland, lasting 2 minutes) could be made over 450 times while one jet makes a non-stop journey from Sydney to San Francisco, a total of 7,475 km (4,645 miles).

The first car

The first petrol-driven car took to the roads in 1885. It had 3 wheels and a tiller to steer. Its top speed was 16 km/h (10 mph). Just 100 years later there are enough vehicles in the world for every tenth person to own one. If they all met in one traffic jam, it would go round the world 34 times.

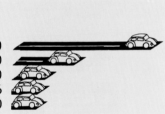

DID YOU KNOW?

Concorde travels faster than the speed of sound, cruising at 2,333 km/h (1,500 mph). It flies between London and New York in 3 hours, a distance of 5,536 km (3,500 miles). This is over twice as fast as an ordinary passenger plane.

Widest and narrowest

The widest road in the world is the Monumental Axis in Brasília, Brazil. It is 250 m (820 ft) wide, which is wide enough for 160 cars side by side. It is over 500 times wider than the narrowest street, which is in Port Issac, Britain. At its narrowest it is a mere 49 cm (1½ ft) and is known as 'squeeze-belly alley'.

World famous train

The Orient Express once ran between Paris and Istanbul. It now makes a shorter trip from London to Venice. It offers luxury travel at £1,500* for a return ticket. This is twice the price of a return plane ticket to Sydney, Australia, a city 14 times further away from London than Venice.

Busiest rail network

About 18½ million people use trains in Japan every day. If one train carried them all, it would have about 370,000 carriages and would stretch for over 3,300 km (2,000 miles).

Fastest train

The French railway system operates the TGV train, which achieved a top speed of 515 km/h (320 mph) without passengers in 1990. Its average speed on the Paris to Lyon passenger route is 212.5 km/h (132 mph).

Top 5 railway countries
(km of track)

USA	296,497
Former USSR	144,900
Canada	120,000
Germany	83,244
India	61,478

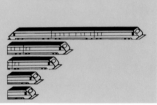

Amazing But True

The Boeing 747 (Jumbo Jet) is the largest and most powerful plane. It can carry up to 500 passengers. It stands as high as a 6-storey office block and weighs over 370 tonnes. It has a maximum speed of 969 km/h (602 mph) and a wing-span of over 70 m (232 ft).

The bicycle

An early form of bicycle, called a hobbyhorse or walk-along, was popular in the mid-17th century. It had no pedals. We had to wait almost 200 years for their invention.

Top holiday countries
(number of visitors)

France	51,462,000
USA	39,772,000
Spain	34,300,000
Italy	26,679,000
Hungary	20,510,000
Austria	19,011,000
UK	18,021,000
Germany	17,045,000
Canada	15,258,000
Switzerland	13,200,000

Money*

World's largest mint

The largest mint – the factory where coins are made – is in the USA. It can make 22 million coins a day using almost 100 stamping machines. It covers an area of 4½ hectares (11 acres). At full production it could produce a pile of coins 5 times higher than Mount Everest in just one day.

Earliest coins

Coins found in Lydia (Turkey) date from the reign of King Gyges in the 7th century BC. These coins below were found in Sicily and date to the 5th century BC.

Highest value note

A few, very rare, $10,000* notes exist in America. They are not in general circulation.

*See page 96

Amazing But True

In 1989, Britain's Abbey National Building Society handed over a cheque worth £1,425,000,000* to the newly created Abbey National plc. It was the largest cheque ever written.

Military spending

The USA spends $300 billion* on defence in a year – more than the people in most countries earn collectively in the same period. The USA and the former USSR used to spend more on arms than all the rest of the world.

Highest paid job

Michael Milken, an American working for Drexel Burnham Lambert Inc., earned $15,000* a day in salary and bonuses in 1987 – an annual income of $550 million.

Sunken treasure

Almost 2,000 Spanish galleons lie off the coast of Florida and the Bahamas. They were sunk in the 16th century, most of them carrying large amounts of gold. This area is the largest untapped storehouse of treasure in the world.

Golden Beatle

Paul McCartney, songwriter and ex-Beatle, earns an estimated £25 million a year from his records. This is about £45* a minute or £70,000 a day.

The Chinese one kwan note printed in the 14th century was 92.8 x 33 cm (9 x 13 in). It is 73 times larger than the smallest note, the 10 bani issued in Romania in 1917.

Income Tax

Many governments take a certain amount of money from the salaries of their citizens. This is called Income Tax. It was introduced in Britain in 1799 by the Prime Minister, William Pitt. He needed money to pay for the war against Napoleon. The war ended over 150 years ago, but Income Tax has remained.

Different money

Coins and notes are not the only form of money. Teeth of animals, metal bracelets and necklaces, shells, axe heads, knives, blocks of salt and even blocks of tea leaves have been used. The word *cash* comes from an Indian word meaning compressed tea and the word *salary* comes from the Latin word for salt. Both were used to pay people in the past.

Honesty rules

In 1972, $500,000* was found by Lowell Elliot in Indiana, USA. The money was dropped by a criminal escaping by parachute. Resisting the temptation to keep the money, he tracked down the owner and returned every cent.

Powerful banks

The world's most wealthy bank is Citicorp, based in New York. Only the US Government handles more money in a year. The 56 poorest countries each has less wealth than each of the top 500 commercial banks in the world.

Money loses value

When the price of buying things goes up, money becomes worth less. This is called inflation. In Germany after the First World War, the German Mark dropped in value. In 1921, 81 Marks were worth 1 American dollar. Two years later, the same dollar was worth 1 million Marks.

Great Train Robbery

In 1963 over £2½ million* was stolen from a train in Buckinghamshire, England. Only one seventh of the total was ever recovered. It was the costliest train robbery.

*See page 96 **81**

Languages

10 most spoken languages

Chinese	700,000,000
English	400,000,000
Russian	265,000,000
Spanish	240,000,000
Hindustani	230,000,000
Arabic	146,000,000
Portuguese	145,000,000
Bengali	144,000,000
German	119,000,000
Japanese	116,000,000

The first alphabet

The Phoenicians, who once lived where Syria, Jordan and Lebanon are today, had an alphabet of 29 letters as early as 1,700 BC. It was adopted by the Greeks and the Romans. Through the Romans, who went on to conquer most of Europe, it became the alphabet of Western countries.

Turkey

Cyprus

Mediterranean Sea

Phoenicia

Sounds strange

One tribe of Mexican Indians hold entire conversations just by whistling. The different pitches provide meaning.

The Rosetta Stone

The Rosetta Stone was found by Napoleon in the sands of Egypt. It dates to about 196 BC. On it is an inscription in hieroglyphics and a translation in Greek. Because scholars knew ancient Greek, they could work out what the Egyptian hieroglyphics meant. From this they learned the language of the ancient Egyptians.

Many Chinese cannot understand each other. They have different ways of speaking (called dialects) in different parts of the country. But today in schools all over China, the children are being taught one dialect (Mandarin), so that one day all Chinese will understand each other.

Translating computers

Computers can be used to help people of different nationalities, who do not know each others' language, talk to each other. By giving a computer a message in one language it will translate it into another specified language.

World-wide language

English is spoken either as a first or second language in at least 45 countries. This is more than any other language. It is the language of international business and scientific conferences and is used by airtraffic controllers world-wide. In all, about one third of the world speaks it.

Earliest writing

Chinese writing has been found on pottery, and even on a tortoise shell, going back 6,000 years. Pictures made the basis for their writing, each picture showing an object or idea. Probably the earliest form of writing came from the Middle East, where Iraq and Iran are now. This region was then ruled by the Sumerians.

The most words

English has more words in it than any other language. There are about 1 million in all, a third of which are technical terms. Most people only use about 1 per cent of the words available, that is, about 10,000. William Shakespeare is reputed to have made most use of the English vocabulary.

Amazing But True

A scientific word describing a process in the human cell is 207,000 letters long. This makes this single word equal in length to a short novel or about 80 typed sheets of A4 paper.

Many tongues

A Frenchman, named Georges Henri Schmidt, is fluent (meaning he reads and writes well) in 31 different languages.

International language

Esperanto was invented in the 1880s by a Pole, Dr Zamenhof. It was hoped that it would become the international language of Europe. It took words from many European countries and has a very easy grammar that can be learned in an hour or two.

The same language

The languages of India and Europe may originally come from just one source. Many words in different languages sound similar. For example, the word for *King* in Latin is *Rex,* in Indian, *Raj,* in Italian *Re,* in French *Roi* and in Spanish *Rey*. The original language has been named Indo-European. Basque, spoken in the French and Spanish Pyrenees, is an exception. It seems to have a different source which is still unknown.

Number of alphabets

There are 65 alphabets in use in the world today. Here are some of them:

Roman
ABCDEFGHIJKLMNOPQRS

Greek
ΑΒΓΔΕΖΗΘΙΚΛΜΝΞΟΠΡ

Russian (Cyrillic)
АБВГДЕЖЗИЙІКЛМНОП

Hebrew
מעדיף כיום דיור בשירות

Chinese
評定。因此我們制定一種申請房屋計點辦

Arabic
١٨٩٧ وصل إلى إنجلترا أنموذج

Art and entertainment

Most productive painter

Picasso, the Spanish artist who died in 1973, is estimated to have produced over 13,000 paintings, as well as a great many engravings, book illustrations and sculptures, during his long career – he lived to be 91. This means that he painted an average 3½ pictures every week of his adult life.

Most valuable painting

Leonardo da Vinci's *Mona Lisa* is probably the world's most valuable painting. It was stolen from the Louvre, Paris, in 1911, where it had hung since it was painted in 1507. It took 2 years to recover. During that time, 6 forgeries turned up in the USA, each selling for a very high price.

The oldest museum

The Ashmolean Museum in Oxford, Britain, was built in 1679.

The record of records

The *Guinness Book of Records*, first published in 1955, has been translated into 24 languages and has sold over 50 million copies world-wide.

Largest painting by a single artist

The Battle of Gettysburg by Paul Philippoteaux is the size of 10 tennis courts. It took 2½ years to paint (1883) and measures 125 m (410 ft) by 21.3 m (70 ft).

Largest art gallery

The Winter Palace and the Hermitage in St Petersburg, Russia, have 322 galleries showing a total of 3 million works of art and archaeological exhibits. A walk around all the galleries is 24 km (15 miles).

Best-selling novelist

Barbara Cartland, a British authoress, has sold about 500 million copies of her romantic novels world-wide and they have been translated into 17 languages. All her books gathered together would make 5,000 piles, each as high as the Eiffel Tower.

Pop records

The Beatles were the most successful pop group of all time. They sold over 1,000 million discs and tapes. The biggest selling single was *White Christmas*, written by Irving Berlin and sung by Bing Crosby. The most successful album is *Thriller* by Michael Jackson, selling over 40 million copies.

Band Aid

On July 13th, 1985, two pop concerts took place, one in Wembley, London, and the other at the JF Kennedy Stadium, Philadelphia. Fifty well-known bands played to raise money for the starving of Africa. By the end of the year over £50 million* had been raised by the concert, together with a record and a book of the event.

Largest audiences

The largest audience for a single concert was in 1990 when an estimated 2 million people attended a Bastille Day concert by Jean-Michel Jarre. The Rolling Stones attracted record audiences to their 1989 *Steel Wheels* tour of North America. 3.3 million people attended in 30 cities, raising a record £185 million*.

DID YOU KNOW?

The smallest professional theatre in the world is to be found in Hamburg, Germany. *The Piccolo* seats only 30 people. The Perth Entertainment Centre, Australia, has a theatre that holds 80,000, which is a capacity over 2,500 times greater.

William Shakespeare

Shakespeare, commonly thought the world's greatest playwright, wrote 37 plays in all. The longest is *Hamlet*. The role of Hamlet is also the longest written by Shakespeare.

A night at the opera

Richard Wagner had an eccentric patron in Ludwig II, King of Bavaria. He was so impressed by Wagner's music that he built a castle (called Neuschwanstein) in Bavaria for Wagner's operas.

Most expensive film

The most expensive film ever made was *Terminator 2: Judgement Day*. It cost $104 million* to make.

Amazing But True

Wolfgang Amadeus Mozart wrote about 1,000 pieces of music, including many operas and symphonies. He died aged 35, but had been composing since the age of 4. He is thought to be one of the world's greatest composers.

*See page 96

The world of machines

Largest and slowest

The machine that takes the Space Shuttle to its launching pad is called the *Crawler* and for a very good reason. It weighs 3,000 tonnes and travels at a maximum speed of 3 km/h (2 mph). It is 40 m (130 ft) long, and 35 m (115 ft) wide.

Oldest working clock

The mechanical clock in Salisbury Cathedral, Britain, dates back to 1386. It is still in full working order, after repairs were made in 1956, some 600 years later.

Earliest steam engine

Richard Trevithick, a Cornish inventor, built the first steam engine in 1803. The first public railway was opened 23 years later between Stockton and Darlington, Britain. The engine used was designed by George Stephenson.

The sewing machine

The sewing machine was first used in France in the early 19th century. It was made of wood. Isaac Singer invented the first foot treadle machine in 1851. This became so popular that it lead to mass-production of sewing machines.

DID YOU KNOW?

The first motorcycle was designed and built by the firm of Michaux-Perreaux in France in 1869. It ran on steam and had a top speed of 16 km/h (10 mph). The first petrol-driven motorcycle was designed in 1885 by Gottlieb Daimler. Its top speed was 19 km/h (12 mph). Compare this with the 512 km/h (318.6 mph) of the fastest modern bike.

Radio fraud

In 1913, almost 50 years after the first radio transmission, an American was convicted of trying to mislead the public. He had advertised that in a few years his radio company would be able to transmit the human voice across the Atlantic to Europe. The district attorney did not believe him. Two years later a trans-Atlantic conversation took place.

Amazing But True

The Scottish inventor, John Logie Baird, gave the first public demonstration of the television in 1926 in Soho, London. Ten years later there were 100 TV sets in the country. Today there are about 100 million sets in the USA alone.

A mirror on the universe

The inventor of the telescope is thought to be Roger Bacon, a 13th century monk. His instrument was first discovered in detail in 1608 by a Dutchman. Today, the largest telescope is the Keck telescope on Mauna Kea, in Hawaii. It has a 10 m (33ft) mirror made up of 36 segments, all joined together to make the correct curve.

Powerful computer

The fastest and most powerful computer is the liquid-cooled Cray 2, which has a main memory capacity of 32 million bytes. If all the people in China could each make a calculation in a second, it would take the entire population to keep up with this computer.

Most powerful fire-engine

A fire-engine designed to tackle aircraft fires can squirt 277 gallons of foam a second out of its 2 turrets. It is the 8-wheeled Oshkosh firetruck. It could fill an olympic-sized swimming pool in only 30 minutes.

Most accurate clock

The Olsen clock in Copenhagen town hall, Denmark, will lose half a second every 300 years. It took 10 years to make. An atomic clock in the USA is accurate to within 1 second in 1,700,000 years.

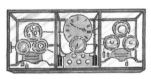

Amazing But True

The fastest official record for typing is 216 words in one minute or 3½ words per second. An electronic printer in the USA can type over 3,000 times faster: that is 700,000 words a minute or 12,000 a second.

The longest cars

In 1927, 6 Bugatti 'Royales' were made in France. They were each 6.7 m (22 ft) long. A custom built Lamrooster measures 15.24 m (50 ft), has 10 wheels and a pool in the back.

World speed records

Steam locomotive	1938	202.77 km/h	(126.00 mph)
Helicopter	1986	400.87 km/h	(249.09 mph)
Motorcycle	1978	512.73 km/h	(318.60 mph)
Aircraft	1976	3,529.00 km/h	(2,192.9 mph)
Command module	1969	39,897.00 km/h	(24,791.5 mph)

World map

Alaska

Canada

Greenland

Finland
Sweden
Iceland   Norway
Britain   6
Ireland   2   3
8   5
France 9   10
Portugal   16
Spain   Italy   17

United States of America

ATLANTIC OCEAN

Bermuda

Tunisi

Bahamas
Mexico

Morocco

Algeria   Lib

Cuba   Dominican Republic
Belize   Puerto Rico
Guatemala   Honduras   Haiti   Dominica
El Salvador   Nicaragua   Barbados
Costa Rica   Trinidad and Tobago
Panama   Venezuela   Guyana
Colombia   Surinam
French Guiana

Western Sahara
Cape Verde
Mauritania   Mali   Niger
Gambia   Senegal
Guinea-Bissau   32   Nigeria
Guinea
Sierra Leone   Benin   34
Liberia   Togo   36
Ivory Coast   Gabon
Ghana

PACIFIC OCEAN

Ecuador

Peru

Congo

Angol

KEY TO NUMBERS
1 Denmark
2 Germany
3 Poland
4 Slovak Republic
5 Czech Republic
6 Netherlands
7 Belgium
8 Luxembourg
9 Switzerland
10 Austria
11 Hungary
12 Romania
13 Yugoslavia
14 Bosnia-Herzegovina
15 Croatia
16 Slovenia
17 Andorra
18 Bulgaria
19 Albania
20 Greece

Brazil

Bolivia   Paraguay

Chile

Uruguay

Argentina

Falkland Islands

Namibia

Botswana

South Africa

21 Syria
22 Lebanon
23 Israel
24 Jordan
25 Kuwait
26 Bahrain
27 Qatar
28 United Arab Emirates
29 Bangladesh
30 Cambodia
31 Singapore
32 Burkina
33 Chad
34 Cameroon
35 Central African Republic
36 Equatorial Guinea
37 Uganda

ARCTIC OCEAN

Russian Federation

Kazakhstan

Mongolia

47
48

49

Turkey

50 51

52 53 55

54

N. Korea

Japan

China

S. Korea

22 21
23 24

Iraq

Iran

Afghanistan

Bhutan

Taiwan

25 26
27 28

Pakistan

Nepal

Laos

Hong Kong

Egypt

Saudi
Arabia

Oman

India

29

Burma

Vietnam

Philippines

Sudan

30

Yemen

Djibouti

Thailand

Brunei

Ethiopia

Maldives

Sri Lanka

Malaysia

Papua New Guinea

Zaire

Somalia

31

Indonesia

Solomon
Islands

37
38
39

Kenya

Seychelles

INDIAN OCEAN

Tanzania

Comoros

41
40

Mauritius

Fiji

42

Reunion

Madagascar

Australia

Mozambique

Swaziland

Lesotho

New Zealand

38 Rwanda
39 Burundi
40 Malawi   48 Moldavia
41 Zambia   49 Georgia
42 Zimbabwe   50 Armenia
43 Estonia   51 Azerbaijan
44 Latvia   52 Turkmenistan
45 Lithuania   53 Uzbekistan
46 Belorussia   54 Tajikistan
47 Ukraine   55 Kyrgyzstan

Countries of the world facts

Country	Capital	Population	Area (sq km)	Area (sq miles)
Afghanistan	Kabul	16,430,000	648,000	250,000
Albania	Tiranë	3,300,000	29,000	11,000
Algeria	Algiers	25,660,000	2,382,000	919,500
American Samoa	Pago Pago	47,000	197	76
Andorra	Andorra	60,000	500	193
Angola and Cabinda	Luanda	10,020,000	1,247,000	481,500
Anguilla	The Valley	8,000	96	37
Antigua and Barbuda	St John's	77,000	442	171
Argentina	Buenos Aires	32,710,000	2,767,000	1,068,000
Armenia	Yerevan	3,300,000	30,000	11,500
Aruba	Oranjestad	62,500	193	75
Australia	Canberra	17,340,000	7,678,000	2,964,000
Austria	Vienna	7,820,000	84,000	32,500
Azerbaijan	Baku	7,000,000	87,000	33,500
Bahamas	Nassau	253,000	14,000	5,500
Bahrain	Manama	520,000	600	232
Bangladesh	Dacca	118,740,000	144,000	55,500
Barbados	Bridgetown	255,000	430	166
Belgium	Brussels	9,840,000	31,000	12,000
Belize	Belmopan	188,000	23,000	9,000
Belorussia	Minsk	10,000,000	207,500	80,000
Benin	Porto Novo	4,736,000	113,000	43,500
Bermuda	Hamilton	61,000	50	19
Bhutan	Thimphu	1,550,000	47,000	18,000
Bolivia	La Paz	7,610,000	1,099,000	424,000
Bosnia-Herzegovina	Sarajevo	4,364,500	51,500	20,000
Botswana	Gaborone	1,350,000	600,000	231,500
Brazil	Brasília	153,320,000	8,512,000	3,285,500
Brunei	Bandar Seri Begawan	270,000	6,000	2,500
Bulgaria	Sofia	8,980,000	111,000	43,000
Burkina	Ouagadougou	9,240,000	274,000	106,000
Burma	Rangoon	42,560,000	676,500	261,000
Burundi	Bujumbura	5,458,000	28,000	11,000
Cambodia	Phnom Penh	8,440,000	181,000	70,000
Cameroon	Yaoundé	11,834,000	475,000	183,500
Canada	Ottawa	26,603,000	9,976,000	3,851,000
Cape Verde	Praia	370,000	4,000	1,500
Cayman Islands	Georgetown	27,000	300	116
Central African Republic	Bangui	3,039,000	623,000	240,500
Chad	Ndjamena	5,687,000	1,284,000	495,500
Chile	Santiago	13,390,000	757,000	292,000
China	Peking	1,155,800,000	9,597,000	3,704,500
Colombia	Bogotá	33,610,000	1,139,000	439,500
Comoros	Moroni	551,000	2,000	772
Congo	Brazzaville	2,271,000	342,000	132,000
Costa Rica	San José	2,994,000	51,000	19,500
Croatia	Zagreb	4,760,500	56,500	22,000
Cuba	Havana	10,625,000	115,000	44,500
Cyprus	Nicosia	710,000	9,000	3,500
Czech Republic	Prague	10,400,000	79,000	30,500
Denmark	Copenhagen	5,150,000	43,000	16,500

Country	Capital	Population	Area (sq km)	Area (sq miles)
Djibouti	Djibouti	409,000	22,000	8,500
Dominica	Roseau	83,000	751	290
Dominican Republic	Santo Domingo	7,170,000	49,000	19,000
Ecuador	Quito	10,850,000	284,000	109,500
Egypt	Cairo	53,223,000	1,001,000	386,500
El Salvador	San Salvador	5,252,000	21,000	8,000
Equatorial Guinea	Malabo	348,000	28,000	11,000
Estonia	Tallinn	1,600,000	45,000	17,500
Ethiopia	Addis Ababa	53,380,000	1,222,000	471,500
Falkland Islands	Stanley	2,000	12,000	4,500
Fiji	Suva	780,000	18,000	7,000
Finland	Helsinki	5,030,000	337,000	130,000
France	Paris	57,050,000	551,000	212,500
French Guiana	Cayenne	100,000	91,000	35,000
Gabon	Libreville	1,172,000	268,000	103,500
Gambia	Banjul	861,000	11,000	4,000
Georgia	Tbilisi	5,460,000	69,700	27,000
Germany	Berlin	79,360,000	357,000	138,000
Ghana	Accra	15,028,000	239,000	92,000
Greece	Athens	10,060,000	132,000	51,000
Greenland	Godthåb	57,000	2,186,000	844,000
Grenada	St George's	80,000	344	133
Guadeloupe	Basse-Terre	344,000	2,000	772
Guam	Agana	132,000	541	209
Guatemala	Guatemala City	9,197,000	109,000	42,000
Guinea	Conakry	5,756,000	246,000	95,000
Guinea-Bissau	Bissau	965,000	36,000	14,000
Guyana	Georgetown	800,000	215,000	83,000
Haiti	Port-au-Prince	6,486,000	28,000	11,000
Honduras	Tegucigalpa	5,105,000	112,000	43,000
Hong Kong	Hong Kong	5,750,000	1,000	386
Hungary	Budapest	10,340,000	93,000	36,000
Iceland	Reykjavík	260,000	103,000	40,000
India	Delhi	849,640,000	3,288,000	1,269,000
Indonesia	Jakarta	187,760,000	1,904,000	735,000
Iran	Tehran	57,730,000	1,648,000	636,000
Iraq	Baghdad	19,580,000	435,000	168,000
Ireland	Dublin	3,520,000	70,000	27,000
Israel	Jerusalem	4,970,000	21,000	8,000
Italy	Rome	57,050,000	301,000	116,000
Ivory Coast	Abidjan	11,998,000	322,000	124,500
Jamaica	Kingston	2,420,000	11,000	4,000
Japan	Tokyo	123,920,000	372,000	143,500
Jordan	Amman	4,140,000	98,000	38,000
Kazakhstan	Alma-Ata	16,691,000	2,717,500	1,049,000
Kenya	Nairobi	24,032,000	583,000	225,000
Kiribati	Tarawa	70,000	717	277
Korea, North	Pyongyang	22,190,000	121,000	47,000
Korea, South	Seoul	43,270,000	98,000	38,000
Kuwait	Kuwait City	2,100,000	18,000	7,000
Kyrgyzstan	Bishkek	4,400,000	76,500	29,500

Country	Capital	Population	Area (sq km)	Area (sq miles)
Laos	Vientiane	4,260,000	237,000	91,500
Latvia	Riga	2,680,000	25,000	9,500
Lebanon	Beirut	2,740,000	10,000	4,000
Lesotho	Maseru	1,774,000	30,000	11,500
Liberia	Monrovia	2,607,000	111,000	43,000
Libya	Tripoli	4,545,000	1,760,000	679,500
Liechtenstein	Vaduz	30,000	160	62
Lithuania	Vilnius	3,700,000	65,000	25,000
Luxembourg	Luxembourg	370,000	3,000	1,000
Madagascar	Antananarivo	11,197,000	587,000	226,500
Malawi	Lilongwe	8,289,000	118,000	45,500
Malaysia	Kuala Lumpur	18,330,000	330,000	127,500
Maldives	Malé	220,000	300	116
Mali	Bamoko	8,156,000	1,240,000	478,500
Malta	Valletta	360,000	300	116
Martinique	Fort-de-France	340,000	1,000	386
Mauritania	Nouakchott	2,025,000	1,031,000	398,000
Mauritius	Port Louis	1,075,000	2,000	772
Mexico	Mexico City	86,154,000	1,973,000	761,500
Moldavia	Chişinău	4,400,000	33,700	13,000
Monaco	Monaco	30,000	2	0·8
Mongolia	Ulan Bator	2,250,000	1,567,000	605,000
Morocco	Rabat	25,061,000	447,000	172,500
Mozambique	Maputo	15,656,000	783,000	302,000
Namibia	Windhoek	1,781,000	824,000	318,000
Nauru	Nauru	9,350	21	8
Nepal	Kathmandu	19,600,000	141,000	54,500
Netherlands	Amsterdam	15,060,000	37,000	14,500
Netherlands Antilles	Willemstad	190,000	800	309
New Caledonia	Noumea	170,000	22,000	8,500
New Zealand	Wellington	3,380,000	269,000	104,000
Nicaragua	Managua	3,871,000	130,000	50,000
Niger	Niamey	7,732,000	1,267,000	489,000
Nigeria	Lagos	108,542,000	925,000	357,000
Norway	Oslo	4,260,000	324,000	125,000
Oman	Muscat	1,560,000	212,000	82,000
Pakistan	Islamabad	115,520,000	804,000	310,500
Panama	Panama City	2,418,000	77,000	30,000
Papua New Guinea	Port Moresby	3,770,000	462,000	178,500
Paraguay	Asunción	4,400,000	407,000	157,000
Peru	Lima	22,000,000	1,285,000	496,000
Philippines	Manila	62,870,000	300,000	116,000
Poland	Warsaw	38,240,000	313,000	121,000
Portugal	Lisbon	10,580,000	92,000	35,500
Puerto Rico	San Juan	3,599,000	9,000	3,500
Qatar	Doha	380,000	11,000	4,000
Réunion	Saint-Denis	592,000	3,000	1,000
Romania	Bucharest	23,190,000	238,000	92,000
Russian Federation	Moscow	148,500,000	17,075,500	6,591,000
Rwanda	Kigali	7,181,000	26,000	10,000
St Kitts and Nevis	Basseterre	44,600	265	102
St Lucia	Castries	150,000	600	232
St Vincent-Grenadines	Kingstown	120,000	389	150
San Marino	San Marino	20,000	61	24

Country	Capital	Population	Area (sq km)	Area (sq miles)
São Tomé and Principe	São Tomé	121,000	1,000	386
Saudi Arabia	Riyadh	14,870,000	2,150,000	830,000
Senegal	Dakar	7,327,000	196,000	75,500
Seychelles	Victoria	70,000	440	170
Sierra Leone	Freetown	4,151,000	72,000	28,000
Singapore	Singapore	2,710,000	600	232
Slovak Republic	Bratislava	5,300,000	49,000	19,000
Slovenia	Ljubljana	1,950,000	20,500	8,000
Solomon Islands	Honiara	320,000	29,000	11,000
Somalia	Mogadishu	7,497,000	638,000	246,500
South Africa	Pretoria	35,282,000	1,221,000	471,500
Spain	Madrid	38,960,000	505,000	195,000
Sri Lanka	Colombo	16,990,000	66,000	25,500
Sudan	Khartoum	25,204,000	2,506,000	967,500
Surinam	Paramaribo	420,000	163,000	63,000
Swaziland	Mbabane	770,000	17,000	6,500
Sweden	Stockholm	8,560,000	450,000	174,000
Switzerland	Berne	6,710,000	41,000	16,000
Syria	Damascus	12,120,000	185,000	71,500
Taiwan	Taipei	19,910,000	36,000	14,000
Tajikistan	Dushanbe	5,000,000	143,000	55,000
Tanzania	Dar-es-Salaam	25,635,000	945,000	365,000
Thailand	Bangkok	56,080,000	514,000	198,500
Togo	Lomé	3,531,000	56,000	21,500
Tonga	Nuku'alofa	90,000	800	309
Trinidad and Tobago	Port of Spain	1,230,000	5,000	2,000
Tunisia	Tunis	8,074,000	164,000	63,500
Turkey	Ankara	56,100,000	781,000	301,500
Turkmenistan	Ashkhabad	3,600,000	488,000	188,500
Tuvalu	Funafuti	10,000	26	10
Uganda	Kampala	18,795,000	236,000	91,000
Ukraine	Kiev	51,700,000	604,000	233,000
United Arab Emirates	Abu Dhabi	1,590,000	87,000	33,500
United Kingdom	London	57,410,000	244,000	94,000
USA	Washington DC	249,920,000	9,363,000	3,614,000
Uruguay	Montevideo	3,100,000	176,000	68,000
Uzbekistan	Tashkent	20,000,000	447,500	172,500
Vanuatu	Vila	150,000	15,000	6,000
Vatican City	Vatican City	1,000	0.4	0·1
Venezuela	Caracas	19,320,000	912,000	352,000
Vietnam	Hanoi	66,230,000	330,000	127,500
Virgin Islands	Road Town	17,000	130	50
Western Sahara	Ad Dakhla	179,000	267,000	103,000
Western Samoa	Apia	200,000	3,000	1,000
Yemen	Sana'a	11,280,000	528,000	204,000
Yugoslavia	Belgrade	10,337,500	102,000	39,500
Zaire	Kinshasa	35,562,000	2,345,000	905,000
Zambia	Lusaka	8,073,000	753,000	290,500
Zimbabwe	Harare	9,369,000	391,000	151,000

Index

* **Currency conversion chart (correct on October 8th, 1992)**

	US$	Sing.$	NZ$	Aust.$	Can.$	£ Sterling
US$	1.0	1.59	1.85	1.39	1.24	0.57
Singapore $1	0.63	1.0	1.16	0.88	0.77	0.36
New Zealand $1	0.54	0.86	1.0	0.75	0.67	0.31
Australian $1	0.72	1.14	1.33	1.0	0.89	0.42
Canadian $1	0.81	1.29	1.50	1.12	1.0	0.47
£1 Sterling	1.73	2.75	3.18	2.38	2.13	1.0

WEATHER FACTS

Anita Ganeri

Consultants: Roger Hunt and Bob Riddaway

CONTENTS

Illustrated by Tony Gibson

**Additional illustrations by
Martin Newton and Ian Jackson**

Designed by Teresa Foster

Additional designs by Tony Gibson

Additional research by Chris Rice

What is weather?

Looking at weather

The weather is a vital part of our daily lives and it changes all the time. Meteorologists study the following to try to work out what will happen next:

1. Atmospheric or air pressure
2. Air temperature
3. Wind speed and direction
4. Cloud types and amounts
5. Sunshine amounts
6. Precipitation (rain, snow, sleet or hail)
7. Humidity (amount of water vapour in air)
8. Visibility (the furthest point you can see on a certain day)

Where it happens

The atmosphere is like a giant blanket of air around the Earth. It is divided into layers. Weather happens in the troposphere, the layer directly above the ground. Above the Equator the troposphere is about 16 km (10 miles) deep. Mount Everest, the highest point on Earth, reaches about half way up the troposphere.

DID YOU KNOW?

Without the weather to spread the Sun's heat around the world the Tropics would get hotter and hotter and the Poles colder and colder. Nothing would be able to live on the Earth.

Heavy air

The air presses down all over the Earth. This is called air or atmospheric pressure. The weight of air pressing down on each 1 sq m (10 sq ft) of the Earth's surface is greater than that of a large elephant. Air also

presses down on our bodies but we do not feel it because breathing balances out the effect. Air pressure is greatest at ground level and gets less the higher up you go. Aircraft are specially pressurized so people can breathe.

Barometers

Barometers measure air pressure. On an aneroid barometer a needle on a dial moves as the air pressure changes. Pressure is measured in millibars (mb). At sea level pressure is usually between 900-1050 mb. Pressure can also be measured in mm (in) of mercury with a mercury barometer.

Amazing But True

In 1654 Otto von Guericke, a German scientist, showed just how strong air pressure can be. He fitted two halves of a hollow sphere, about 56 cm (22 in) across, together so tightly that they were completely airtight. Then he pumped all the air out of them. The air pressure outside was so strong that it took 16 horses to pull the two halves apart.

Air masses

Air masses are huge masses of air which are warm, cold, dry or moist depending on the nature of the land or sea they pass over. They cover vast areas, often some 1,000,000 sq km (386,000 sq miles), about the same size as Egypt. Air masses move over the Earth's surface and help spread the Sun's heat around the world.

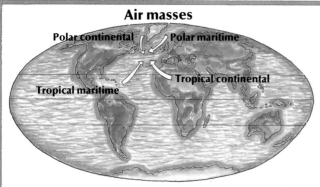

Air masses

Air masses are named after the type of climate they come from. There are four main kinds:

Polar continental (cP)
Forms over very cold land like North Canada. Cold and dry in winter, warm in summer.

Polar maritime (mP)
Forms over cold Northern seas like the Arctic Ocean. Cool and showery.

Tropical continental (cT)
Comes from warm inland places like the Sahara Desert. Is hot and dry.

Tropical maritime (mT)
Forms over warm oceans near the Equator. It is warm, moist and brings unsettled weather.

Fronts

A front is a boundary between air masses of different temperatures. At every front there is a band of cloud. When a front passes there is a change in temperature and wind direction and it usually rains. The three types of front are cold, warm and occluded*.

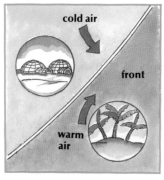

Highs and lows

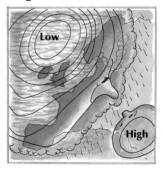

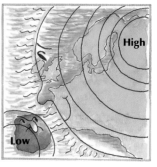

Pressure is different all over the world. Lows are areas of low pressure with the lowest pressure at the centre. Highs are areas of high pressure with the highest pressure at the centre. The way these move from day to day causes the changes in the weather. Lows usually bring wet, cloudy weather. Highs bring sunnier, dry weather.

Finding the lows

If you stand with your back to the wind in the northern hemisphere the nearest low will be on your left. In the southern hemisphere it is on your right.

*An occluded front is where a cold front catches up with a warm one.

The Sun

Energetic Sun

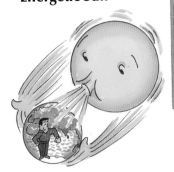

Highest recorded temperatures		
Africa	58°C	Azizia, Libya
America	57°C	Death Valley, California
Asia	54°C	Tirat Tsvi, Israel
Australia	53°C	Cloncurry, Queensland
Europe	50°C	Seville, Spain
Antarctica	14°C	Esperanza, Palmer

All the Earth's heat and light comes from the Sun. More heat and light reaches the Earth from the Sun in one minute than the whole world can produce in a year. Sunlight travels at about 300,000 km (186,000 miles) per second. It takes about 8½ minutes to reach the Earth.

Life support

The Sun keeps the temperature of most of the Earth's surface at −51°C to 49°C (−60°F to 120°F). Most living things can only survive at 0°C to 49°C (32°F to 120°F). If the amount of sunlight reaching the Earth was cut by a tenth, the oceans would turn to ice and life on Earth would die.

Effect on the weather

The Sun is the key to the world's weather. Its rays filter through the atmosphere and warm the Earth's surface which, in turn, heats the air above. The Equator is hot because the Sun shines directly overhead. The Poles are cold because the rays hit the Earth at wider angles.

DID YOU KNOW?

The light given off by a piece of the Sun's surface the size of a postage stamp is more than 500 60-watt light bulbs. It could light all the rooms in 48 average-sized homes.

The snug Earth

The Earth absorbs sunlight and then releases it into the air again as heat. The heat is trapped by water vapour and clouds in the atmosphere and reflected back to Earth. The atmosphere acts like an enormous blanket around the Earth, keeping in the warmth.

Cold mountains

People used to think that the closer you went to the Sun, the hotter it would be. But as hot air rises it expands and cools, so the higher you go the colder it is. Air cools by 3°C (5.5°F) for every 305 m (1,000 ft) it rises. This is why the tops of mountains are cold.

Lowest recorded temperatures

Antarctica	−88°C	Vostok
Asia	−68°C	Oimekon, USSR
America	−63°C	Snag, Yukon
Europe	−55°C	Ust'Schchugor, USSR
Africa	−24°C	Ilfrane, Morocco
Australia	−22°C	Charlotte Pass, NSW

Solar power

Solar panels are used to collect the Sun's heat. Water in them absorbs the heat and is used to warm homes. Electricity can also be made from sunlight. In 1982 the car *The Quiet Achiever* was driven right across Australia on sunshine power alone.

Hottest and coldest

At Dallol, Ethiopia the mean (average) shade temperature over a year is 34.4°C (94°F), making it the hottest place in the world. The coldest place in the world is Vostok in Antarctica where the mean temperature over a year is a freezing −57.8°C (−72°F).

Sunspots

Sunspots are dark patches on the Sun's surface. A single spot may be 8 times the Earth's diameter. They become very active every 11 years. Meteorologists think that sunspot activity may alter weather patterns by affecting the Earth's magnetic fields.

Thermometers

Thermometers are used to measure temperature. They are placed in the shade, 1.5 m (5 ft) off the ground. In direct sunshine and on the ground, the temperature recorded may be much higher than that off the ground.

Amazing But True

Solar ponds are lakes of salty water which collect the Sun's heat in their deepest, saltiest layers. The temperature can reach boiling point.

Scientists in New Mexico, USA proved this by boiling eggs in a solar pond. The eggs only took about five minutes to cook.

101

Water on the move

The world's water

About 70% of the Earth is covered with water. Most of this lies in the oceans. The Pacific Ocean alone covers almost half the world. Much of the rest of the water is in the ice sheets, glaciers and underground.

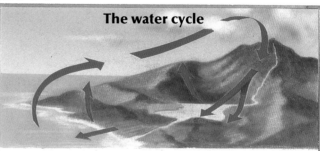

The water cycle

No new water is ever made. The rain you see has fallen millions of times before. In the water cycle the water on the Earth is used again and again. The Sun heats the oceans and lakes and millions of gallons of water rise into the air as invisible water vapour.

This is called evaporation. As the vapour rises, it cools and turns back into liquid water. This is called condensation. It falls as rain and snow and is carried back to the ocean by rivers and streams. Then the cycle begins all over again.

Water's disguises

There are 3 forms of water in the air:
1 The gas water vapour.
2 Liquid water droplets.
3 Solid ice crystals.
It changes from one form to another by evaporation, freezing, melting and condensation.

Watery air

The amount of water vapour in the air is called humidity. All air contains some water vapour but the amount varies greatly. Warm air can hold more vapour than cold air. In the Tropics the air is hot and sticky and contains nearly as much water vapour as the air in a sauna. It can be very uncomfortable.

DID YOU KNOW?

If all the water in the air fell at the same time, it would cover the whole Earth with 25 mm (1 in) of rain. This amount of rain would fill enough buckets to reach from the Earth to the Sun 57 million times.

Dew point

As air cools at night there is a point when it cannot hold any more water vapour and condensation begins. This is called the dew point and dew forms on the ground. It evaporates in the morning when the air warms up.

Dew traps

Farmers in Lanzarotte, Canary Islands, collect dew to water their crops. The dew traps look like moon craters, 3 m (10 ft) wide and 2 m (6 ft) deep. A layer of volcanic ash inside makes a good surface for condensation. Vines planted in the craters can live on the dew if it does not rain.

Rivers in the sea

Oceans have a great effect on climate. They absorb the Sun's heat and spread it around the world in currents. These are huge rivers in the sea driven by the winds. Warm and cold currents heat or cool the air above them causing hotter or cooler types of weather.

The oceans

The oceans supply most of the water for the water cycle. In a year up to 2,000 mm (79 in) of water evaporates from the Pacific and the Indian Oceans. It would take over a million years for the oceans' total water supply to pass through the air.

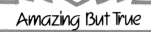

Amazing But True

The West Wind Drift carries over 2,000 times more water than the Amazon, the world's largest river. It flows three times as fast as the Gulf Stream and about 2½ times faster than the fastest man can swim.

The Gulf Stream

The warm Gulf Stream, one of the strongest currents, speeds east across the Atlantic at 178 km (111 miles) a day. It then turns north and divides, bringing mild weather to Europe. New York is only 160 km (100 miles) north of Lisbon in Portugal but in January it is cold at −1°C (31°F) while Lisbon is sunny at 10°C (50°F).

Clouds

How clouds form

Clouds form when warm air rises and cools down enough for some of the water vapour in it to condense into tiny water droplets or ice crystals. Billions of these make up a cloud. Water vapour can also condense on to smoke or dust specks in the air.

Warm air rising

Warm air expands and cools

Cloud forms

Two basic shapes

There are two basic cloud shapes caused by the two ways in which air can rise. 'Heap' (cumuliform) clouds form when bubbles of warm air rise quickly and then cool. 'Layer' (stratiform) clouds form when a large, spreading mass of air rises very slowly.

Amazing But True

The tallest cloud is the giant cumulonimbus. It can reach a height of 18 km (11 miles) which is twice as high as Mount Everest and can hold more than ½ million tonnes of water.

Water music

People in Chile's dry Atacama Desert collect water from sea fog. They use fog harps which are wooden frames strung with nylon threads. Water from the fog condenses on to the threads. More than 18 litres (32 pints) of water can be collected on 1 sq m (3 sq ft) of thread in a day.

Fog

Fog is really low cloud which forms when air near the ground cools. Sea fog forms when warm air from the land flows over cold seas. In the Arctic fog can rise up from the sea like steam rising from hot water. It is called sea smoke.

Fog danger

Fog reduces visibility and causes accidents on land and at sea. In 1962 two trains crashed in thick fog in London. 90 people were killed and many more injured.

DID YOU KNOW?

For centuries sailors lost at sea have used clouds to guide them to land. Fleecy clouds on the horizon often form above islands.

Cloud messengers

There are three families of clouds. They were given Latin names by Luke Howard in 1804. They are cirrus ('curl of hair'), cumulus ('heap') and stratus ('layer'). There are 10 main types of clouds made up of combinations of these families. Clouds are also grouped by their height above the ground. Each cloud carries a message about the weather to come so weather men use clouds to help them make forecasts.

Cirrus

High, ice-crystal clouds which look like wispy curls of hair. Often signs of bad weather to come.

Cirrostratus

Sheets of thin, milk-coloured cloud which form high up and often bring rain within 24 hours.

Altostratus

Layers of thin, grey cloud which can grow into rain clouds. Often form haloes round the Sun.

Stratocumulus

Uneven rolls or patches of cloud across the sky. Usually a sign that drier weather is on the way.

Cumulus

Clearly defined puffs of fluffy cloud like cauliflowers. They appear in sunny, summer skies.

Cirrocumulus

Often called a 'mackerel sky' – the ripples of cloud look like fish scales. Unsettled weather.

Altocumulus

Fluffy waves of grey cloud which can bring showers or break up to give sunny periods.

Nimbostratus

Thick, dark grey masses of cloud which bring rain or snow. 'Nimbus' means rain in Latin.

Stratus

Low, grey blanket of cloud which often brings drizzle. It can cover high ground and cause hill fog.

Cumulonimbus

Towering clouds which usually bring thunderstorms with rain, snow or hail.

Rainfall

Out of the clouds

Raindrops form in clouds when tiny water droplets join together or larger ice crystals melt. A raindrop must contain as many as 1,000 droplets for it to be heavy enough to fall. When water falls as rain or snow it is called precipitation.

Greatest average annual rainfalls		
Continent	MM	Place
Oceania (Pacific islands)	11,684	Mt Wai-'ale-'ale, Hawaii
Asia	11,430	Cherrapunji, India
Africa	10,277	Debundseha, Cameroon
S. America	8,991	Quibdo, Colombia
N. America	6,655	Henderson Lake, British Colombia
Europe	4,648	Crkvice, Yugoslavia
Australia	4,496	Tully, Queensland

Raindrops and drizzle

Raindrops are usually about 1.5 mm (0.06 in) round. They never grow bigger than 5 mm (0.2 in) which is about the size of a pea. Drops less than 0.5 mm (0.02 in) round are called drizzle. Raindrops are not tear-shaped, as is often thought, but look like flat-bottomed circles.

From dry to worse

From 1570-1971 Calama, Chile held the record for being the driest place in the world. It had had no rain at all for 400 years. But on 10 February 1972 torrential rain fell causing terrible floods. The whole town was surrounded by water and its electricity supply was cut off. Many buildings were badly damaged.

DID YOU KNOW?

The amount of water that falls to Earth each year as rain, snow and hail is equivalent to 10 million gallons for every person in the USA. This is enough for each person to have 900 baths a day.

Least average annual rainfalls		
Continent	MM	Place
S. America	0.8	Arica, Chile
Africa	2.5	Wadi Halfa, Sudan
N. America	30.5	Bataques, Mexico
Asia	45.7	Aden, South Yemen
Australia	119.3	Millers Creek
Europe	162.5	Astrakhan, USSR
Oceania	226.0	Puako, Hawaii

Greatest observed rainfalls

Time	MM	Place
1 min	31	Unionville, USA
15 min	198	Plumb Point, Jamaica
12 hours	1,340	Belouve, Reunion
24 hours	1,869	Cilaos, Reunion
1 month	9,299	Cherrapunji, India
1 year	26,459	Cherrapunji, India

Amazing But True

On 9 February 1859 a shower of fish fell in Glamorgan, Wales. They covered an area about the size of three tennis courts laid end to end. No one knew where they came from.

Smell of rain

Many people claim to be able to smell rain. This may be because our sense of smell is keener when the air is moist and also because of the gases given off by wet soil and plants.

Rain forests

In the tropical rain forests of South America it rains nearly every day. Each year at least 2,030 mm (80 in) and as much as 3,810 mm (150 in) of rain can fall. The air is always moist and sticky.

Rain gauge

Rain gauges measure the depth of rain which would cover the ground if none of it drained away or evaporated. The simplest type is a funnel connected to a tank which collects and measures the day's rainfall.

Differences in rainfall

Rain does not fall evenly over the Earth. The place with the highest number of rainy days each year is Mt Wai-'ale-'ale on the island of Kauai in Hawaii. Here it rains on as many as 350 days each year.

The record for the greatest average annual rainfall belongs to Tutunendo in Colombia, South America with an annual average of 11,770 mm (463 in). This would cover about nine average-sized adults standing on each other's shoulders. It is 14,713 times as much as the average annual rainfall in Arica in Chile.

Dust Bowl

Drought is caused by a lack of rain. The Dust Bowl in America was created by years of drought from 1930-1940. The soil was so dry it was blown away by the wind and farmers were ruined. The Dust Bowl reached from Texas right to the Canadian border.

Ice and snow

What is snow?

Snow crystals form when water freezes on to ice pellets in a cloud, making them bigger. As they fall through the cloud they collide with other snow crystals and become snowflakes. Snow often melts as it passes through warmer air and falls as rain.

World snowfall records			
City	Date		Amount
London	19 January	1881	4.5 m snow drifts
New York	6 February	1978	65 cm snow
Sydney	28 June	1836	Only snow on record
Jordan	2 March	1980	38 cm in Amman
Ireland	1 April	1917	25 m drifts

Snow wonder

Most snow crystals have six sides. Billions and billions have fallen to Earth but no two have ever been seen to be identical. The shape of the crystals depends on the air temperature. In colder air, needle and rod shapes form. Complicated shapes form in warmer air.

Palace of ice

In 1740 the Empress of Russia built a palace of ice as a home for a newly-married prince who had disobeyed her. Everything in it was carved from ice, even the pillows on the bed. Luckily for the prince his chilly home melted in the spring.

Snowball fight

Snow is more likely the higher you go. Some mountains are always covered in snow. In November 1958 rain fell in the New York streets while security guards on top of the Empire State Building enjoyed a snowball fight.

Greatest snowfall

The most snow to fall in a year was at Paradise, Mount Rainier, USA from 1971-1972. Some 31,102 mm (1,224 in) of snow fell, enough to reach a third of the way up the Statue of Liberty in New York.

DID YOU KNOW?

Metal pipes often burst when the water inside them turns to ice. This is because water expands when it freezes. It also becomes lighter. If ice did not float on water the seas would gradually turn to ice and no life would be able to survive on Earth.

What is hail?

Hail only falls from cumulonimbus clouds. Ice crystals are tossed up and down in the cloud as many as 25 times. Water freezes on to the crystals in layers, like the skins of an onion, until they are heavy enough to fall as hailstones. They are usually about the size and shape of peas.

Amazing But True

In 1930 five German pilots bailed out of their aircraft into a thundercloud over the Rhön mountains in Germany. They became the centres of hailstones and were bounced up and down in the cloud. Covered by layers of ice, they eventually fell frozen to the ground. Only one of the pilots survived.

Lucky escape

The sea between Denmark and Sweden can freeze over and the ice can be strong enough for cars to cross it. In 1716 the King of Sweden led his army over the ice to invade Denmark. The lucky Danes were saved by the ice melting.

Hail damage

Hail can badly damage crops and houses. Hailstones as big as cricket balls fell in Dallas, USA in May 1926 causing $2 million of damage in just 15 minutes. Farmers in Italy often shoot firework rockets into clouds to try to shatter the hailstones.

Jack Frost

At night the ground cools and, in turn, cools the air around it. If the temperature falls below freezing point dew freezes and is called frost. Hoar frost often forms around keyholes and delicate fern frost on windows.

The biggest hailstone

A hailstone the size of a melon fell in Coffeyville, Kansas, USA on 3 September 1970. It weighed 750 g (1.67 lb) and was 44.5 cm (17.5 in) round.

109

Thunder and lightning

Thunderstorms

Thunderstorms usually happen when the air is warm and humid. Huge cumulonimbus clouds form in the sky and gusty winds begin to blow. A thunderstorm often lasts for less than an hour but it produces the most dramatic type of weather.

Storm survival

Lightning always takes the quickest path to the ground. Tall trees and buildings are most at risk. Very few people are struck by lightning but it is dangerous to stand near a tree in a storm. It is safest to be in a car as the lightning will go into the ground through the rubber tyres.

DID YOU KNOW?

There are about 16 million thunderstorms a year throughout the world. About 1,800 storms rage at any moment day or night.

Unlucky strike

Lightning has hit the Empire State Building in New York as much as 12 times in 20 minutes and as often as 500 times a year. Most tall buildings have lightning conductors to carry the electricity safely to the ground.

Lightning

Electricity builds up in a thunder cloud and is released as a brilliant flash of lightning. A 'leader' stroke zig-zags to the ground. It forms a narrow path for the 'return' stroke (the one we see) to race up. Lightning can go from clouds to the ground or from cloud to cloud.

Thunder

Lightning can heat the air in its path to 30,000°C (54,000°F) which is 5 times hotter than the Sun's surface. This air expands at great speed and causes the booming noise we call thunder. Thunder can be heard at least 16 km (10 miles) away.

1, 2, 3, 4, 5 . . .

Lightning and thunder happen at exactly the same time but you see lightning first because light travels faster than sound. If you hear a thunderclap 5 seconds after you see a flash, the storm is about 2 km (1.2 miles) away.

Lightning birth?

Lightning may have been one of the causes of life on Earth. Scientists in the USA sent artificial lightning through a mixture of gases similar to those in the atmosphere. Amino acids formed which are believed to be the basic ingredients found in all forms of life on Earth.

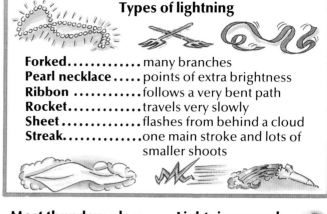

Types of lightning

Forked............many branches
Pearl necklace .....points of extra brightness
Ribbon ....follows a very bent path
Rocket............travels very slowly
Sheet ....flashes from behind a cloud
Streak.............one main stroke and lots of smaller shoots

Flash lighting

There are about 6,000 flashes of lightning every minute in the world. If the electricity from these could be collected and stored it would be enough to light every home in Britain and France for ever.

Most thundery place

Bogor in Java has at least 220 thundery days a year and has had as many as 322. It has at least 25 severe storms a year with lightning often striking a small area every 30 seconds for up to half an hour.

Ball lightning

'Fireballs' may or may not exist. There have been many reports of pear-shaped balls of fire floating into houses and then exploding. In 1980 a motorist in Britain saw a flashing ball of fire pass his car. It then exploded quite harmlessly.

Lightning speed

Lightning can travel at a speed of up to 140,000 km/s (87,000 miles/s) on its return journey. A rocket travelling at this speed would reach the Moon in 2½ seconds.

Amazing But True

The only person to survive being struck by lightning seven times was an American, Roy C. Sullivan. He lost his big toenail in 1942, his eyebrows in 1969 and had his hair set on fire twice. The other times he suffered slight burns.

World winds . . . 1

What is wind?

Wind is simply moving air. The Sun heats up some parts of the Earth more than others and the wind spreads this heat more evenly around the world. The map shows the main world and local winds.

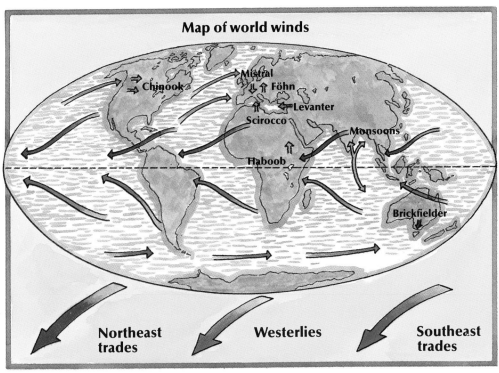

Map of world winds

Chinook

Mistral

Föhn

Levanter

Scirocco

Haboob

Monsoons

Brickfielder

Northeast trades

Westerlies

Southeast trades

How does it blow?

Air moves because of differences in pressure around the world. Warm air is light and rises leaving an area of low pressure as at the hot Equator. Cold air is heavier and sinks, causing high pressure, as at the icy Poles. Air flows from high to low pressure but it does not flow in a straight line from the Poles to the Equator. It is swung sideways by the Earth's spin.

In a spin

The Earth spins on its axis and this affects the direction of the wind. In the northern hemisphere winds are swung to the right, and in the southern to the left. This is called the Coriolis effect.

cold air

warm air

cold air

DID YOU KNOW?

In the northern hemisphere winds flow from west to east. This means that an aircraft flying from New York to London could arrive about ½ hour early because it has the wind behind it. But it could be delayed by ½ hour on the way back when flying into the wind.

112

Trade winds

The trade winds are steady winds flowing towards the Equator. In the 18th century sailing ships used them as guides for crossing the Atlantic Ocean. Columbus might never have discovered America in 1492 without the trade winds' help.

Jet streams

Jet streams are very strong winds blowing about 10 km (6 miles) above the Earth. They can be up to 4,000 km (2,500 miles) long but no more than 500 km (310 miles) wide. They were not discovered until World War II when pilots found their air speed reduced when they were flying against the jet stream.

Sea breezes

On a hot, sunny day the land heats up more quickly than the sea. Because of this air rises over the land and cool sea breezes rush in to replace it.

By evening sea breezes can reach 200 km (322 miles) inland. At night land cools down more quickly than the sea so the breeze blows out from land to sea.

Local winds

Winds affect the weather and are given special names in many parts of the world.

Brickfielder	Very hot NE summer wind that blows dust and sand across Australia.
Chinook	Warm, dry wind of the Rocky Mountains, USA. Welcomed by cattlemen because it can remove snow cover very quickly. Named after a local Indian tribe.
Föhn	Warm, dry European wind that flows down the side of mountains.
Haboob	The Arabic name for a violent wind which raises sandstorms, especially in North Africa.
Levanter	Pleasant, moist E wind that brings mild weather to the Mediterranean.
Mistral	Violent, dry, cold, NW wind that blows along the coasts of Spain and France.
Scirocco	Hot, dry S wind that blows across North Africa from the Sahara. Becomes very hot and sticky as it reaches the sea.

Amazing But True

Rising air currents called thermals can delay the fall of a parachutist. On 26 July 1959 an American pilot ejected from his plane at 14,400 m (47,000 ft) and took 40 minutes to fall through a thunder cloud instead of the expected 11 minutes.

World Winds . . . 2

The Beaufort Scale

The Beaufort Scale was invented in 1805 by Admiral Beaufort to estimate wind speed.

The original scale was for use at sea but it has been adapted for use on land.

The Beaufort Scale for use on land

Force	Strength	Kph	Effect
0	Calm	0-1	Smoke rises vertically
1	Light air	1-5	Smoke drifts slowly
2	Light breeze	6-11	Wind felt on face; leaves rustle
3	Gentle breeze	12-19	Twigs move; light flag unfurls
4	Moderate breeze	20-29	Dust and paper blown about; small branches move
5	Fresh breeze	30-39	Wavelets on inland water; small trees move
6	Strong breeze	40-50	Large branches sway; umbrellas turn inside out
7	Near gale	51-61	Whole trees sway; difficult to walk against wind
8	Gale	62-74	Twigs break off trees; walking very hard
9	Strong gale	75-87	Chimney pots, roof tiles and branches blown down
10	Storm	88-101	Trees uprooted; severe damage to buildings
11	Violent storm	102-117	Widespread damage to buildings
12	Hurricane	Over 119	Devastation

DID YOU KNOW?

A wind that blows as fast as the fastest man can run (43 kph/27 mph), is only a 'strong breeze' on the Beaufort Scale. A wind as fast as a running cheetah (113 kph/70 mph), the world's fastest animal, registers as a 'storm'.

Blowing in the wind

Wind speed and strength must be allowed for when new buildings are designed. The bridge over the Tacoma Narrows in the USA shook so violently in strong winds that it was nicknamed 'Galloping Gertie'. It eventually collapsed during a severe storm.

Windblown

Ship designers are now going back to building sailing ships to take advantage of the wind. In August 1980, a Japanese tanker, the *Shinaltoku Maru*, was launched. As well as an engine it had two square sails, controlled by computer.

Wind chill is the cooling effect of the wind on the skin. The stronger the wind the more heat is lost from the body and the colder a person feels. If human skin were exposed to winds of 48 kph (30 mph) in a temperature of −34°C (−30°F) it would freeze solid in 30 seconds.

Wind power

Windmills were once used to grind wheat to make flour. Today they are being used to generate electricity. The windmill at Tvind, Denmark is over 50 m (164 ft) high with three blades, each weighing over 5 tonnes. It can produce enough electricity to light up about 120 homes.

Windiest place

The windiest place in the world is the George V Coast in Antarctica. Here gales of 320 kph (200 mph) have been recorded.

Highest recorded gust

On 12 April 1934 a gust of wind blowing at 371 kph (231 mph) was recorded at Mount Washington, USA. This is some 251 kph (155 mph) stronger than Beaufort Scale 12, three times as strong as a hurricane.

Hat trick

Because wind funnels through mountains it may be stronger in a pass than on a peak. At Pali Lookout near Honolulu, a sightseer can throw his hat over the cliff and the wind will immediately throw it back .

Wind palace

The Wind Palace in Jaipur, India was specially built in the 1760s by the king so that the wind would cool it naturally. The palace is little more than a screen with balconies. The ladies of the court could sit behind these and watch the busy city down below.

Hurricanes

Tropical terrors

Hurricanes begin over warm, tropical oceans. They are like giant spinning wheels of storm clouds, wind and rain and can be up to 500 km (310 miles) across with winds whirling at up to 300 kph (190 mph). They sweep westwards over warm tropical seas, dying down when they reach land.

Stormy eyes

A hurricane has a centre or 'eye'. It can be up to 32 km (20 miles) across. Here the weather is surprisingly calm with low winds and clear skies. As the 'eye' passes overhead there is a lull in the storm for a few minutes or at the most a few hours.

Hurricane map with local names

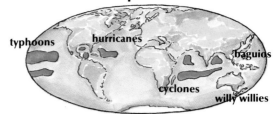

typhoons   hurricanes   baguios

cyclones   willy willies

Hurricanes turn anti-clockwise north of the Equator and clockwise to the south.

I name you . . .

Hurricanes were first given names in the 19th century by Clement Wragge, an Australian weather man. Nicknamed 'Wet Wragge', he used the names of people he had quarrelled with for very violent storms. Today an alphabetical list of names is drawn up each year for the coming year's hurricanes.

DID YOU KNOW?

If all the energy from one hurricane in a single day could be converted into electricity, it would be enough to supply the whole of the USA for three years. This is equivalent to the amount of energy needed to power 1,095 cars an incredible 36,000 times around the world.

5 of the worst recent hurricanes

Name	Date		Location	Effect
Unnamed	November	1970	Bangladesh	1 million dead
Tracey	December	1975	Darwin, Australia	90% of people homeless
David	August	1979	Dominica, W. Indies	2,000 dead; 20,000 homeless
Frederic	August	1979	Alabama, USA	£250 million damage
Allen	August	1980	Haiti	½ million homeless

Tornadoes

Terrible twisters

Tornadoes are funnel-shaped storms which twist as hot air spins upwards. At the centre winds can reach 644 kph (400 mph). Tornadoes leapfrog across land causing great damage when they touch the ground. They can suck up anything in their path, even people. Mid-West America has the most tornadoes.

Tornado on tour

On 26 May 1917, a single tornado sped 471 km (293 miles) across Texas, USA. It travelled at 88-120 kph (55-75 mph) for about 7 hours and 20 minutes.

Most destructive

Tornadoes are much smaller than hurricanes but much more violent. The tornado which hit Missouri, USA in March 1925 was only 274 m (900 ft) across. It killed 800 people and uprooted trees, swept cars over rooftops and hurled aside trains.

Train thief

A tornado in Minnesota, USA in 1931 lifted an 83-tonne train 25 m (80 ft) into the air and dropped it in a ditch. Many of its 117 passengers died.

Highest waterspout

Waterspouts are like tornadoes but these funnels of water form over sea. The highest seen was in 1898 in Australia. It was 1,528 m (5,015 ft) high and 31 m (10 ft) across.

Picked clean

Several chickens had all their feathers plucked off by a tornado in Bedfordshire, England in May 1950 . . . and they survived!

Amazing But True

On 4 September 1981 a tornado hit Ancona in Italy. It lifted a baby asleep in its pram 15 m (50 ft) into the air and set it down safely 100 m (328 ft) away. The baby was still sleeping soundly!

Climate and the seasons

What is climate?

Climate is the usual pattern of weather a place has measured over a very long time. How hot or cold a place is depends on how far north or south of the Equator it is (its latitude). Ocean currents, winds and mountains also affect climate.

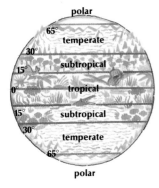

Climates of the world

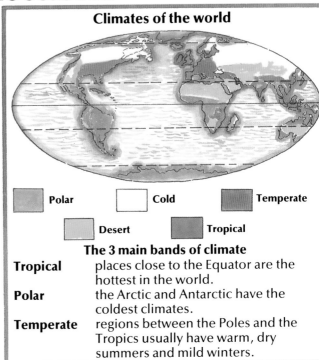

	Polar		Cold		Temperate
	Desert		Tropical		

The 3 main bands of climate

Tropical   places close to the Equator are the hottest in the world.

Polar   the Arctic and Antarctic have the coldest climates.

Temperate   regions between the Poles and the Tropics usually have warm, dry summers and mild winters.

Land and sea

Coasts have a maritime climate. Sea temperature does not change much during the year so summers are cool but winters mild. Land far from the sea heats up and cools down more quickly so summers are hotter but winters colder. This is a continental climate.

DID YOU KNOW?

Temperate climates are thought to be the most pleasant to live in as they do not usually have extremes of hot or cold. Only 7% of the Earth's land surface has a temperate climate, yet nearly half the world's population lives in these areas.

City climates

In many places with a temperate climate the west end of a city is more fashionable than the east. This is because the wind usually blows from the west bringing fresh air to the west end and carrying smoke and pollution to the eastern side.

Extreme climates

Hottest and driest

Deserts are the hottest and driest places on Earth. In some deserts rain never falls. During the day it can be hot enough to fry an egg on the sand and at night cold enough for water to freeze.

Coldest

The Antarctic is the coldest and windiest place in the world with temperatures falling well below −50°C (−60°F). Even in midsummer, temperatures stay below freezing point.

Wettest

Near the Equator much of the land is covered in dense rain forest. The temperature is about 27°C (80°F) all year round. Heavy rain falls here every day.

Seasons

The seasons are caused by the Earth moving around the Sun and tilting at an angle to the Sun. They change as each half of the Earth leans towards or away from the Sun. When it is summer in the northern hemisphere it is winter in the south.

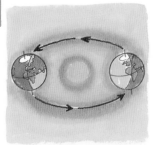

Tropical season

Summer and winter are unknown in places near the Equator as the Equator never tilts away from the Sun. Some places have dry seasons and wet or monsoon seasons, others just hot and wet.

Most pleasant climate

Quito in Equador has earned the name 'Land of eternal spring' because of its climate. Temperatures never fall below 8°C (46°F) at night and reach 22°C (72°F) in the day. Every month about 100 mm (4 in) of refreshing rain falls.

Mountain sides

Mountains can affect the climate far away from them by diverting winds and rain. The sheltered (leeward) side of a mountain has dry weather because the air releases its rain as it rises up over the other (windward) side and cools.

119

Special effects

Rainbows

If sunlight shines through drops of water it breaks up into its 7 main colours – red, orange, yellow, green, blue, indigo and violet. When sunlight hits raindrops or water spray a rainbow appears. To see a rainbow you must have your back to the Sun. From the ground you only see part of a full circle of colours.

Long bow

Rainbows usually only last for a few minutes. But a rainbow seen in Wales on 14 August 1979 was said to have lasted for three hours.

DID YOU KNOW?

Sometimes double rainbows can form. In a single bow red is always at the top and violet at the bottom. In the second fainter bow the colours are always the other way round.

St Elmo's fire

'St Elmo's fire' is a type of lightning which clings to ships' masts and the wing tips of aircraft. It is bluish-green or white and was named after a 4th century Italian bishop, Elmo, the patron saint of fire. Sailors prayed to him for protection at sea and took 'St Elmo's fire' to be a sign of good luck whenever it appeared.

Rings round the Sun

Whitish haloes round the Sun or Moon appear when light is bent by ice crystals in clouds high up in the atmosphere. Haloes are thought to be signs that rain is on its way and this is often

true. The Zuni Indians of North America believed that when the Sun was 'in his tepee' (that is, inside a halo) rain was likely to follow shortly afterwards.

Diamond dust

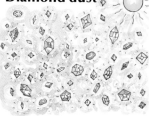

In very cold climates when temperatures drop to below −30°C (−22°F) water droplets in fog may freeze and the air fills with ice crystals. These fall slowly to the ground sparkling in the sunshine and are called ice fog or 'diamond dust'. It is dangerous if breathed in.

Mirages

Mirages are optical illusions. Light is bent as it passes through layers of air with different densities so distant objects look distorted.

Mirages are often seen over hot deserts or roads where a layer of heavy cold air lies over a layer of light warm air. Water may seem to appear on roads but this is really only the light from the sky reflected as if in a mirror. A similar reflection causes oases to appear in the desert.

Fata Morgana

One of the most beautiful mirages is the Fata Morgana, named after a fairy in a story. The mirage appears in the Strait of Messina, Italy as a town in the sky. Then a second town appears piled on top of the first, then a third. Each has splendid palaces and tall towers. People dressed in white seem to walk through the streets. No-one is sure what the mirage reflects but it may be one of the small fishing villages on the coast.

Amazing But True

Some fabulous animals were seen in the Gobi Desert by an American explorer, Roy Chapman Andrews. They looked like giant swans wading in a lake on legs 4½ m (15 ft) long. As Andrews went nearer, the water disappeared and the creatures changed shape. The giant swans were really antelopes grazing on the grass.

Red skies

At sunrise and sunset the sky is often a rich orange-red colour. This is because the short blue light waves in sunlight are scattered by dust in the air and only the longer red waves can get through. The colour of the sky is thought to show what the weather will be like. A red sky at night is said to be a sign of a fine day to come and a red sunrise a sign of bad weather.

Measuring the weather

Weather watching

There are about 10,000 weather stations all over the world in cities, at airports and on weather ships. Working together they watch the weather very closely. Every few hours they measure

humidity, wind speed and direction, pressure and temperature and check rain gauges. All this information is translated into an international code and sent round the world for forecasters to use.

Eureka

The Eureka weather station in Canada is the most remote in the world. It is 960 km (600 miles) from the North Pole – further north than any Eskimos live. Built in 1947, it has many luxuries including a greenhouse where staff grow plants during the 5 months when there is constant daylight.

Radiosonde

The weather high up in the atmosphere affects the weather on Earth. To measure it, balloons are sent up carrying instruments which radio information back to the ground. The balloons reach heights of 35-40 km (20-25 miles) and then burst. Small parachutes carry the instruments safely back to the ground.

Satellites

Satellites show weather patterns which cannot be seen from the ground. There are two types of weather satellites. Polar orbitting

satellites circle the Earth while geo-stationary satellites stay in a fixed place 35,000 km (22,000 miles) above the Equator. Cameras on board send back photographs of clouds.

Weather firsts

The first weather satellite was *Tiros I*, launched on 1 April 1960. It circled the Earth every two hours at heights of 700-1500 km (420-900 miles) and sent back pictures of cloud and snow cover.

Radar

Using radar, weathermen can see if rain is on the way. Each radar covers an area of about 200 km (124 miles) and picks up echo signals of the rain. On the radar screen the white patches are rain.

Storm tracking

In the USA radar is used to follow storms minute by minute so that tornado warnings can be given. In 1985 the Wimbledon tennis championships were saved by radar which saw a terrible storm coming. The groundstaff were warned in time to cover the courts.

Instruments for measuring weather

Weather	Instrument		Units
Atmospheric pressure	Barometer		Millibars
Temperature	Thermometer		°C/°F
Rainfall	Rain gauge		mm
Sunshine	Campbell Stokes recorder		Hours
Wind speed	Anemometer		Kph
Wind direction	Wind vane/ wind sock		Compass points

Cloud cover

The amount of cloud covering the sky is measured in eighths (oktas) from 1 to 8 oktas. 0 oktas means the sky is clear, 8 means it is completely covered. The height of a cloud is measured by how far its base is above sea level.

Anemometer

Anemometers measure wind speed. The most common type looks like a toy windmill. Three cups are fixed to a central shaft and the stronger the wind blows the faster they spin round. The wind speed in kph (mph) is shown on a dial, just like a car's speedometer.

Forecasting the weather

Sign language

People were predicting the weather long before forecasts appeared on T.V. or in newspapers. They looked for 'signs' in the way plants and animals behave. When the pressure drops – a sign of bad weather – sheeps' wool uncurls and ants move to higher ground. Pine cones open when rain is about.

Weather maps

A forecaster is like a detective gathering information and clues. Detailed information about the weather at a certain time of the day is collected and plotted on a map, called a synoptic chart. From this the forecaster, using a computer, can work out very accurately what the next day's weather should be like.

Amazing But True

Animals can indicate the weather, often very accurately. The Germans used to keep frogs as live barometers because they croak when the pressure drops.

Isobars

Isobars are lines drawn on a synoptic chart joining together areas of equal pressure. The further apart they are, the lighter the wind. When they are close together the pressure is usually low and the wind is strong.

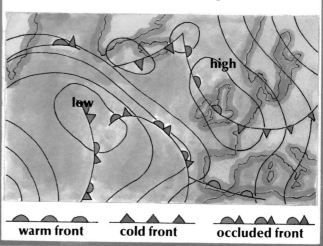

| warm front | cold front | occluded front |

Early warning

As long ago as the 5th century BC the Greeks sent out weather forecasts to their sailors. In the 4th century BC calendars of weather facts and forecasts called 'peg' calendars were put up on important buildings in many Greek cities and were very popular.

DID YOU KNOW?

The more observations there are the more accurate the forecasts will be. Ideally scientists would need frequent reports for every 15 cm^2 (2.3 in^2) of the Earth's surface. This means a report for each piece of the Earth just big enough to stand on.

Forecast factory

An English man, L. R. Richardson, was one of the first people to try to forecast the weather using mathematical equations. He worked out though that he would need a staff of 64,000 to do all the sums quickly enough.

Record forecasts

The U.S. Weather Service makes about 2 million forecasts a year. It also sends out storm and flood warnings and nearly 750,000 forecasts for aircraft. It claims that its one day forecasts are accurate more than three quarters of the time.

Computer age

Because computers can do difficult sums very quickly they have made forecasting much more accurate. The two largest computers are at the weather centres in Washington, USA and Bracknell, UK. The Bracknell computer can handle 400 million calculations a second.

False alarm

In 1185 an astronomer, Johannes of Toledo, predicted that the following year a terrible wind would bring famine and destruction to Europe. People were so frightened that some built new homes underground. But nothing happened!

Who uses forecasts?

Forecasts are used everyday to help us decide what to wear and where to go. They are vital to pilots, sailors and farmers who need to know exactly what weather to expect. If cold weather is on the way more electricity is made and chemists stock more cold cures. Dairies make more ice-cream if hot weather is expected.

Two types of forecast

There are two types of forecast – short and long range. Computers help forecasters produce short range charts for up to a week ahead. Long range forecasting is less accurate and is often done by looking at past weather records. In India forecasts have been made of the next year's monsoon so that famine can be prevented if the rain fails as often happens.

Weather wear and tear

Wear and tear

Rain, wind and frost are always wearing away the Earth's surface. This is called weathering. Rain collects in cracks in the rocks. If it freezes it expands and cracks the rocks apart with a force of 90 kg (200 lb) per 6 sq cm (1 sq in) to form crevices. The wind carries away small pieces of rock chipped off when crevices form.

Wind on sand

Sand blown by the wind helps to shape deserts. Wind blowing constantly from one direction piles the sand up into sanddunes. As more sand is blown across the top of a dune and trickles down the other side, the dune rolls forward like a wave. Small dunes can move more than 15 m (50 ft) a year and can bury whole villages as they pass. The two main types of dune are barchan and seif. The much larger seif dunes can be up to 400 km (250 miles) long.

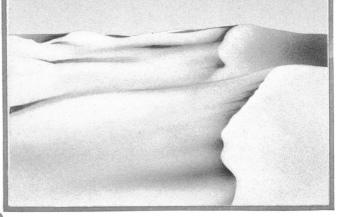

DID YOU KNOW?

Weathering is very slow. The height of some mountains is lowered by about 8.6 cm (3½ in) every 1,000 years. At this rate a mountain only as tall as the Eiffel Tower would take over 3 million years to wear right down.

Highest dunes

The highest measured sanddunes in the world are in the Sahara Desert. They can reach a height of 430 m (1410 ft) – nearly as high as the Empire State Building in New York, USA.

Sand saucers

Huge 'saucers' have been scooped out of the Sahara Desert by windblown sand. The Qattara Depression in Egypt is a huge hollow area below sea-level which is almost the size of Wales.

Fairy forest

Trees growing very high up on mountain sides have to grow close to the ground for protection from the strong cold wind. They are forced to grow sideways and become twisted. These are called krummholz trees or elfin wood. Some fir and pine trees grow so close to the ground that you can step right over them.

Irrigation

In places with little rainfall, water is stored in reservoirs and tanks and used for crops and for drinking. In the USA irrigation accounts for nearly half of the water used. The world's longest irrigation canal is in the USSR. It is 850 km (528 miles) long, over twice as long as Britain's River Thames.

Weather and crops

Temperature and rainfall are the most important influences on growing crops. There is an ideal climate for every crop and farmers have to consider their local climate before choosing which are the best crops to grow.

Weather beaters

Scientists are now at work creating crops which can survive in harsh climates. These include potatoes and sugar beet which can live through droughts and barley which is not killed by frost.

Ice slice

Glaciers are huge rivers of ice which move slowly down mountain slopes. In the last Ice Age rocks in the underside of the ice scraped and tore away deep valleys like the Norwegian fjords.

Crops and climate

	Crop	Ideal climate
	oranges	warm and sunny
	rice	warm and wet
	maize	warm and wet in summer
	oats	quite cool and wet
	potatoes	cool and wet

Living with the weather

Weather wear

People wear clothes suited to the climate they live in. In hot places like the Middle East they wear long, loose robes specially folded so that cool air is trapped inside. In the desert people wear turbans and veils to protect their heads and faces from the Sun and sand. Fur is worn in cold places because it is very good at keeping out the cold.

Aches and pains

There may be some truth in the saying that people can feel the weather in their bones. Some people find that they have aches and pains when the air is humid. Others get headaches before a thunderstorm.

Body guard

The body protects itself from too much heat or cold by perspiring or shivering. Shivering is caused by the muscles twitching and giving off heat. Perspiration is the body's own air-conditioner. It evaporates off the skin and cools it down.

Lifestyles

Weather affects the way people live. In the desert people such as the Bedouins of the Sahara live a nomadic life. They move from place to place in search of water and fodder for their animals. They live in tents to make moving house easier.

Windcatchers

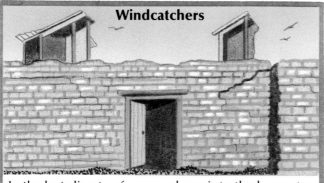

In the hot climate of Pakistan many houses have windcatchers on their roofs. These trap the wind and direct it down into the house to keep it cool. They are a simple but very effective system of natural air-conditioning.

Sleepy head

Animals react to changes in the weather. Some hibernate in winter when food is short. Their pulse and breathing rates slow down to save energy. A hibernating hedgehog only breathes once every 6 seconds – 200 times slower than its normal breathing rate.

Water frog

The water-holding frog which lives in the Central Australian Desert only has a drink every five to six years. This is how often rain falls. Then the frog comes to the surface and absorbs about half its own weight in water so it looks like a small balloon. This supply keeps the frog alive during the droughts.

Amazing But True

As you go higher, the air becomes thinner. Most people need to breathe faster and deeper to take in sufficient oxygen. Andean Indians however, who live in mountain villages, have extra large lungs which enable them to breathe more air at a normal rate.

Skin shield

People who live in hot climates have darker skins to protect them from the Sun. Their skin contains a lot of melanin, a brown pigment which acts as a shield against the Sun's harmful ultra-violet rays. Fair-skinned people tend to get sunburnt easily as they are not so well protected.

Ice house

Eskimos used to build their homes out of snow to make use of the arctic climate they live in. Igloos are quick to build. Blocks of snow are made into a circular base then more circles are added on top, each smaller than the last. An air hole is left at the top and an entrance tunnel built. Snow is such a good insulator that it keeps the inside of the igloo warm and snug though the outside walls stay frozen.

Changing the weather

Warmly wrapped

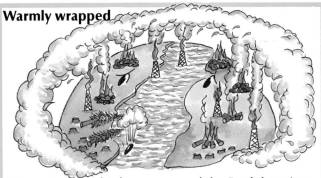

Most scientists think that the Earth is getting warmer. Burning coal, oil and forests increases the amount of carbon dioxide gas in the atmosphere. This acts like a giant blanket round the Earth keeping in warmth which would otherwise escape. If the amount of carbon dioxide in the air were doubled, the Earth's temperature might rise by about 2°C (4°F).

Fog clearing

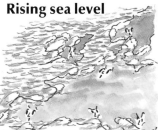

Fog can cause accidents and delays at airports. Many airports today have huge pipes along the sides of the runways. Fuel is pumped into them and burned. This raises the air temperature so that the fog evaporates and planes can take off and land safely.

Acid rain

The rain which falls on parts of Europe and North America can be more acid than lemon juice. Acid rain falls when gases and chemicals from factories dissolve in water in the air to form weak acids. Pollution carried by the wind can fall as acid rain hundreds of kilometers away and destroy forests, crops and life in lakes and rivers.

Rising sea level

If the Earth's temperature increased by 2°C (3.6°F), the oceans would also get warmer and the water would expand. This would cause the sea level to rise by about 0.6 m (2 ft).

Traffic trouble

In many big cities the air is being polluted by exhaust fumes from cars, buses and lorries. When these fumes react with sunlight it can form a kind of fog called 'photochemical smog'. This can damage people's health, stone buildings and plants. In Los Angeles, Mexico City and Tokyo, it is a very serious problem.

Pea-soupers

Smog is a mixture of smoke and fog. Until the 1960's London had terrible smogs called pea-soupers which were coloured green by smoke from factories and coal fires. The worst pea-souper was in December 1952. Some 4,000 people died from chest diseases.

Making rain

Scientists have tried to make rain by sprinkling particles like ice crystals into clouds to encourage raindrops to form. This method, called cloud seeding, is not very successful.

DID YOU KNOW?

The ozone layer is a layer of concentrated ozone gas about 24 km (15 miles) up in the atmosphere. It protects us from the Sun's harmful ultra-violet rays. However, this vitally important layer is being destroyed through the use of aerosol cans containing CFC's. The use of safe gases is being increased.

Rain forests

Every three seconds a piece of South American rain forest the size of a football pitch is cut down. This may lead to changes in rainfall and temperature around the world. Trees 'breathe out' water vapour which is turned into rain in the water cycle. Destroying the forests means that less water vapour is made and less rain falls. Burning the trees increases the amount of carbon dioxide in the air and may be making the Earth warmer.

Weather of the past

Ice Ages

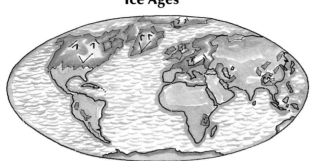

The Earth's climate changes very slowly over the centuries. It is made up of warm periods (interglacials) and cold periods (glacials) or Ice Ages. We live in an interglacial which began about 10,000 years ago. The last glacial was 19,000 years ago when a third of the Earth lay under an ice sheet some 244 m (800 ft) thick.

How Ice Ages happen

Ice Ages may have been caused by changes in the Earth's orbit round the Sun. Even the tiniest difference in the Earth's path can alter the amount of heat the Earth receives from the Sun, and can plunge it into a freezing Ice Age.

DID YOU KNOW?

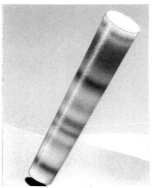

A change in climate may have been the reason for dinosaurs becoming extinct about 65 million years ago. Some people believe that the Earth became very cold as a result of a meteor striking the Earth, causing a dust cloud to block out the Sun's heat. Dinosaurs were probably cold-blooded and could not adapt.

Ice cores

One way of finding out about past climates is by drilling holes in glaciers and pulling out long cores of ice. Distinct layers can be seen in the ice. The darker the ice the colder the climate was. An ice core 366 m (1200 ft) long can tell us about the weather of the past 1400 years.

Climate clues

Scientists find clues about the Earth's past in fossils, soils and trees. Every year a tree grows a new ring. If the ring is wide the weather was

moist and warm, if narrow then it was dry and cold. Tree ring dating gives the most reliable picture of the weather of the past. Bristlecone pines in the USA give the longest record. Some are over 4,000 years old.

Viking voyages

From AD 1000-1200 the world's weather became warmer. The arctic ice melted and the Vikings were able to sail north from Scandinavia to Greenland which was about 1-4°C (2-7°F) warmer than today. They also sailed across the Atlantic to North America. Today's storms and icebergs would make this route very dangerous for the light, wooden Viking boats.

Frost fairs

During the Little Ice Age, the River Thames in London froze over in winter and fairs were held on the ice. The first was in 1607. Tents were set up and there were swings, foodstalls and sideshows. In the winter of 1683 the ice was 26 cm (10 in) thick. The last frost fair was in 1813. It only lasted a few days but the ice was strong enough for an elephant to walk on.

Little Ice Age

From about AD 1400 the Earth's climate became much colder and the 'Little Ice Age' began. In the winter of 1431 every river in Germany froze over. The cold weather lasted until about 1850. Arctic pack ice stretched towards the equator and the temperature was about 2-4°C (4-7°F) lower than today.

Saharan seasons

About 450 million years ago the Sahara Desert was covered in ice. But from about 4000-2000 BC it was covered in grass and trees. Cave paintings from Tassili, Algeria, which date from that time, show people hunting and lions, buffalo and elephants roaming wild.

Amazing But True

London, England, was a very different place 50 million years ago. It had a hot, humid climate and was covered in marshy swamps and tropical jungle where hippos, turtles and crocodiles lived.

Weather gods

Weather power

Good harvests depend on good weather. Early farmers, such as the Sumerians, who lived 7,000 years ago, thought gods ruled the weather. These gods were worshipped with prayers and sacrifices. People today still pray for fine weather and for a good harvest.

Blood-thirsty Sun

The Aztecs believed that the Sun god, Huitzilopochti, was a warrior who fought against the power of night so that the Sun could be reborn every morning. He had to be kept strong and people were sacrificed to provide him with human hearts and blood which were thought to be his favourite food.

Some early primitive people thought that evil spirits lived in the clouds who sent down hail to destroy their crops. They used to shoot arrows into the clouds to frighten the spirits away.

Wind worship

The Ancient Greeks gave the winds names and characters. The Tower of the Winds in Athens, built in 100 BC, shows one of the eight main winds on each wall. Each is dressed for the weather it brings.

Boreas (North)
Notos (South)
Zephyros (West)
Apeliotes (East)
Kaikas (North East)
Euros (South East)
Lips (South West)
Skiros (North West)

Re and Nut

Like the Aztecs, the Ancient Egyptians believed that the gods ruled everything in nature. Their most important god was Re, the Sun god whose mother, Nut, was the sky goddess. Nut was held up by the god of air who stood over the god of Earth.

Sun kings

Many people have worshipped the Sun as the source of life itself. The Ancient Egyptians even believed that their Pharoah was the son of the Sun god, and in Japan the Emperor was thought to be a direct descendant of the Sun goddess.

Thunderous Thor

Thor was the Norse god of thunder. He was thought to be very strong, and to have wild, red hair and a beard. Thor raced across the sky in a chariot pulled by two giant goats, and he brewed up storms by blowing through his beard. He lived in a great hall called Bilskirnir, which means lightning.

Dragon breath

The Chinese believed that dragons formed clouds with their breath and brought rain. The rain fell when the dragons walked over the clouds and storms raged when they fought with each other.

Hot dog days

The Romans called the hottest days of summer 'dog days'. They linked the weather with the stars, and at this time Sirius, the Dog star, was the brightest in the sky.

Chinese calendar

In the 3rd century BC the Chinese divided the year into 24 festivals connected with the weather. Each season had six festivals telling people what weather to expect so that they could sow and harvest their crops at the right times.

Rainbow god

The Kabi people from Queensland in Australia worship a god called Dhakhan who is half fish and half snake. Dhakhan lives in deep water holes in the ground. He appears as a rainbow in the sky when he moves from one hole to the next.

Dancing in the rain

The Hopi Indians of North America perform special rain dances like the buffalo and snake dances. As they dance they pray to the gods to send them rain.

Water everywhere

There are many stories about a great flood which nearly destroyed mankind. The Bible tells of Noah and the Ark. In the Babylonian poem 'Gilgamesh' a violent storm drowns the Earth. In the Greek myth Zeus sends the flood to punish people for being so wicked.

Freaks and disasters

Iced turtle

During a severe hailstorm on 11 May 1894 near Vicksburg, USA, gophar turtle the size of a brick fell with the hail. It had been bounced up and down in a thunder cloud and coated in layer after layer of ice.

Worst weather disasters

Disaster	Location	Date	Deaths
Drought/famine	Bengal, India	1943-4	1,500,000
Flood	Henan, China	1939	1,000,000
Hurricane	Bangladesh	1970	1,000,000
Smog	London, UK	1952	2,850
Tornado	Missouri, USA	1925	800
Hail	Moredabad, India	1888	246
Lightning	Umtali, Zimbabwe	1975	21

Desert snow

Snow fell in the Kalahari Desert in Africa on 1 September 1981 – the first time in living memory. Temperatures dropped as low as −5°C (23°F).

Food from the sky

The sky over Turkey rained down food in August 1890. A type of edible lichen fell with the rain which the local people collected and made into bread.

Hot and cold

On 22 January 1943 a freezing cold winter's day in South Dakota, USA, was transformed into a balmy spring one. At precisely 7.30 in the morning the temperature rose an amazing 27°C (49°F) in just two minutes.

Amazing But True

On 14 October 1755 rain the colour of blood fell in Locarno, Switzerland, and red snow fell over the Alps. This odd colouring was caused by dust from the Sahara Desert in North Africa which had been carried over 3,000 km (1,850 miles) by the wind.

Leg strike

Lightning can fuse or melt metal together. On 10 August 1975, umpire in England was struck by lightning. He was not hurt but the knee joint in his false metal leg was welded quite solid!

Out of the blue

Thirty workers picking peppers in Arizona, USA, were knocked down by a flash of lightning which appeared out of a clear sky. Three died and many were injured.

About turn

A tornado in the USA picked up a railway engine, turned it round in mid-air and put it down again on a parallel track running in the other direction.

Watery walkways

In 1929, the captain of a ship bound for Uruguay reported seeing the unique sight of two large clouds connected by waterspouts. This is difficult to believe, but may not be impossible.

Pennies from heaven

In June 1940 a shower of silver coins fell in Gorky*, Russia. A tornado uncovered an old treasure chest, lifted it into the air and dropped some 1,000 coins on a nearby village.

DID YOU KNOW?

There have been many reports of showers of fish and frogs. On 16 June 1939, a shower of tiny frogs fell at Trowbridge in England. Strong winds had sucked the frogs up from ponds and streams nearby and they then fell with the rain.

Wild weather

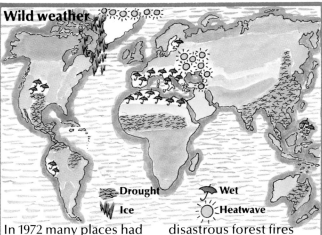

Drought
Ice
Wet
Heatwave

In 1972 many places had unusual weather. On the Arctic coast the temperature reached 32°C (90°F) for several days. In the USSR a heatwave caused disastrous forest fires and in India the monsoon rains failed. In Peru and the Philippines, however, there was very heavy rain and flooding.

Television weather maps

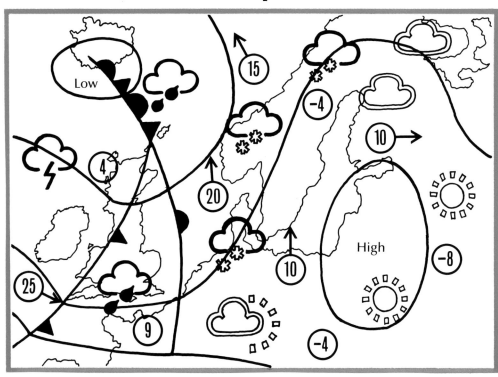

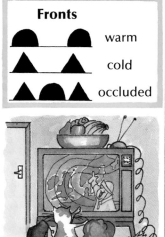

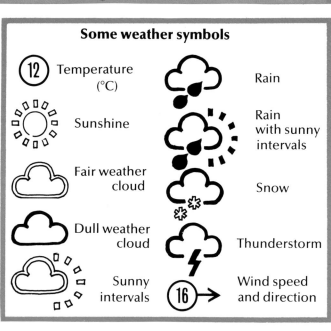

Fronts

warm

cold

occluded

Some weather symbols

(12) Temperature (°C)

Sunshine

Fair weather cloud

Dull weather cloud

Sunny intervals

Rain

Rain with sunny intervals

Snow

Thunderstorm

(16) → Wind speed and direction

Weather calendar

1st century BC Hero of Alexander (Ancient Greece) was probably the first to discover that air had weight.

1607 The first Frost Fair was held on the frozen river Thames in London with tents, sideshows and foodstalls.

1611 Johann Kepler (Germany) was the first person to describe the six-sided shape of snowflakes.

1643 Evangelista Torricelli (Italy) invented the first barometer for measuring air pressure.

1654 Grand Duke Ferdinand of Tuscany invented the first sealed thermometer for measuring temperature.

1718 Gabriel Daniel Fahrenheit (Germany) devised the Fahrenheit scale (°F) for measuring temperature.

1722 Reverend Horsley (Britain) invented the first modern rain gauge. The earliest mention of a rain gauge is in Indian writings from 400 BC.

1742 Anders Celsius (Sweden) devised the Celsius or Centigrade scale (°C) for measuring temperature.

1752 Benjamin Franklin (USA) invented the lightning conductor for use on high buildings.

1783 Horace-Bénédict de Saussure (Switzerland) made the first hair hygrometer for measuring humidity.

1802 Luke Howard (Britain) named the three families of clouds – cirrus, cumulus and stratus.

1805 Admiral Sir Francis Beaufort (Britain) devised the Beaufort Scale for measuring wind speed at sea.

1843 Lucien Vidie (France) made the first aneroid ('non-liquid') barometer for measuring air pressure.

1846 John Robinson (Britain) invented the cup anemometer for measuring wind speed and direction.

1851 The first published weather maps were sold to the public at the Great Exhibition in London.

1856 The first national storm warning system was started in France after storms destroyed ships during the Crimean War.

1930 Pierre Molchanov (USSR) launched a radiosonde for measuring weather in the upper atmosphere.

c.1945 John von Neumann (USA) built a computer known as *Maniac*. It was once used for weather forecasting.

1960 The first specialized weather satellite, *Tiros 1*, was launched by the USA. It provided a unique, global view of weather conditions.

1988 Public became aware that burning fossil fuels could lead to global warming.

Weather record breakers

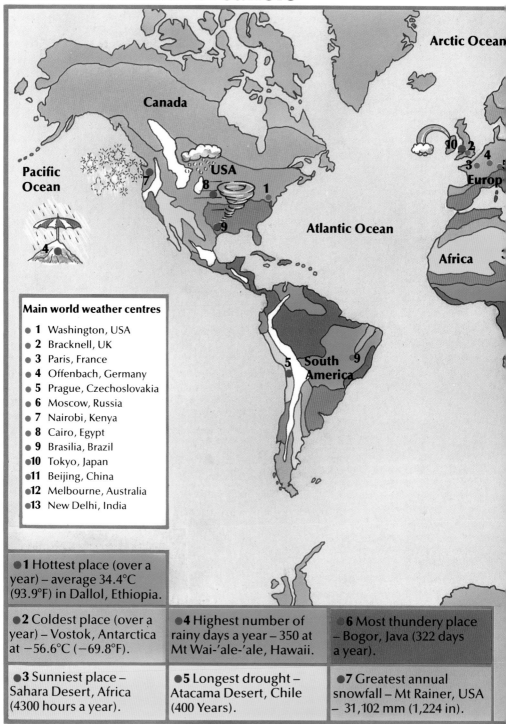

Arctic Ocean

Canada

Pacific Ocean

USA

Atlantic Ocean

Europe

Africa

South America

Main world weather centres

- 1 Washington, USA
- 2 Bracknell, UK
- 3 Paris, France
- 4 Offenbach, Germany
- 5 Prague, Czechoslovakia
- 6 Moscow, Russia
- 7 Nairobi, Kenya
- 8 Cairo, Egypt
- 9 Brasilia, Brazil
- 10 Tokyo, Japan
- 11 Beijing, China
- 12 Melbourne, Australia
- 13 New Delhi, India

●1 Hottest place (over a year) – average 34.4°C (93.9°F) in Dallol, Ethiopia.

●2 Coldest place (over a year) – Vostok, Antarctica at −56.6°C (−69.8°F).

●4 Highest number of rainy days a year – 350 at Mt Wai-'ale-'ale, Hawaii.

●6 Most thundery place – Bogor, Java (322 days a year).

●3 Sunniest place – Sahara Desert, Africa (4300 hours a year).

●5 Longest drought – Atacama Desert, Chile (400 Years).

●7 Greatest annual snowfall – Mt Rainer, USA – 31,102 mm (1,224 in).

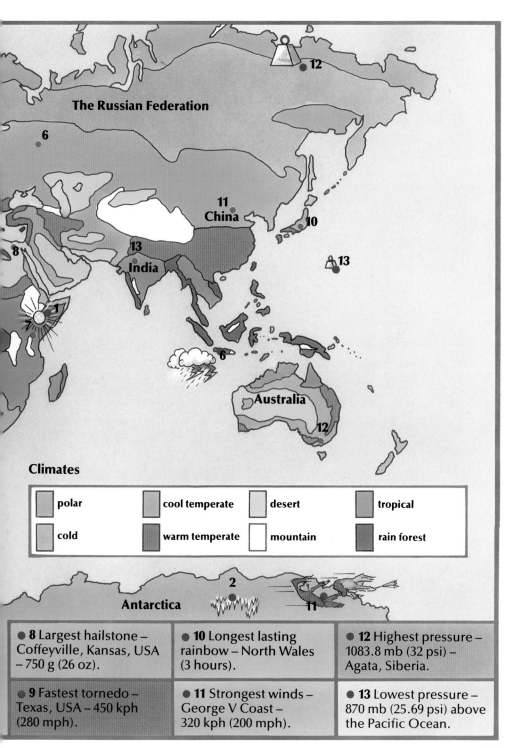

The Russian Federation

6

11
China

10

13
India

8

1

13

6

Australia

12

Climates

polar	cool temperate	desert	tropical
cold	warm temperate	mountain	rain forest

12

2
Antarctica

11

● **8** Largest hailstone – Coffeyville, Kansas, USA – 750 g (26 oz).	● **10** Longest lasting rainbow – North Wales (3 hours).	● **12** Highest pressure – 1083.8 mb (32 psi) – Agata, Siberia.
● **9** Fastest tornedo – Texas, USA – 450 kph (280 mph).	● **11** Strongest winds – George V Coast – 320 kph (200 mph).	● **13** Lowest pressure – 870 mb (25.69 psi) above the Pacific Ocean.

Glossary

Air mass Huge mass of cold or warm air which moves around the world. Can be dry or moist.

Air pressure Due to the weight of the atmosphere pressing down on the Earth's surface.

Anemometer Instrument used to measure wind speed.

Atmosphere The blanket of air around the Earth.

Barometer Instrument used to measure air pressure.

Celsius Degrees (°C) used for measuring temperature. Also called Centigrade.

Climate The general weather of a place over a long period of time.

Cloud A mass of tiny water droplets or ice crystals.

Cold front Boundary between two different air masses where cold air pushes warm air away to bring colder weather.

Condensation When water vapour cools and turns into liquid water.

Coriolis effect The bending of the winds caused by the Earth spinning on its axis.

Dew point The temperature at which the air cannot hold any more water vapour and condensation begins.

Evaporation When liquid water is heated and turns into water vapour.

Fahrenheit Degrees (°F) used for measuring temperature.

High (anticyclone) Area of high pressure. Brings dry weather.

Humidity The amount of moisture in the form of water vapour there is in the air.

Hygrometer Instrument used to measure humidity.

Isobars Lines drawn on a weather map, joining places of equal pressure.

Jet stream Strong wind 5-10 km up in the atmosphere.

Low (depression) Area of low pressure. Often brings wet weather.

Meteorology The scientific study of the atmosphere and weather.

Meteorologists Scientists who study the atmosphere and weather.

Millibar Unit (mb) used to measure air pressure.

Occluded front Combination of warm and cold fronts as a cold front overtakes a warm front.

Precipitation Water which falls from a cloud as rain, snow or hail.

Radiosonde Instruments attached to a balloon for measuring the weather in the upper atmosphere.

Synoptic chart Weather map using isobars to show highs, lows and fronts.

Thermometer Instrument used to measure temperature.

Troposphere The lowest level of the atmosphere, directly above the ground, where weather happens.

Warm front Boundary between two different air masses where warm air pushes cold air away to bring warmer weather.

Water vapour Water in gas form which is in the atmosphere and helps make the weather.

Weather The state of the atmosphere at a certain time and place. Includes temperature, humidity, wind, cloud and precipitation.

Index

SPACE FACTS

Struan Reid

CONTENTS

Illustrated by Tony Gibson

**Additional illustrations by
Martin Newton**

Designed by Teresa Foster

Additional designs by Tony Gibson

Consultant: Sue Becklake

What's it all about?

Astronomy

What is a star? How big is the Universe? Where did the Sun and Earth come from? These are some of the questions that people have been asking for thousands of years. Astronomy is the science that tries to answer these questions and the job of the astronomer is to try and understand the Universe.

Delayed timing

Light from the Sun takes over eight minutes to reach us, travelling a distance of 150 million km (93 million miles). It takes eleven hours to reach the furthest planet in our Solar System, which is Pluto.

A special measurement

The Universe is so enormous that astronomers use a special measurement known as a light year. This is the distance light travels in one year, or 9.5 million, million km (about 6 million, million miles). Light travels at a speed of 300,000 km (186,000 miles) per second.

One of the family

The Earth on which we live is one of a family of nine planets travelling round the Sun. Together they are known as the Solar System. The Sun itself is one very ordinary star in our galaxy, the Milky Way, which contains about 100,000 million stars altogether.

Sun · Mercury · Venus · Earth · Mars · Jupiter · Saturn · Uranus · Neptune · Pluto

One among many

Our own galaxy measures about 950,000 million, million km across. It is only one among millions of other galaxies. All the galaxies and the space around them make up the Universe.

As far as we can see

THE END OF THE UNIVERSE?

The furthest distance astronomers can see into the Universe is about 15,000 million light years, although this is not necessarily the edge of the Universe. It might not even have a boundary.

Amazing But True

If it was possible to travel in a spacecraft at the speed of light, you could go round the Earth seven times in just one second.

The light reaching us now from our nearest star set off over four years ago. At present rocket speeds it would probably take thousands of years to get to the nearest star and back.

The scale of the Universe

The distances in the Universe are so great that it is difficult to imagine them. If the Sun was the size of a ball 1.8 m (6 ft) across, then Pluto, the most distant planet in our Solar System, would be the size of a pea 7.6 km (4.7 miles) away. But our nearest star would be about 52,000 km (32,313 miles) away.

We've only just begun

The exploration of space by satellites and spacecraft is helping scientists learn more about our neighbouring worlds in the Solar System and about the Universe as a whole. But so far we have only been able to explore two other planets in our Solar System with unmanned spacecraft.

Future meetings

In the future we may be able to travel as far as the stars and land on their planets. Some stars may have planets on which other beings live whom we may be able to visit or contact by radio.

Now read on

This book tells you about some of the discoveries that have been made and the possible plans for the future, some of which may happen in your own lifetime.

Going up Our Universe at different heights

A 1 km: low altitude.

B 10,000 km: high.

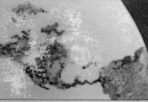

C 1 million km: Earth-Moon system.

D 10 million, million km: 1 light year.

E 100,000 light years: Milky Way galaxy.

F 15,000 million light years: limits of the observable Universe.

The Solar System

The Sun's family

All the planets surrounding the Sun are members of the Sun's family, known as the Solar System. The Sun lies at the centre of the family and orbiting (circling) round it are the planets and their moons and also the asteroids.

The Sun's diameter of 1,392,000 km (865,000 miles) is about 109 times that of Earth's and 10 times that of Jupiter's. If the Sun were represented by a beach ball with a 50 cm (20 in) diameter, Mars would be the size of a small pea about 55 m (180 ft) away and Jupiter would be the size of a golfball 280 m (919 ft) away.

Orbits of the planets

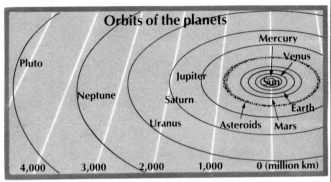

Pluto
Neptune
Uranus
Jupiter
Saturn
Asteroids
Mercury
Venus
Sun
Earth
Mars

4,000   3,000   2,000   1,000   0 (million km)

Birth in a cloud

Many scientists think that the Solar System was formed from a cloud of gas and dust about 4,600 million years ago. The Sun formed in the centre while the planets grew from balls of gas round it.

Merry-go-round

All the members of the Solar System move about other objects. The moons are circling their parent planets, the planets circle the Sun, while each spins about its axis at the same time. The Sun also spins and the whole Solar System is travelling round the galaxy it lies in.

Messenger of the gods

Named after the speedy messenger of the Roman gods, Mercury travels round the Sun at the fastest speed of all the planets, about 172,248 kph (107,030 mph).

Gas condenses

Sun born

Planets form

Solar System born

The Sun gives off huge amounts of deadly radiation, but we are protected from the worst blasts by a magnetic cage called the magnetosphere that surrounds the Earth. Inside this cage, two doughnut-shaped belts trap the electric particles. These are called the Van Allen belts after their discoverer, James Van Allen.

Brightest and faintest

Viewed from Earth, by far the brightest of the planets visible to the naked eye is Venus. It is often called the "evening star". The faintest planet is Pluto. It can only be seen through a telescope.

Data

Planet	Rotational period (round axis)	Orbital period (round Sun)
Mercury	58.7 days	88 days
Venus	243 days	224.7 days
Earth	23.93 hrs	365.25 days
Mars	24.62 hrs	687 days
Jupiter	9.92 hrs	11.9 years
Saturn	10.23 hrs	29.5 years
Uranus	17 hrs	84 years
Neptune	18 hrs	165 years
Pluto	6.4 days	248 years

The unique planet

The Earth is a very special planet because it is the only place in the Solar System, and the only known place in the entire Universe, to support life. If it was closer to the Sun it would be too hot to support life and if it was further away it would be too cold.

Fast spinner

Jupiter is the fastest spinning planet in our Solar System. If you could stand on the equator of the planet, you would be travelling at a speed of 45,500 kph (28,273 mph), compared with the Earth's speed of 523 kph (325 mph).

149

The Sun

One among millions

The Sun is a star, one of 100,000 million stars in our galaxy, the Milky Way. Although it is a very ordinary star in the galaxy, it is very important in our Solar System; without it there would be no life on Earth.

Sizing up the Sun

If the Sun was the size of a large orange, the Earth would be the size of a tiny seed about 10 m (33 ft) away.

Great ball of fire

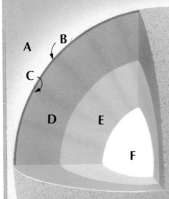

The Sun is mainly made up of the lightest gas, called hydrogen. It burns up 700 million tonnes of hydrogen every second in nuclear reactions at its centre. Scientists believe the Sun loses 4 million tonnes of gas every second, which is about the weight of one million elephants.

A Corona (outer part of the Sun's atmosphere) – 2 million°C.

B Chromosphere (9,600 km/6,000 miles deep) – 4,000°C to more than 50,000°C at the top.

C Photosphere (400 km/249 miles deep) – 6,000°C.

D Convective zone (where gases move round).

E Radiative zone.

F Solar interior – 15 million°C. Nuclear reactions take place here.

Amazing But True

One second of the energy given off by the Sun is 13 million times greater than the average amount of electricity used each year in the USA. All the Earth's oil, coal and wood supplies would fuel the Sun for only a few days.

A long car drive

The distance of the Sun from Earth is just under 150 million km (93 million miles). This distance is called an astronomical unit. If you drove a car at 88 kph (55 mph) from the Earth to the Sun it would take 193 years.

Dangerous heat

The temperature at the centre of the Sun reaches 15 million °C (27 million °F). If a pinhead was this hot, it would set light and destroy everything for 100 km (60 miles) around it.

DID YOU KNOW?

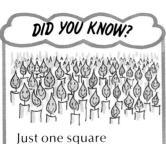

Just one square centimetre of the Sun's surface shines with the brightness of 232,500 candles.

Deadly breeze

The Sun gives off a stream of particles charged with electricity. This is called the solar wind and is estimated to blow more than twice as far as Pluto, the furthest planet in the Solar System.

Light shows

Glowing coloured lights, called aurorae, can sometimes be seen in the skies of the north and south poles. They happen when the electric particles from the Sun bump into the gases in the Earth's atmosphere and make them glow.

Fiery fountains

Fountains of burning hydrogen and helium gas called solar prominences flare up in the Sun's chromosphere. The greatest solar prominence ever recorded reached a height of 402,000 km (250,000 miles), more than the distance from Earth to the Moon.

The Sun's beauty spots

Areas of gas that are cooler than the rest of the surface appear as dark patches on the Sun and are called sunspots. They only seem dark in comparison to the brilliant surrounding surface. Eight Earths can fit into the area of one sunspot.

Why a battle ended

Eclipses of the Sun take place when the Sun, Moon and Earth are all lined up so that the Moon blocks out the sunlight. In 585BC an eclipse happened in the middle of a battle between the Lydians and Medes. The armies made peace.

The Moon

Data

Diameter at the equator: 3,476 km

Mass: 0.0123 (Earth = 1. It would take 81 Moons to equal the mass of the Earth.)

Surface gravity: 0.17 (Earth = 1)

Distance from Earth
furthest: 406,700 km
nearest: 356,400 km
average: 384,000 km

Rotational period round Earth: 27.3 Earth-days

Phases of the Moon

From Earth, the Moon seems to change shape, from a sliver to a full Moon and back to a sliver again. This is because we see different amounts of the Moon's sunlit side as it moves round the Earth. The different shapes are called phases and the Moon goes through its phases in 29.5 days.

Pockmarked surface

About 500,000 Moon craters can be seen through the most powerful telescopes. It would take someone about 400 hours to count all of them – and just those on the face that we can see.

Our nearest neighbour

The Moon is the closest neighbour to Earth. Its average distance from Earth is only 384,000 km (239,000 miles). A train travelling at 161 kph (100 mph) would take 99.5 days to cover the distance.

DID YOU KNOW?

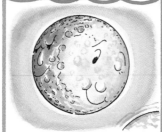

The Moon takes just over 27 days to travel round the Earth. It always keeps the same half facing the Earth. The far side of the Moon had never been seen until the USSR spacecraft Luna 3 took the first photographs of it in 1959.

A Scottish crater

The largest crater we can see on the Moon is called Bailly and covers an area of about 67,300 square km (26,000 square miles). If Bailly was brought down to Earth, Scotland could sit comfortably inside it.

Seas without water

The dark areas you can see on the Moon's surface are called "seas". There is no water there but millions of years ago they were covered by volcanic lava. Some are very big. The Ocean of Storms is larger than the Mediterranean.

As dry as dust

The Moon has no atmosphere and contains no water. Its soil is so dry that nothing will grow in it. But scientists have found that with air and water, plants can grow in Moon soil on Earth.

Dead quiet

The Moon is a completely silent place. Noises cannot be heard as there is no air to carry sound from one place to another.

Precious stones

The various Apollo astronauts who landed on the Moon brought back to Earth a total of 382 kg (842 lb) of Moon rocks and dust. Divided into the total cost of the Apollo space programme, the samples of Moon rock and dust cost around $67,000 per gram ($1,896,000 per ounce).

Staying the same

Unlike the Earth, which has been continuously worn away, the surface of the Moon has not been attacked by wind and water. The rocks brought back to Earth by astronauts had probably been lying in the same position on the surface of the Moon for 3,000 million years without moving a fraction.

Amazing But True

Footprints left on the Moon by the Apollo astronauts will probably be visible for at least 10 million years.

Moonquivers

There are earthquakes on the Moon known as moonquakes, but they are very weak compared to our earthquakes. About 3,000 occur each year, but all the moonquakes in one year would produce enough energy for just a small fireworks display.

Gravity and tides

The pull of gravity of the Earth on the Moon keeps the Moon circling round the Earth. But the Moon's gravity also pulls the water in the Earth's seas towards it, causing the Earth's tides. If the Moon was closer to Earth the pull of its gravity would be much stronger and the tides would flood the coastlines of the world.

Mercury, Venus and Mars

Data

Planet	Diameter at the equator	Mass	Orbital speed (round Sun)	Surface temperatures	Satellites
Mercury	4,878 km	0.055 (Earth=1)	47.9 km/sec	350°C	0
Venus	12,100 km	0.815	35.0 km/sec	480°C	0
Mars	6,780 km	0.107	24.1 km/sec	–23°C	2

The inner planets

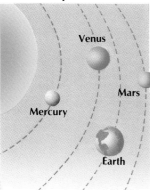

Mercury, Venus and Mars, along with the Earth, form a group of four rocky planets unlike the others. They are known as the inner planets because they are the nearest to the Sun.

Hotter than a desert

Mercury is the closest planet to the Sun. Because of this, it has scorching daytime temperatures of up to 350°C (662°F). This is over seven times hotter than the hottest temperature ever recorded on Earth – 57.7°C (136°F) at Azizia, Libya in 1922.

Freezer cold

The temperature on Mercury at night can plunge to –170°C (–274°F) because there is no blanket of atmosphere to trap the heat. This is more than seven times colder than the temperature inside the freezer compartment of a refrigerator.

DID YOU KNOW?

Mercury has a core of iron, slightly bigger than our Moon. At recent world production figures for iron, it would take about 6,500 million years to mine all the iron in Mercury's core.

Not really an atmosphere

Although Mercury is surrounded by a thin layer of helium gas, there is so little of it that the amount collected from a 6.4 km (4 mile) diameter sphere would be just enough to fill a child's small balloon.

Clouds of acid

Although Venus and Earth are about the same size, their atmospheres are completely different. Venus' atmosphere is made up mostly of carbon dioxide gas, which is poisonous, and contains sulphuric acid in its clouds.

Deep atmosphere diving

Venus' atmosphere is so thick that at the planet's surface the pressure is 90 times that on Earth. On Earth, the atmospheric pressure measures 1.03 kg cm^2 (14.7 lb in^2). On Venus, the same area has a pressure of 600 kg (1,323 lbs). This is the pressure a diver would experience at 80 m (264 ft) beneath the sea.

Back-to-front

Venus rotates east to west, in the opposite direction to all the other planets. This means that the Sun rises in the west and sets in the east.

Amazing But True

There is so little water in the Martian atmosphere that if all of it was collected together it would fit into the Serpentine Lake, London.

Mountain high

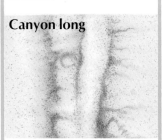

One of the highest mountains in the Solar System is found on Venus. It is called the Maxwell Montes and is more than 2 km (1.2 miles) higher than Mt. Everest.

Canyon long

Mars has the largest canyon in the Solar System, called the Mariner Valley. It is 13 times longer than the Grand Canyon in the USA and would stretch from one side of the USA to the other.

Midget moons

Mars has two tiny moons, called Phobos and Deimos. Deimos is so small and its gravity so weak that people could launch themselves into space by reaching a speed of 36 kph (22 mph).

Greenhouse effect

The atmosphere on Venus traps the heat rather like a greenhouse so that the temperature reaches about 500°C (932°F).

Jupiter and Saturn

Data	Jupiter	Saturn
Diameter at the equator	143,000 km	120,000 km
Mass	318 (Earth=1)	95
Orbital speed (round Sun)	13.1 km/sec	9.7 km/sec
Cloud top temperatures	–150°C	–180°C
Number of satellites	16	21

Sizing up Jupiter

Jupiter is much smaller than the Sun. If the Sun's diameter was equal to a giant tractor tyre 175 cm (69 in) in diameter, then Jupiter would be the size of a ball 18 cm (7 in) in diameter and the Earth would be the size of a small marble about 1 cm (0.4 in) in diameter.

Similar planets

Jupiter and Saturn are members of a group of four planets, known as the "gas giants", which are very different from the inner planets. They have small rocky centres, surrounded by liquid hydrogen and covered with thick, cloudy atmospheres.

The giant planet

Jupiter is the largest planet in our Solar System. Jupiter is more than 1,300 times bigger than Earth and bigger than all the other planets put together.

The Great Red Spot

The reddish patch on Jupiter is known as the Great Red Spot and was first recorded in the 17th century. It is the biggest hurricane in the Solar System with swirling clouds about 38,500 km (24,000 miles) long by 11,000 km (7,000 miles) wide. It is as big as three Earths.

Fat stomach

Jupiter spins round very quickly on its axis, taking less than 10 hours to make one turn. This forces the equator to bulge out so that the planet looks like a squashed ball.

Heart pressure

The core of Jupiter is about the size of Earth and has a temperature of about 30,000°C (54,000°F). The pressure at the core is more than 30 million times higher than the Earth's atmosphere. If anyone flew to Jupiter and then landed on the surface, they would be crushed by the pressure straight away.

Amazing But True

Jupiter is so big that if a bicyclist set out to travel non-stop once round it at a speed of 9.6 kph (6 mph), the journey would take more than five years (1,935 days) to complete.

Inside-out moon

The most explosive object in the Solar System is one of Jupiter's moons, called Io. Geologists estimate that the volcanoes on its surface throw up enough material every 3,000 years to cover the entire surface with a thin layer about 1 cm (0.4 in) thick. So Io is continually turning itself inside out.

Speedy moon

The fastest-moving moon in the Solar System, known as J3, travels at a speed of about 113,600 km (70,400 miles) per hour. A person travelling at this speed could fly from Bombay in India to Port Said in Egypt in 2 minutes 11 seconds.

DID YOU KNOW?

Saturn is the second biggest planet in the Solar System and it is 95 times heavier than Earth. The volume of Saturn is 744 times that of Earth.

Hurricane winds

The winds that blow round Saturn's equator are ten-times stronger than the average hurricane on Earth, travelling at 1,770 kph (1,100 mph).

Record rings

Saturn is one of the most beautiful planets in the Solar System. It is surrounded by rings made up of millions of icy particles. The ice particles are like tiny mirrors and are very thin compared to their 275,000 km (171,000 miles) diameter. They are only about 100 m (300 ft) thick. On this scale, a gramaphone record 1.5 mm (0.06 in) thick would be 4 km (2.5 miles) across.

Lighter than water

Saturn is composed mostly of hydrogen and helium gas and liquid, like Jupiter. But it is smaller than Jupiter. It has the lowest density of all the planets in the Solar System. If it was the size of a tennis ball it would be able to float in a bucket of water.

Uranus, Neptune and Pluto

Data	Uranus	Neptune	Pluto
Diameter at the equator	52,000 km	49,000 km	Approx. 2,400 km
Mass	14.54 (Earth=1)	17.2	0.002?
Orbital speed round Sun	6.8 km/sec	5.4 km/sec	4.7 km/sec
Surface temperatures	−210°C	−220°C	−230°C
Satellites	15	2	1

Little and large

Uranus and Neptune are a second pair of "gas giants", though smaller than Jupiter and Saturn. Pluto is a small, solid planet, probably more like the rocky inner planets (Mercury, Venus, Earth and Mars). They are all far too cold for anything to live on their surfaces.

Green with methane

The atmospheres surrounding Uranus and Neptune contain hydrogen and helium, like those of Jupiter and Saturn. But their atmospheres also contain methane gas, which makes them look green from Earth.

Amazing But True

One of the strangest things about Uranus is that it rolls round the Sun on its side, while all the other planets spin round like tops. This means that either Uranus' northern or southern hemisphere

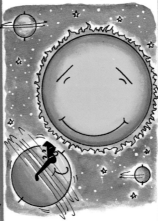

will face the Sun and will receive almost constant sunlight, while the other remains in darkness. This creates the Solar System's longest seasons, summers and winters about 21 years long.

New discovery

People used to think that the furthest planet in the Solar System was Saturn. But in 1781 an astronomer called Sir William Herschel discovered a faint planet which was later named Uranus. It was the first planet to be discovered since the Ancient Greeks.

Blacker than black

In 1977, astronomers discovered that Uranus has a set of narrow rings. There are now thought to be 10 of these. They are made of about the darkest material known in the Solar System.

Not quite a twin

Neptune was first seen in 1846. It is almost the twin of Uranus, but it is slightly smaller and it does not have Uranus' tilt.

Uranus

Neptune

Old first birthday

A baby born on Pluto (if that was possible) would have to wait 147 Earth years before it reached its first birthday.

Long plane journey

The average distance of Neptune from the Sun is 4,500 million km (2,800 million miles). This is 30 times the distance between Earth and the Sun. If an aeroplane flew at 1,770 kph (1,100 mph), it would take 289 years to travel from Neptune to the Sun.

DID YOU KNOW?

A person on Neptune would never live for one Neptune year. The Neptune year is the time it takes Neptune to travel once round the Sun – 164.8 Earth years.

The smallest planet

Pluto was discovered in 1930. With a diameter of 2,400 km (1,500 miles) it is smaller than our Moon, making it the smallest and lightest planet in the Solar System.

Stretched orbit

Pluto has a very strange path round the Sun. While the routes of the other planets are almost circles, Pluto's is more elongated. Because of its strange orbit, Pluto is closer to the Sun between 1979 and 1999 than Neptune, making Neptune the furthest planet from Earth during those years.

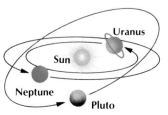

Uranus

Sun

Neptune

Pluto

Cosy companion

Pluto has a very close companion, a moon called Charon which was discovered in 1978 and which lies only 20,000 km (12,500 miles) from Pluto. Its diameter is about 800 km (500 miles), making it the largest moon compared to its planet in the Solar System.

Spaced out

For most of the time, Pluto is the furthest planet from Earth. An aeroplane travelling at a speed of 1,810 kph (1,125 mph) would take about 370 years to travel from Earth to Pluto.

Asteroids, comets and meteors

Stone belt

Between the inner planets (Mercury, Venus, Earth and Mars) and the outer planets (Jupiter, Saturn, Uranus, Neptune and Pluto) lies a belt of about 40,000 much smaller irregular planets known as asteroids.

The main comets

Name	Orbital period round Sun (years)
Schwassmann – Wachmann	16.1
Halley	76.03
D'Arrest	6.2
Encke	3.3
Pons – Winnecke	6.3
Finlay	6.9
Faye	7.4
Tuttle	13.61
Crommelin	27.9

Big lump

The largest asteroid is called Ceres. It measures about 1,000 km (620 miles) in diameter and if it arrived on Earth it could fit on to the surface of France.

Dirty snowballs

Comets are balls of icy particles and dust that come from the furthest parts of the Solar System and travel round the Sun. A comet glows slightly and reflects the light of the Sun. Scientists think that about 100,000 million comets may circle the Sun.

Roaring tail

When a comet approaches the Sun, a huge tail appears behind it. This is made up of gas and dust released from the comet by the heat of the Sun. The comet's tail points away from the Sun because the solar wind blows it away.

Wrapping up Earth

The Great Comet of 1843 had a tail about 330 million km (200 million miles) long. If this tail was wrapped round Earth it would circle the equator about 8,000 times.

Lighter than air

The density of a comet is far less than that of water or air. If all the comets were put together they would weigh no more than the Earth.

Life boat

According to astronomers Chandra Wickramasinghe and Sir Frederick Hoyle, life may have originated far out in space and been brought to Earth aboard a comet which crashed on to the surface.

Signs in the sky

The appearance of Halley's Comet in the sky through the centuries has been regarded as an important sign. It was seen in England in 1066 before the Battle of Hastings and William the Conqueror's battle cry was "A new star, a new king".

Streaking rocks

Meteors are small pieces of rock that enter the top of Earth's atmosphere. They do not manage to travel far down and reach the Earth's surface, but burn up about 80 km (50 miles) up in the sky, producing streaks of light known as "shooting stars".

Jumbo meteorite

Meteorites are large chunks of rock that reach the Earth's surface without burning up. Scientists think that they come from asteroids. The largest known meteorite in the world fell to Earth at Hoba West in Namibia, Africa. It measures 2.7x2.4 m (9x8 ft) and weighs about 60 tonnes, as much as 9 elephants.

Explosive impact

One of the most famous meteorite craters on Earth is the Arizona Crater in the USA. It was formed about 22,000 years ago and the force of the explosion when the meteorite hit Earth equalled 1,000 Hiroshima atomic bombs.

Iron from space

Eskimos in Greenland used iron tools for centuries, even though they could not smelt iron. They mined iron in almost pure form from three large meteorites that had fallen on Greenland hundreds of years ago.

DID YOU KNOW?

Meteors burn up in the atmosphere and filter down to Earth as dust. The total weight of the Earth increases in weight from this dust by about 25 tonnes each day, which adds up to 9,125 tonnes each year.

The life of stars

Millions of suns

The stars you can see in the night sky are really distant suns. Our Sun is only one very ordinary star among millions of others. The next nearest star to our Solar System is called Proxima Centauri and is 4.25 light years away.

A star is born

Stars are born from the huge clouds of gas and dust known as nebulae that float in the Universe. They begin to grow when part of a cloud forms into a small lump. This grows smaller and hotter until a nuclear reaction starts and the star is born.

Long journey

A car travelling from our Solar System at 88.5 kph (55 mph) would take 52 million years to drive to Proxima Centauri. This is equal to about 722,000 average lifetimes.

Hot heart

The heart of a star is extremely hot and reaches a temperature of about 16 million °C (29 million °F). A grain of sand that hot would kill a person up to 161 km (100 miles) away.

Long-distance call

One of the largest stars known is called Betelgeuse. It has a diameter of 1,000 million km (621 million miles), or about 730 times greater than the Sun. If you made a telephone call from one side to the other, your voice, travelling at the speed of light, would take 55 minutes to reach the other end of the line.

What is a star?

A star shines with its own light. It is made up mostly of hydrogen gas and held together by its own gravity. Reactions in the heart of stars, like those in nuclear bombs, generate heat and light.

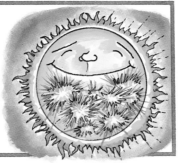

162

Star death

When the hydrogen gas at the centre of a star is burned up, it begins to die. It then swells up to a red giant star. When our Sun begins to die it will swell up until it is beyond the Earth's orbit, destroying the entire planet and destroying Mercury and Venus as well.

Little heavyweight

A red giant star then collapses into a ball about the size of the Earth. This is known as a white dwarf star and its gravity is so strong that a large cupful of its material weighs about 500 tonnes, which is about the weight of two Boeing 747 jumbo jets put together.

Neutron stars

If a star is much bigger than the Sun, the collapse goes beyond the white dwarf stage and does not stop until the star is about 10 km (6.25 miles) across. This is called a neutron star and a pinhead of its material would weigh about 1 million tonnes. This is about the same weight as two of the world's largest supertankers put together.

Amazing But True

A 4 kg (9 lb) baby would weigh 40,000 million kg (90,000 million lb) on the surface of a neutron star because the gravity is so strong.

Pulsating stars

Some neutron stars spin round very fast, as much as 642 times a second, sending out a beam of radio waves. This type of neutron star is called a pulsar. The first pulsar was discovered in 1968 by a British astronomer called Antony Hewish. He thought it was a message coming from another planet, until more were discovered.

Shrinking to nothing

A dying star at least three times bigger than the Sun goes on shrinking beyond the neutron star stage. Its gravity is so strong that it drags everything back to the star. The star has become a black hole. Black holes are impossible to see because even light cannot escape from them.

163

Groups of stars

Star families

Some of the stars in our galaxy, like our Sun, are alone with no star companions. But because stars are normally born in groups which gradually drift apart, many are found in pairs or sometimes larger numbers.

Pairs of stars

Double, or binary, stars consist of two stars which circle round each other. Close pairs of stars may take only a day or even less to complete their circuits, but pairs that are far apart may take over a hundred years.

Star clusters

As well as binary stars and small groups, there are larger groups called star clusters. There are two types of cluster, known as open and globular. Open clusters are found in the spiral arms of our galaxy and usually contain several hundred young stars. Globular clusters are found near the centre of our galaxy and are much more compact groups containing up to a million older stars.

The Seven Sisters

About 1,000 open clusters are in our galaxy. The Pleiades is one such cluster, containing about 400 stars. It is also known as the Seven Sisters and can easily be found in the night sky without a telescope.

Amazing But True

There are about 120 globular clusters in our galaxy. Globular clusters are so tightly packed at their centres that if our Earth was placed in the middle of one the nearest stars would only be light days away, rather than light years. Our night sky would always be as bright as if there was a full moon shining.

The heaviest giants

Plaskett's star, lying about 2,700 light years away from us, is really made up of two giant stars that orbit each other every 14 days. Astronomers think that the largest of the two stars is so big that it is about 55 times heavier than the Sun. A star this weight would be the size of about 18 million Earths or 1,460 million Moons.

A gang of stars

As well as double stars, there are star systems with three or even more members, though not many of these are known. A well-known example, called Castor, contains six stars. Only three stars can be seen with a telescope, two bright and one dim, but each is really a close double star.

DID YOU KNOW?

A nova (meaning "new star") is a star that suddenly flares up to be many times brighter than it was. A really brilliant nova may have been a star which could hardly be seen even with a large telescope. It then suddenly becomes visible to the naked eye but gradually fades again.

Eclipsing stars

Some pairs of stars move round each other so that, seen from Earth, they block out each other's light. These are known as eclipsing binaries and the amount of light we can see goes down during each eclipse.

Mystery giant

One of the most mysterious eclipsing binary stars is called Epsilon Aurigae. The two stars revolve round each other every 27 years. One of the stars has never been directly seen but some astronomers believe it may be the largest star known, with a diameter 2,800 times that of the Sun. If it was placed in the middle of our Solar System, the edge of this star would reach as far as Uranus.

Throbbing stars

Eclipsing stars are not the only ones whose brightness goes up and down. There are some stars called the Cepheid variables that actually swell and shrink regularly. As they throb in and out their brightness also rises and falls.

The brightest star

Eta Carinae is an unusual variable star. Astronomers think that it may be a slow nova star. In 1843 it flashed its record brilliance which has been estimated to have been up to six million times brighter than the Sun, making Eta Carinae the most brilliant star ever recorded.

Nebulae

Dusty space

Although the stars in the night sky look close together, they are really separated by huge stretches of space. This space contains very small gas and dust particles known as interstellar matter.

Gas and dust clouds

Some of the interstellar matter in space has collected together to form clouds called nebulae (from the Latin for clouds). There are three types of nebula.

Dark nebulae do not shine but, by blocking out the light from the stars behind, they appear as darker patches in the sky.

Reflection nebulae also do not shine but reflect the light from nearby stars.

Many glowing nebulae contain young, hot stars which make the gases glow.

Star nurseries

The oldest stars in our galaxy are concentrated in the central bulge. The younger stars, like our Sun, lie further from the centre in the spiral arms. This is the area where stars are born and objects like the Orion, Lagoon and Trifid nebulae are star birthplaces. The dark spots inside may be baby stars.

Galactic babies

Every 18 days, about 20 times a year, our galaxy gives birth to a new star. Every half second a human birth occurs on Earth.

Giant explosions

Some nebulae are formed from the remains of giant star explosions called supernovae. The outer layers of the star are thrown off as clouds of gas which glow. The Crab Nebula is the most famous example of this type and is believed to have been formed in 1054, when Edward the Confessor was King of England.

The Orion Nebula is so huge that if the distance between the Earth and the Sun was represented by 2.5 cm (1 in), the Orion Nebula would be 20.3 km (12.6 miles) in diameter.

Blowing bubbles

A huge cloud of gas called the Cygnus Superbubble lies about 6,500 light years away from our Solar System. Astronomers believe that this superbubble was formed from a number of supernovae explosions over the last three or four million years.

Death and life

Supernovae explosions are so powerful that they are brighter than 1,000 million Suns. This type of nebula represents the end of a star's life and new stars will be born from the clouds of gas to continue the cycle of life and death.

A veil of gas

The Veil Nebula lies about 2,500 light years away from us and is probably formed from the remains of a supernova explosion. Astronomers have worked out that the explosion took place about 50,000 years ago, when primitive humans lived on Earth.

Amazing But True

The Orion Nebula in our galaxy is a glowing nebula. It lies about 1,600 light years away from us but it is so bright that it can be seen with the naked eye. It is many times thinner than the air we breathe. If a sample 2.5 cm (1 in) in diameter could be taken all the way through the nebula, the material collected would weigh less than a small coin.

Smoke signals

Ring nebulae are formed from the puffs of gases given off by dying stars when they reach the red giant stage near the end of their lifetimes. The expanding, glowing gases form rings round the stars.

The Milky Way

Our galaxy

Stars are not scattered randomly throughout the Universe, but are grouped together in giant clouds known as galaxies. The Milky Way is the name of the galaxy our Solar System lies in, in one of the spiral arms.

Star town

The Milky Way contains at least 100,000 million stars. Huge distances lie between each one. If each star was the size of the full-stop at the end of this sentence, there would be one star every 21 cm^2 (3.26 in^2), covering an area of about 40 km (15.5 square miles). This is the size of a small town.

Giant catherine wheel

Because we live inside the Milky Way, it is difficult to see its shape. Astronomers have worked out that the Milky Way is in the shape of a giant spiral measuring about 100,000 light years in diameter. Two starry arms wind round the centre several times like a catherine wheel.

DID YOU KNOW?

The word galaxy comes from the Greek word for milk, "gala". The Ancient Greeks thought the Milky Way was formed from spilt milk from the breast of the goddess Hera when she suckled the baby Herakles (Hercules).

Pot belly

The centre of the Milky Way measures about 20,000 light years from one side to the other and bulges up and down. About 40,000 million of the galaxy's stars are concentrated in the centre.

Star crashes

Stars at the centre of the Milky Way probably collide once every 1,000 years. If the car collision rate on Earth was the same we would have to wait two million years before the first crash, and there would not have been a single one so far in car history.

Cutting it down to size

If our Solar System could fit into a tea cup, the Milky Way would be the size of North America.

Galactic fog

We cannot see deep into the heart of the Milky Way because of huge clouds of gas and dust that block the view. To see the centre from Earth would be like trying to see the Moon through a thick cloud of smoke.

Greedy guts

Some astronomers think that a very powerful black hole lies at the centre of the Milky Way, equal in weight to four million Suns. Such a black hole would be so powerful that it would capture and destroy the equivalent of 3.3 Earths every year.

Galaxy drive

Our Solar System lies in one of the arms of the Milky Way, about 33,000 light years from the centre of the galaxy. If you drove a car from Earth at 161 km (100 miles) per hour it would take a total of about 221,000 million years to reach the centre of the Milky Way.

Amazing But True

Our galaxy is so huge that a flash of light travelling at its natural speed of 1,100 million km (670 million miles) per hour would take 100,000 years to go from one side of the galaxy to the other.

Changing shape

The stars of the Milky Way move continuously round the centre, but they do not turn like a solid wheel. Stars near the centre travel one circuit in only 10 million years, yet out near our Solar System a single

circuit takes about 225 million years. Every time our Solar System moves once round the galaxy, the central stars turn 100 times. This means that the shape of the Milky Way is changing slowly the whole time.

Happy cosmic birthday

A cosmic year is the time it takes our galaxy to cover one complete circuit, about 225 million years. One cosmic year ago, the Earth was at the beginning of the Triassic period, when giant reptiles were replacing sea creatures as the main form of life.

Galaxies

A drop in the ocean of space

Most astronomers believe that galaxies were formed about 14,000 million years ago, about 1,000 million years after the Big Bang (the explosion that formed the Universe). The galaxy we live in is called the Milky Way. There are probably thousands of millions of other galaxies.

The Earth is the third closest planet to the Sun and one of the smaller planets of the Solar System.

The Solar System is tiny when seen in its galaxy, the Milky Way.

The Milky Way itself is insignificant when pictured with the other galaxies.

Types of galaxies

Galaxies come in various shapes. Four main types have been named according to their shapes: spirals, ellipticals, barred spirals and irregular galaxies.

The largest galaxies have diameters of about 500,000 light years but the smallest have diameters of a few thousand light years.

Spiral

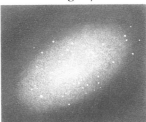

Elliptical

Barred spiral

Irregular

DID YOU KNOW?

Galaxies are found in groups or clusters. Many clusters of galaxies are known, some of which contain hundreds of members loosely held together by the force of gravity. The Virgo cluster of galaxies, more than 60 million light years away from us, contains at least 1,000 galaxies. Our cluster consists of only about 20 galaxies.

Carry on counting

An average galaxy contains about 100,000 million stars. To count all the stars would take a thousand years at the rate of three a second.

Outshining the Sun

The galaxy known as M87 is the brightest in the Virgo cluster. A mysterious jet of gases streams out of its centre about 5,000 light years into space. The brightest point in this jet shines with the strength of 40 million Suns.

Second-rate galaxy

Our galaxy, the Milky Way, is a member of a cluster known as the local group which contains about 20 other galaxies. A galaxy called the Andromeda Spiral is the largest member of the group, with the Milky Way coming a poor second.

Older than humans

The Andromeda Spiral is estimated to be 2.2 million light years from the Milky Way. It is the most distant object visible to the naked eye, yet it is still one of the nearest galaxies to us. When you look at Andromeda you are seeing light that started its journey towards you when mammoths first lived on the Earth's surface.

Amazing But True

Some galaxies are powerful sources of radio waves as well as light. These are known as radio galaxies. Astronomers now think that the radio waves could be caused by huge explosions inside the galaxies.

Calling all quasars

In 1963 radio waves were discovered to be coming from objects that looked like faint stars. These are now called quasars and about 1,300 have so far been discovered. They seem to be small compared to galaxies but up to a thousand times brighter than normal galaxies.

To the edge of time

The most distant object ever seen in the Universe through a telescope is a quasar known as PKS2000-330 and it is thought to be 13,000 million light years away from us. It is racing

away from our galaxy at a speed of about 273,000 km/sec (170,000 miles/sec), about two-thirds the distance from the Earth to the Moon each second.

Origins of the Universe

The Big Bang theory

Most astronomers now believe that the Universe began with a huge explosion, often referred to as the "Big Bang". A tiny point of incredible energy blew apart, scattering hot gases in every direction. Out of this material the galaxies, stars and planets were formed.

Disappearing stars

When their light is examined with special equipment, most stars show something known as red shift. This indicates that the stars are moving away from us and shows that the Universe is still expanding with the force of the Big Bang. When the Universe was 9.5 million years old, it was expanding at nearly the speed of light – 300,000 km (186,000 miles) per second.

The age of the Universe

Once astronomers had measured the speed at which the galaxies are moving outwards, they could work backwards to decide how long ago the Universe began. They now generally agree that it started about 15,000 million years ago. If each year was equal to one second, the seconds would add up to almost 475 years.

Time chart

Millions of years		Event
0		Big Bang
1,000		Galaxies begin to form.
4,000		Stars develop within galaxies.
10,000		Our Solar System forms.
11,000		Life begins to form on Earth.
14,650		Human beings (Homo sapiens) first appear on Earth.
15,000		Today

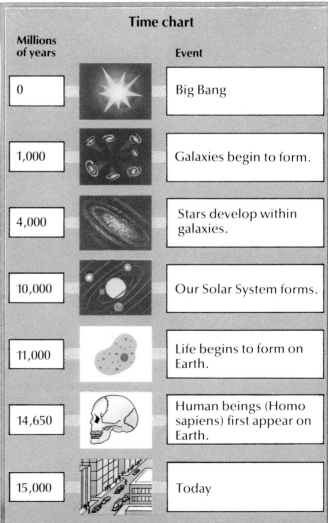

A hot pinhead

Astronomers think that the temperature one second after the Big Bang was so hot that it measured about 10,000 million °C. Just a pinhead amount of this very high temperature, with a radius of 1 mm (0.03937 in), would equal over 18 times the entire energy output of the Sun since it was born about 5,000 million years ago.

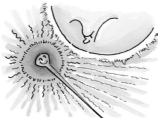

Starting all over again

Some astronomers believe that the outward-speeding galaxies could slow down and then fall back towards the centre. Finally they would collide and create a new explosion. The cycle would be repeated about every 80,000 million years, which means that the next Big Bang could take place in about 65,000 million years' time. This is known as the Oscillating Universe theory.

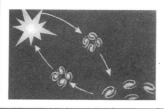

Radio astronomers used to think that the crackling noises picked up on their equipment were caused by pigeon droppings on their radio antennae. But they have now found that space is filled with faint radio waves. These are the dying radio echoes of the Big Bang.

Staying the same

Some astronomers believe that although the Universe is expanding it always looks the same. This is because new galaxies are formed at the centre to replace those that are moving outwards. This is known as the Steady State theory.

Some of the particles that make up living things have been found in outer space. One of them is alcohol. Astronomers estimate that a huge cloud in the constellation of Sagittarius contains enough ethyl alcohol to make 10,000 million, million, million, million bottles of whisky.

The mysterious neutrino

Among the most mysterious ingredients of the Universe are neutrinos. They are unimaginably tiny particles, freed one second after the Big Bang. These particles travel at the speed of light and can pass right through Earth without even slowing down. Millions will pass through this page, and through you, in the time it takes you to read it.

Early astronomy

Farming astronomers

People in ancient times used the position of the Sun and the Moon in the skies to tell them the season of the year, so that they could plan the planting and harvesting of their crops. They built stone monuments thousands of years ago that served as giant calendars, some of which can still be seen in parts of the world today.

Stone calendar

Stonehenge in England was started nearly 4,000 years ago and has different pairs of stones which can be lined up with sunrise and moonrise on different days throughout the year. This monument may have been used to find midsummer and midwinter before the invention of the calendar.

A giant clock

The Great Pyramid of Cheops was built by the Ancient Egyptians in about 2,550BC. It is probably the world's oldest astronomical observatory and as well as being a tomb it was designed to tell the time in hours, days, seasons and even centuries.

Nearly right

The distance around the Earth was first accurately measured by a Greek astronomer called Eratosthenes, who lived from about 276 to 194BC. His figure of about 40,000 km (24,856 miles) almost matched the modern measurement of 40,007 km (24,860 miles).

Using a telescope

In the early 17th century, the Italian scientist Galileo Galilei was the first person to use a telescope in astronomy. Among his discoveries, he first saw four of Jupiter's moons and argued that the planets circled the Sun in the same way as these moons circled Jupiter.

DID YOU KNOW?

The first person to claim that the Earth revolves round the Sun was a Greek astronomer called Aristarchos of Samos, who lived from about 310 to 250BC. But as everyone believed the Sun moved round the Earth, this idea was not accepted.

The Ptolemaic theory

In about AD150, a Greek astronomer known as Ptolemy stated that the Earth lay stationary at the centre of the Universe and the Sun, the Moon and the five known planets (Mercury, Venus, Mars, Jupiter and Saturn) all moved round it. Most people believed this for the next 1,400 years.

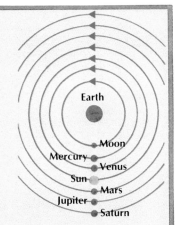

The Copernican theory

In 1543, a Polish clergyman called Nicolas Copernicus stated that the Sun was at the centre of the Universe and not the Earth. The Earth turned on its axis once a day and travelled round the Sun once a year. But Copernicus still believed that the planets moved round in circles, which is wrong.

Going round in ellipses

Finally, in 1609, Johannes Kepler of Germany worked out the correct movement of the planets. He calculated that the planets moved round the Sun in ellipses (flattened circles) not circles.

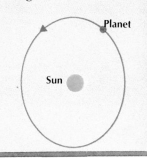

The world is round

In the 6th century BC, the Greek mathematician Pythagoras claimed that the Earth was a sphere rotating on its axis. But most people thought that the Earth was flat and so few agreed with him.

The pull of gravity

The story that the English astronomer Sir Isaac Newton worked out his Law of Universal Gravity in 1687 after watching an apple fall to the ground is probably true. He realized that the force which pulled down the apple was the same as the force which keeps the Moon in its path round the Earth and all the planets in their paths round the Sun.

Amazing But True

In the 6th century BC a Greek philosopher called Heraclitus estimated that the Sun measured only about one-third of a metre (1 ft) across. In fact, it is nearly 1.4 million km (870,000 miles) across.

Modern astronomy

Above the clouds

Many astronomers today work in large observatories built high in mountain ranges. Here they are above most of the clouds and away from the dazzle of street lights so that they can see the night sky more clearly.

Amazing But True

A telescope in the Lick Observatory, USA also serves as a tomb. The refracting telescope is mounted on a pillar that contains the remains of James Lick, who paid for the observatory and who died in 1876.

Increasing the light

Astronomers can see many thousands of stars that are invisible to the naked eye by using telescopes. These are used to magnify distant objects, such as nebulae, and also to collect more light coming from them and reaching the eye.

Lenses and mirrors

Telescopes collect light from stars using either a lens (a refracting telescope) or a mirror (a reflecting telescope). The larger the lens or mirror in a telescope, the more light it can collect and so the more powerful it is. The largest modern telescopes are usually reflectors.

The big one

The world's largest reflecting telescope was built in the 1970s near Zelenchukskaya in the Caucasus Mountains, USSR. Its largest mirror weighs 70 tonnes and

Odd one out

One of the strangest telescopes is buried 1,500 m (1 mile) down a mine in South Dakota, USA. At the bottom is a tank containing 400,000 litres (88,000 gallons) of tetrachloroethylene (cleaning fluid). This is used to stop neutrinos, tiny particles given off by the Sun, so that they can be counted by astronomers.

measures 6 m (236 in) across. It is powerful enough to spot the light from a single candle 24,000 km (15,000 miles) away.

Giant cameras

Photographs of stars and planets were first taken through a telescope in 1840. Photography is now so important in astronomy that many observatories have telescopes which have been designed not to be looked through and can only take photographs.

Colour information

In the 19th century, astronomers first began to study the light from the Sun and stars by splitting it up into its different colours. This is known as spectroscopy. From the colours astronomers can tell the temperature and types of gases in the stars and so what the stars are made of.

Radio telescopes

Radio telescopes are designed to pick up radio waves coming from distant radio sources. The first true radio telescope was built in 1937. The main type of radio telescope today looks like a giant dish. The radio waves are focused on to the telescope's receiver, above or below the dish.

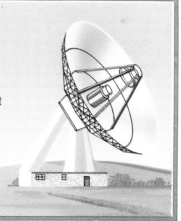

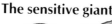

DID YOU KNOW?

Some radio telescopes, known as interferometers, consist of two or more medium-sized radio telescopes. This is like using a single radio dish several kilometres wide and so gives a much clearer picture of the skies.

The sensitive giant

The world's largest radio telescope is at Arecibo in Puerto Rico. Its dish measures 305 m (1,000 ft) across, wider than three football fields. It can pick up signals as weak as one-hundredth of a millionth of a millionth of a watt. (An ordinary light bulb is 100 watts.)

A faint glimmer

Radio waves from space are very weak. It has been calculated that if the energy reaching us from a quasar – a mysterious type of galaxy that sends out radio waves – were collected by a radio telescope for 10,000 years, there would only be enough to light a small bulb for a fraction of a second.

Astronomy in orbit

Blanket atmosphere

A lot of information from stars never reaches astronomers on the ground because of the blanket of atmosphere that surrounds the Earth. Now that telescopes can be placed above the atmosphere, astronomers can detect invisible waves of energy from stars known as ultra-violet and X-rays which never reach the Earth's surface.

Light bulb power

Most satellites are powered by solar cells, which convert sunlight into electricity. On average, a scientific satellite needs only about 250 watts of power. This is about the amount of power used in two ordinary house light bulbs.

Eyes in the sky

Before satellites carrying telescopes were launched into space, there were three ways of looking at the stars from above the Earth's surface – from aeroplanes, balloons and rockets. These are all still used, as well as satellites.

Homes in the sky

A space station is a kind of giant satellite where people can live for many days on end without returning to Earth. The Russian Salyut and the latest Mir series and the American Skylab were launched to carry out scientific experiments and to discover the effect on people of long periods in space.

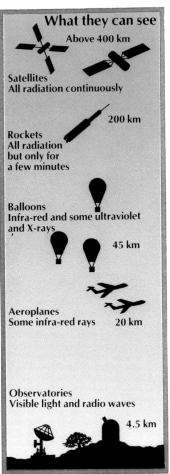

What they can see

Above 400 km

Satellites
All radiation continuously

200 km

Rockets
All radiation but only for a few minutes

Balloons
Infra-red and some ultraviolet and X-rays

45 km

Aeroplanes
Some infra-red rays   20 km

Observatories
Visible light and radio waves

4.5 km

A long time in space

The longest time anyone has spent non-stop in space is nearly 237 days. This was achieved in 1984 by three Russian cosmonauts called Kizim, Solovyov and Atkov in Salyut 7.

The first space station

The first space station, called Salyut 1, was launched by Russia in 1971. Salyut 6 spent five years in space, the longest time a space station has spent in orbit. It re-entered the Earth's atmosphere and broke up in 1982.

In space, far from the pull of gravity of planets, objects have no weight. This is known as weightlessness. People get a little taller in space because the discs in their backbones are no longer squashed down by the pressure of gravity and their backs stretch a little.

As big as a house

The total size of Skylab, with the Apollo Command and Service modules attached, was about 331.5 cu m (11,700 cu ft), about the same as a small, two-bedroom house.

Spinning and swimming

Small animals were also kept on board Skylab. Two spiders adapted to weightlessness and spun normal webs. Minnows born on Earth swam in a tank in small circles, but those born in space swam normally.

The space ferry

The Space Shuttle is designed mainly as a ferry to carry people and equipment such as satellites into space. The cost of the entire shuttle programme so far, $9,900 million, amounts to about $2 for every human being in the world.

The space telescope is so accurate that if it was placed on Earth it could see a small coin 700 km (435 miles) away. This is about the distance between London, England and Basle, Switzerland. The space telescope should also be able to see if there are any planets circling nearby stars in our galaxy.

The space telescope

The USA is planning to launch a telescope into space using the Space Shuttle. The space telescope will orbit about 600 km (373 miles)

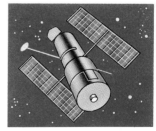

above the Earth and is designed to detect objects 50 times fainter or seven times further away than anything which can be seen from Earth.

Missions to the Moon

Orbiting football

Sputnik 1 was launched by the Russians in October 1957 and was the first spacecraft to go into orbit round the Earth. This marks the real beginning of the Space Age and the race to reach the Moon. Sputnik 1 weighed only 84 kg (185 lb), about the weight of an adult, and was the size of a large ball.

Unmanned probes		
Spacecraft	**Date**	**Results**
Luna 2 (USSR)	12 Sep 59	First man-made object to hit the Moon.
Luna 3 (USSR)	4 Oct 59	Flew behind the Moon and took the first photographs of the far side.
Rangers (USA)	1964-65	Photographed the Moon before crashing into the surface.
Luna 9 (USSR)	31 Jan 66	Made the first soft-landing on the Moon and sent back photographs.
Surveyors (USA)	1966-68	Collected information about the surface of the Moon in preparation for manned landings.
Orbiters (USA)	1966-67	Photographed the Moon's surface for possible landing sites.
Luna 16 (USSR)	12 Sep 70	Made soft-landing, collected soil and returned it to USSR.
Luna 17 (USSR)	10 Nov 70	Landed Lunokhod 1, a roving vehicle for experiments controlled from Earth. It travelled for nearly a year.

Flying high

On April 12th 1961, the Russian astronaut Yuri Gagarin became the first person to travel in space. His spacecraft, called Vostok, circled Earth once, reaching a height of 327 km (203 miles), and then landed on Earth again. The flight lasted about 89 minutes and proved that people could travel in space.

Off target

A mistake of only 1.6 kph (1 mph) in the Apollo's top speed would have led to it missing the Moon by about 1,600 km (1,000 miles). This is about the distance between Moscow and Berlin.

DID YOU KNOW?

The first living creature in space was a dog called Laika, launched in a spacecraft by the USSR in 1957. It died when its oxygen ran out.

A year in space

The world's most travelled person is the Russian astronaut Valery Ryumin. His total time in space is 362 days, nearly a year. During his space trips he went round the world 5,750 times, covering 241 million km (150 million miles), more than the distance from Earth to Mars and back again.

Man on the Moon		
Spacecraft	**Date**	**Results**
Apollo 11 (USA)	16-24 July 69	Landed the first man on the Moon.
Apollo 12 (USA)	12-24 Nov 69	32 hour stay on the Moon.
Apollo 13 (USA)	11-17 Apr 70	Explosion in the spacecraft. Astronauts returned to Earth before landing.
Apollo 14 (USA)	31 Jan-9 Feb 71	Highland area of the Moon explored.
Apollo 15 (USA)	26 July-7 Aug 71	A car called a Lunar Rover taken to the Moon. Astronauts travelled 28 km (17.4 miles).
Apollo 16 (USA)	16-27 Apr 72	Another Lunar Rover taken on mission.
Apollo 17 (USA)	7-19 Dec 72	The last and longest stay on the Moon.

Amazing But True

On Earth, an astronaut in his spacesuit weighs about 135 kg (300 lb). But on the Moon he is six times lighter at only 23 kg (50 lb) because the Moon has much less gravity than the Earth.

Big booster

The total power developed by the USA Saturn V booster rocket, used for all the Apollo missions to the Moon, was almost 4,082,000 kg (9,000,000 lb) of thrust. This is equal to the power of 50 Boeing 747 jumbo jets.

Lunar rubbish

The Apollo astronauts left the remains of six lunar landers, three lunar rover vehicles and more than 50 tonnes of litter on the Moon. The total cost of the Apollo missions to the Moon is estimated at $25,000 million, making this some of the most expensive rubbish in history.

Visiting the planets

Automatic equipment

Since 1962, America and Russia have been launching unmanned spacecaft to investigate the other planets in our Solar System. They carry cameras to take pictures and equipment to measure the magnetic fields and radiation of the planets. They also measure the temperature of the planets.

Probes to the planets

Spacecraft	Launch date	Mission
Mariner 2 (USA)	27 Aug 62	First successful fly-by of Venus.
Mariner 4 (USA)	28 Nov 64	First successful fly-by of Mars.
Venera 4 (USSR)	12 Jun 67	First entry into Venus atmosphere.
Mariner 9 (USA)	30 May 71	First successful Mars orbiter.
Pioneer 10 (USA)	3 Mar 72	First successful fly-by of Jupiter.
Venera 8 (USSR)	27 Mar 72	Returned first data from Venus surface.
Pioneer 11 (USA)	6 Apr 73	Jupiter probe. First fly-by of Saturn.
Mariner 10 (USA)	3 Nov 73	First TV pictures of Venus and Mercury.
Venera 9 (USSR)	8 Jun 75	First pictures from surface of Venus.
Viking 1 (USA)	20 Aug 75	First successful Mars landing.
Viking 2 (USA)	9 Sep 75	Returned data from Mars surface.
Voyager 2 (USA)	20 Aug 77	Fly-by of Jupiter, Saturn, Uranus, Neptune.
Voyager 1 (USA)	5 Sep 77	Fly-by probe of Jupiter and Saturn.
Pioneer-Venus 1 (USA)	20 May 78	Orbited Venus.
Pioneer-Venus 2 (USA)	8 Aug 78	Analysed atmosphere and clouds of Venus.
Venera 13 (USSR)	30 Oct 81	First colour pictures of Venus surface. First soil analysis.
Venera 14 (USSR)	4 Nov 81	Repeated Venus soil analysis.
Venera 15 (USSR)	June 1983	Orbited and mapped Venus surface.
Venera 16 (USSR)	June 1983	Orbited and mapped Venus surface.

A clearer picture

Mariner 10 took about 4,300 close-up photographs of Mercury during its three visits from 1974. Before this, telescopes on Earth could hardly see the surface of Mercury.

Voyager 1 passed Saturn's moon Titan at a distance of only 4,000 km (2,500 miles) from the surface. It was more than 1,524 million km (946 million miles) from Earth. Such accuracy is like shooting an arrow at an apple 9.6 km (6 miles) away and the arrow passing within 2.54 cm (1 in) of the apple.

Goodbye

Pioneer 10 is expected to become the first man-made object to leave our Solar System. It crossed Neptune's path in 1983 and it will eventually disappear into the depths of space.

Look out

In 1968 a piece of Russian rocket broke a house window in Southend-on-Sea, Essex, England. In 1978 two French farmers were nearly hit by a 20 kg (44 lb) piece of a Russian rocket which landed in a field.

Six hour fly-by

The Voyager spacecraft travelled under Saturn's ring system at almost 69,000 kph (43,000 mph). At this speed, a rocket would take just six hours to travel from the Earth to the Moon. This is about the time it takes to travel from London to Bahrain by jet aeroplane today.

Metal message

Pioneer 10 and 11 carry metal plaques with messages for any aliens that might intercept the probes. Each plaque shows a map of the Solar System, the location of our Sun and sketches of human beings.

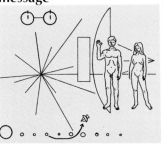

DID YOU KNOW?

By 1990 there will be about 7,000 pieces of space debris orbiting the Earth, consisting of discarded rocket stages and fragments of rockets and satellites that have broken up.

Mapping it out

In less than two years from 1978, the Pioneer-Venus spacecraft mapped 93 per cent of Venus' surface. More was mapped of Venus in that time than had been mapped of Earth up to the year 1800.

Making music

Voyager 1 and 2 carry long-playing records containing electronically coded pictures of the Earth, spoken greetings, sound effects and a selection of music from around the world.

The future in space

A new space age

The human race is about to enter a new age of travelling and living in space. Shuttles will one day make journeys into space as common as ordinary aeroplane flights today. Space cities holding thousands of people will circle the Earth, metals will be mined and future wars may be fought in space.

Living on the Moon

By the beginning of the next century, the first bases on the Moon with people living in them should have been started. Because of the expense of transporting goods to the Moon, edible plants will have to be grown on it and as many things as possible, such as water, oxygen and rubbish, will have to be recycled.

Space cities

Plans have been suggested for building giant colonies in space, housing thousands of people. The land areas would be on the inside surfaces of giant cylinders or wheels which would spin round to provide gravity similar to the Earth's. Inside, people could walk around as freely as on Earth and grow their own food.

Terraforming Mars

Some scientists believe that the atmosphere of Mars could be warmed up so that people could live and work there. In a process called terraforming, plants would be grown round the ice caps to absorb sunlight, warm the surface and melt the ice.

Greening the galaxy

One day special trees might be developed so that they can grow on comets. Seeds from the trees could drift across space to take root on other comets, starting a wave of "greening" throughout the galaxy so that human beings could live on distant planets.

Amazing But True

In order to supply Venus with water, some scientists believe that icy comets could be diverted into the carbon dioxide clouds that surround the planet. There they would be melted to make rivers and lakes.

Space factories

Materials such as special metals and glass and also some medicines that are impossible to make on Earth can be made in space because of the lack of gravity.
Eventually whole industries may be moved from Earth and housed in the space cities.

First space product

The first product ever to be made in space and sold on Earth were tiny balls made of a type of rubber called latex and used to measure microscopic objects. They were all exactly the same size, but latex balls made on Earth can vary in size.

Energy from space

Some scientists believe that the Earth's electricity in the future could come from space. Giant groups of solar cells, which convert sunlight into electricity, would be placed about 35,880 km (22,300 miles) above the equator. The electricity generated by the solar cells would then be beamed down to Earth.

Mining in space

The world is beginning to run short of some essential metals and minerals such as iron and aluminium, but there are plentiful supplies of them elsewhere in the Solar System. One day our Moon and planets such as Mars and the asteroids will be mined for metals.

Starships

The closest star to our Solar System is over four light years away. The journey in a rocket today would take nearly 200,000 years. Future rocket engines have been suggested that would use beams of light for power. These rockets could nearly reach the speed of light, so the same journey would take just over four years.

185

Is there life out there?

We are not alone

Some scientists believe that there are other civilizations in the Milky Way as well as ours. With about 100,000 million stars in our galaxy, it has been estimated that there may be up to one million planets on which there is life of some kind, such as animals or plants.

Am I receiving you?

In 1960, an American astronomer called Frank Drake made the first attempt to pick up possible messages from other stars. He turned a radio telescope towards two stars, called Tau Ceti and Epsilon Eridani. Although he listened for two months, Drake received no messages from the stars.

Strange sights

For centuries there have been reports of strange lights in the sky, craft landing on Earth and creatures emerging from them. Recently, sightings of UFOs (unidentified flying objects) have increased. Most are easily explained, but some remain mysteries.

Are you receiving me?

Since 1974, a radio message beamed from the Arecibo radio telescope in Puerto Rico has been racing towards a cluster of 300,000 stars known as M13. The stars are so far away that even if there are any creatures living in M13, their answer will not reach Earth until about the year 50,000.

The pattern of the Arecibo message

Some famous UFOs

1254. A mysterious coloured ship is supposed to have appeared over St.Albans, England.

1741. Lord Beauchamp saw a small oval ball of fire descending from the sky in England. It then vanished.

1762. A thin UFO surrounded by a glowing ring was spotted by two astronomers near Basle, Switzerland.

1820. A stream of saucer-shaped objects crossed the town of Embrun, France.

1947. A pilot reported seeing gleaming discs flying over the Rocky Mountains, USA. He described them as "skipping like saucers across water" and the name "flying saucer" caught on.

1971. Two men in the USA claimed to have been captured and taken on board a flying saucer where they were examined by tall creatures.

Over the last 30 years over 100,000 people have reported UFO experiences. A public opinion poll carried out in the USA in 1974 showed that more than one in ten people questioned claimed to have seen a UFO.

A vintage year

1952 was a very good year for UFO sightings. There were about 1,500 reports of UFOs from different parts of the world. Most of these sightings have simple explanations, such as aeroplanes, clouds or bright stars, but many remain unexplained.

Swedish sightings

In 1946 in Sweden alone there were about 1,000 reports of UFOs. Most of the reports were of rocket-shaped objects, which have never been identified.

Lines in the sand

At Nazca in Peru there is a plain covered by very straight and wide tracks in the rocky surface up to 8 km (5 miles) long. Seen from above, they look like an airfield. They may be connected with early astronomy, but it is unlikely that they were used as runways by UFOs, as some people claim.

Putting up statues

Some people believe that the giant statues on Easter Island in the Pacific Ocean were put up with the help of visitors from space. But scientists believe that it would have been possible for the islanders to have erected them without any outside help.

DID YOU KNOW?

UFOs are usually seen between 9 pm and 10.30 pm. They have been reported from every country in the world. News of them flows in at an average of 40 sightings every day.

UFO spotting in space

The first UFO seen in space was spotted by the astronaut James McDivitt through the window of the Gemini 4 spacecraft in 1965. He saw an object with arms sticking out of it about 15 km (9.5 miles) from the capsule.

Astronomy lists

Famous observatories

Name	Country	Type
Arecibo	Puerto Rico	Radio
Byurakan	USSR	Optical
Cambridge	England	Radio
Cerro Tololo	Chile	Optical
Flagstaff	USA	Optical
Green Bank	USA	Radio
La Palma	Canary Islands	Optical
Jodrell Bank	England	Radio
Kitt Peak	USA	Optical
Mauna Kea	Hawaii	Optical
Mt Palomar	USA	Optical
Parkes	Australia	Radio
Pulkovo	USSR	Optical
Siding Spring	Australia	Optical
Zelenchukskaya	USSR	Optical

Meteor showers

Name	Date
Quadrantids	Jan 1-5
April Lyrids	Apr 19-24
Aquarids	May 1-8
June Lyrids	June 10-21
Perseids	July 25-Aug 18
Cygnids	Aug 18-22
Orionids	Oct 16-27
Taurids	Oct 10-Dec 5
Leonids	Nov 14-20
Geminids	Dec 7-15

The largest asteroids

Name	Diameter (km)
Ceres	1,000
Pallas	610
Vesta	540
Hygeia	450
Euphrosyne	370
Interamnia	350
Davida	330
Cybele	310
Europa	290
Patientia	280
Eunomia	270
Psyche	250

Future solar total eclipses

Date	Approximate location	Approximate duration
18 March 1988	Indian Ocean, North Pacific	4 minutes
22 July 1990	North Siberia	2 minutes
11 July 1991	Mexico, northern South America	7 minutes
30 June 1992	Uruguay, South Atlantic	5 minutes
3 Nov 1994	Central South America, South Atlantic	4 minutes
24 Oct 1995	South Asia, Central Pacific	2 minutes
9 March 1997	Central Asia	3 minutes
26 Feb 1998	Central Pacific, northern South America	4 minutes
11 Aug 1999	North Atlantic, Central Europe, South Asia	2 minutes

Our local group of galaxies

Leo I	NGC6822
Leo II	NGC185
Large Magellanic Cloud	IC1613
	Wolf-Lundmark
Sculptor	Triangulum
Fornax	NGC147
Milky Way	M32
Small Magellanic Cloud	Andromeda
	NGC205

Major astronomical satellites

OSO 1
7 March, 1962
Orbiting Solar
Observatory

OSO 2
3 Feb, 1965
Orbiting Solar
Observatory

OSO 3
8 March, 1967
Orbiting Solar
Observatory

OSO 4
18 Oct, 1967
Orbiting Solar
Observatory

OAO 2
7 Dec, 1968
Orbiting
Astronomical
Observatory, for
ultraviolet
observations

OSO 5
22 Jan, 1969
Orbiting Solar
Observatory

OSO 6
9 Aug, 1969
Orbiting Solar
Observatory

SAS 1
12 Dec, 1970
Small Astronomy
Satellite, made x-ray
survey of sky

OSO 7
29 Sept, 1971
Orbiting Solar
Observatory

TD-1A
12 March, 1972
European high
energy
astronomy satellite

OAO 3
21 Aug, 1972
Orbiting
Astronomical
Observatory, for
ultraviolet and x-ray
studies

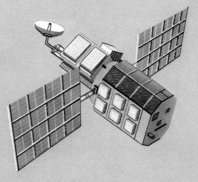

SAS 2
15 Nov, 1972
Small Astronomy
Satellite, made
gamma-ray survey

Ariel V
15 Oct, 1974
UK x-ray satellite

SAS 3
7 May, 1975
Small Astronomy
Satellite, studied
x-ray sources

OSO 8
21 June, 1975
Orbiting Solar
Observatory

HEAO 1
12 Aug, 1977
High Energy
Astronomy
Observatory, made
x-ray survey

IUE
26 Jan, 1978
International
Ultraviolet Explorer,
joint ESA/NASA
satellite

HEAO 2
13 Nov, 1978
High Energy
Astronomy
Observatory
examined
individual x-ray
sources

Ariel VI
2 June, 1979
UK satellite for
cosmic ray and x-ray
studies

HEAO 3
20 Sept, 1979
High Energy
Astronomy
Observatory for
gamma-ray studies

SMM
14 Feb, 1980
Solar Maximum
Mission,
to study the Sun

IRAS
25 Jan, 1983
Infra-red satellite
to provide complete
survey of the sky

189

Space words

Astronomical unit The average distance from Earth to the Sun, about 150 million km (93 million miles).

Constellation A group of stars which appear to make a shape or pattern in the sky. The stars were joined up to make the outlines of mythical animals or people. There are 88 constellations.

Eclipse This occurs when the Earth passes between the Sun and the Moon and light from the Sun is cut off (a lunar eclipse). It also happens when the Moon passes between the Sun and the Earth, casting a shadow on the Earth (a solar eclipse).

Galaxy A giant group of stars held together by gravity. The largest galaxies contain up to a million, million stars.

Gravity All objects in space attract each other by gravity. It is the invisible pull of the Earth which keeps the Moon in orbit round it, and the pull of the Sun which keeps the Earth and the other planets in their orbits round the Sun.

Light year The distance light travels in one year, 9,460,000 million km (5.9 million, million miles).

Nebula A cloud of gas and dust, sometimes dotted with clusters and stars. Stars may be born in nebulae.

Orbit The curved path taken by a natural or man-made object as it moves round another object.

Planet An object which has no light of its own but shines by reflecting a star's light.

Pulsar Very small, fast-spinning star which sends out a flash of radio waves as it spins round.

Quasar An extremely bright and distant object, much smaller than a galaxy but thousands of times brighter.

Radio telescope A special kind of telescope designed to collect radio waves from space.

Red shift The reddening of the light from a star, indicating it is moving away.

Satellite A natural or artificial object that circles round another. The Moon is a natural satellite of the Earth.

Solar System The system of our Sun. It consists of the nine planets and their moons, the asteroids and comets, all of which orbit the Sun.

Solar wind The high-speed stream of electrically-charged atoms of gas sent out by the Sun.

Star A ball of gas which produces its own heat and light from nuclear reactions at its centre.

Universe Everything which is known or thought to exist in space.

Index

191

ANIMAL FACTS

Anita Ganeri

CONTENTS

Illustrated by Tony Gibson and Ian Jackson

Additional illustrations by Pam Corfield

Designed by Tony Gibson and Steve Page

**Consultant: Micheal Boorer,
Education Officer, London Zoo**

What is a mammal?

How many mammals?

There are over 4,000 different kinds of mammals in the world. These are divided into 19 groups called 'orders'. The rodent order is the biggest with about 1,750 species, while the aardvark is the only living member of its order. There are very few mammals in the world compared to other animals and there are hundreds of times more insects than there are mammals.

Central heating

Mammals are warm-blooded. This means that the temperature inside their bodies stays about the same whatever the weather is like outside. Most mammals have a body temperature of about 36°C-39°C (97°F-102°F).

Warm blood allows mammals to be very active and to live in a wide variety of places, from the icy Poles to the hot Tropics. Fur and fat help protect them from the cold and they get rid of excess heat by sweating or panting.

Hair history

Mammals are the only animals with true hair. Hairs are dead cords of a substance called keratin which is also found in nails. What looks like hair on spiders and flies actually contains living parts of the animal. All mammals have some hair, though you would need a magnifying glass to see the fine hair on the lips of a young whale.

Backbones

Mammals are vertebrates which means that they all have backbones. Most of the animals in the world have no backbone. All mammals, except for some sea-cows and sloths, have seven bones in their necks. This includes giraffes whose necks can be 2 m (6½ ft) long and mice who seem to have no neck at all.

DID YOU KNOW?

All mammals breathe air. The distant ancestors of mammals were fish and mammals still have some traces of gills for breathing underwater. The tube running between a mammal's ear and its throat is really a gill-slit.

The kinds of living mammals

Family	Examples	Number of species
Rodents	Rats, mice, squirrels, porcupines	about 1,750
Chiropterans	Bats	about 950
Insectivores (insect eaters)	Shrews, hedgehogs	300
Carnivores (meat eaters)	Dogs, cats, bears, weasels	about 250
Marsupials (pouched mammals)	Kangaroos, possums	about 240
Primates	Bush babies, monkeys, apes	about 180
Ungulates (even-toed)	Cattle, deer, hippos, pigs	about 180
Cetaceans	Whales and dolphins	about 85
Lagomorphs	Rabbits and hares	about 60
Pinnipedes	Seals, sealions, walruses	32
Edentates	Armadillos, sloths, giant anteaters	about 30
Ungulates (odd-toed)	Tapirs, rhinos, horses	15
Pangolins	Scaly anteaters	7
Monotremes (egg layers)	Platypus, spiny anteaters	6
Hyraxes		6
Sirenians	Sea cows and manatees	4
Dermopterans	Flying lemurs	2
Elephants		2
Aardvark		1

Care for the young

All mammals look after their young and feed them on milk. They are the only animals that produce milk. The length of time a baby is looked after by its parents varies from a few weeks for mice to several years for apes.

Earflaps

Mammals are the only animals with flaps around their ears. These direct sound down into the ears. Some sea and burrowing mammals have lost their earflaps as they have become adapted for life in the water or underground.

Poison

Only two types of mammal are poisonous. Some shrews have a slightly poisonous bite. Male platypuses have poisonous spurs on their back legs.

195

The first mammals

Reptile relations

About 250 million years ago most land animals were reptiles. About 200 million years ago some began to develop into mammals. One of the earliest mammals, Megazostrodon, lived 190 million years ago in Africa. It was about 10 cm (4 in) long and looked like a shrew.

Mammals on the move

At the time when the dinosaurs died out, 65 million years ago, mammals began to develop more fully into the three main groups we have today:

Monotremes are those mammals which lay eggs such as the duck-billed platypus.

Marsupials are mammals with pouches. They give birth to tiny babies which crawl into the mother's pouch to feed on milk until they are fully developed.

Placental mammals are the largest group. The baby grows and is nourished inside the mother's body until it is born.

Prehistoric pouches

Millions of years ago, two kinds of giant marsupials lived in Australia. Procoptodon was a huge kangaroo, about 3 m (10 ft) tall, twice the height of a modern kangaroo. Diprotodon was a giant wombat and the largest marsupial ever. It weighed as much as a hippopotamus.

Horse race

The first horses lived about 55 million years ago in the North American forests. Hyracotherium was only the size of a fox and had toes on its feet. Horses grew bigger and developed hooves so they could run faster. Equus, the modern horse, first lived about 2 million years ago.

DID YOU KNOW?

Paraceratherium was the biggest land mammal there has ever been. It lived about 35 million years ago in Asia and Europe and was 8 m (26 ft) tall and 11 m (36 ft) long. It looked like a gigantic rhinoceros but had a long neck like a giraffe. Six people, walking side by side, could easily have passed underneath it.

Super sloth

Megatherium was a type of giant sloth which lived about 15,000 years ago. It was as high as a modern elephant and over 6 m (19 ft) in length. Today's sloths are about a tenth of its size.

First diets

Most early mammals ate insects and worms. Carnivores or meat-eaters first lived about 35 million years ago. The largest carnivore ever lived 20 million years ago. Megistotherium was bigger than a grizzly bear. It attacked and killed huge elephants. One of the fiercest carnivores was Smilodon, the sabre-toothed tiger. It had long pointed teeth for tearing meat apart.

Amazing But True

The first elephants lived 40 million years ago. Moeritherium was only as big as a large pig and had no tusks or trunk. Today's African elephant is 300 times bigger. Deinotherium, which lived 15 million years ago, was much larger than today's elephants. It had tusks which curved back towards its chest. It probably used them like forks to dig up food.

Thunder beast

The giant mammal, Brontotherium, or 'thunder beast', lived 35 million years ago in North America. It was about the size of a hippo and had a forked horn on the end of its nose, perhaps for fending off enemies. This huge creature ate only leaves and fruit.

Little and large

The ancestors of today's camels lived about 10 million years ago. Unlike modern camels, they had no humps. Stenomylus was a tiny animal, only as big as a small deer. Alticamelus was about 3 m (10 ft) tall, with long legs and a long neck, like a giraffe's, for reaching leaves high up in the trees.

Sea giant

A giant whale, Basilosaurus, was the largest prehistoric sea mammal. It was more than 20 m (65 ft) long, about 7 m (13 ft) smaller than a blue whale, the largest sea mammal alive today. It lived 40 million years ago.

Baby mammals

Tail first

The biggest animal baby is a blue whale calf. Unlike most mammals, whales and dolphins are born tail first. Because it is born underwater, the baby has to be pushed quickly to the surface by its mother so that it can breathe. A new-born calf can only stay underwater for about 30 seconds at a time.

Marsupial mother

When a baby kangaroo, or 'joey', is born it is only about the size of a bee and is blind and helpless. The joey crawls into its mother's pouch and stays there for six months, feeding on milk and growing. It comes out of the pouch for the first time after about 28 weeks and leaves the pouch for good after about 33 weeks.

DID YOU KNOW?

All the pet hamsters in the world are descended from the same mother. This was a female wild hamster found with a litter of 12 babies in 1930 in Syria.

Smallest babies

The smallest mammal babies are probably those of the mouse opossums in Central and South America. The new-born babies of some species are only as big as grains of rice.

Egg layer

When the duck-billed platypus was discovered in 1797 people thought that it must be either a duck or a reptile because it was found to lay eggs. The female builds her nest in a river bank tunnel and in it lays soft, sticky eggs. But when the babies hatch they feed on their mother's milk showing that the platypus is in fact a mammal, although a very strange one.

Who am I?

An elephant in the Kruger National Park South Africa chose its own family and now thinks it is a buffalo. It was brought to the park in the 1970s with four other elephants to live near a herd of buffalo.

This elephant soon joined the herd and was accepted as being part of it. It was seen by park rangers drinking from a waterhole with its new buffalo 'family' and running off when a herd of elephants came near.

Mammals and their babies

Mammal	Average pregnancy	Usual number of young
Asian elephant	20 months	1
Indian rhinoceros	18 months	1
Giraffe	15 months	1
Blue whale	11 months	1
Human being	9 months	1
Chimpanzee	8 months	1
Dog	2 months	3-6
Red kangaroo	35 days	1
House mouse	19 days	4-32
American opossum	13 days	10

Most babies

The mammal which has the most young is the common vole. It can have its first litter when it is only 15 days old and has 4-9 babies as often as 15 times a year. In her lifetime, a female vole may have 33 litters, a total of as many as 147 young.

Growing up fast

The striped tenrec in Madagascar is the mammal which grows up the fastest. Two babies born in Berlin Zoo in July 1961 could run almost at once and eat worms by the age of six days. Other mammals can still only drink their mother's milk at this age.

Longest pregnancy

The mammal which has the longest pregnancy (called the gestation period) is an Asian elephant. The pregnancy lasts for 20-22 months, 33 times as long as that of a house mouse. Another female elephant from the herd who is called the 'auntie' helps look after the new baby.

Shortest pregnancy

An American opossum has a pregnancy of only 12-14 days and it may even be as short as eight days. The babies, though, still need to spend another 10 weeks feeding in their mother's pouch before they are fully developed.

Amazing But True

The nine-banded armadillo gives birth to sets of identical quads. Most mammals have babies which look different and are of different sexes. Armadillo quads are always identical and always of the same sex.

Mammal lives

Grand old age

The mammal which lives the longest, after man, is the Asian elephant. The oldest on record was called Modoc. She died in California, USA in July 1975, at the age of 75. During her long career in the circus, Modoc survived two attempts to poison her and a terrible fire. The fire made her a heroine when she dragged the lions' cage out of the big top tent to safety. She starred in several TV series before retiring.

Sea life

Baird's beaked whale is the longest–living sea mammal known. It can live for up to a maximum of about 70 years.

Ancient Nero

Nero, a lion in the Cologne Zoo, West Germany, died at the age of 29 in May 1907. This made him the longest-lived big cat. In the wild lions grow more slowly than in zoos. They usually live for 12-14 years and rarely for 20 years. The oldest tiger was an Indian tigress in the Adelaide Zoo, Australia who lived for 26 years and 3 months.

Oldest horse

The oldest known horse was born in 1760 and died at the age of 62 in Lancashire, Britain. He spent most of his long life towing barges along the canals before he was retired to a farm in 1819. Horses are usually expected to live for about 25-30 years.

Life on the wing

Bats normally live for 10-20 years. The oldest bat known is an Indian flying fox. It died at London Zoo at the age of 31 years and 5 months.

Amazing But True

Lemmings are small, hamster-like rodents from Norway. Their lives seem to go in strange four year cycles. For the first three years the lemmings breed at an ever-increasing rate. Then they seem to panic at the overcrowding and leave their homes in millions to find more space. Their mad rush carries them until they reach rivers or the sea. Even then they plunge in and try to swim across but most drown.

Mammal life-spans

Human being	60-80 years
Asian elephant	70-75 years
Killer whale	50-70 years
Rhinoceros	20-50 years
Hippopotamus	40-50 years
Arabian camel	25-40 years
Chimpanzee	30-40 years
Bottle-nosed dolphin	25-40 years
Zebra	20-30 years
Red deer	Up to 20 years
Giraffe	15-25 years
Koala	15-20 years
Grey kangaroo	15-20 years
Giant anteater	Up to 14 years
Two-toed sloth	8-12 years
European hedgehog	6 years
European rabbit	Up to 5 years
Armadillo	4 years
Rat	4 years
Mole	3-4 years
Long-tailed shrew	12-18 months

Cats and dogs

Domestic cats usually live longer than dogs. The oldest cat was probably a tabby called Puss in Devon, Britain. She died in November 1937, one day after her 36th birthday. The oldest dog was an Australian cattle dog called Bluey who lived for 29 years and 5 months. Dogs usually live for about 8-15 years.

Shortest life

The tiny shrew has the shortest life-span of all the mammals. Most shrews live for only about 12-18 months in the wild. They are born one year, breed the next year and then die. The record life-span for a shrew in captivity is 2 years and 3 months.

What mammals eat

Regular meals

Because they are warm-blooded, mammals can be very active in both hot and cold weather. They need a lot of energy for hunting, finding homes and looking after their young. They get their energy from food and must eat regularly.

The tiny Etruscan shrew has a giant appetite. An adult shrew weighs only 2 g (0.07 oz) but can eat up to three times its own weight in a day and cannot live for more than two hours without food. An adult human being would have to eat a sheep, 50 chickens, 60 large loaves and over 150 apples to match the shrew's meals.

Giant anteater

The South American giant anteater has a 60 cm (24 in) long tongue which it uses to catch ants – its staple diet. It tears open an anthill with its strong claws and pokes its sticky tongue around inside until it is coated with ants, then flicks it out and swallows the ants whole. It can do this twice a second and can easily catch well over 30,000 ants a day.

No drink

Koalas will only eat the leaves of five out of the 350 kinds of eucalyptus tree. The word 'koala' means 'no drink' in the Aborigine language and koalas almost never need to drink water, getting all the liquid they need from the leaves they eat.

Liquid diet

Vampire bats live on a diet of animal blood. They hunt at night and attack animals while they are asleep. The bat's saliva contains a substance which stops the blood from clotting and closing the wound. A great vampire bat weighs about 28 g (1 oz) and drinks about a tablespoonful of blood a day.

Excuse fingers

The aye-aye, a rare lemur in Madagascar, has long, thin middle fingers. It eats wood-boring insects. To catch them, the aye-aye knocks on the tree bark, listens for the insects to move, pokes its skewer-like finger inside and pulls them out.

High table

A giraffe's long neck allows it to reach its favourite food of leaves on branches up to 6 m (20 ft) off the ground. It uses its 40 cm (16 in) long tongue to grip and pull branches down so it can strip off the leaves with its rubbery lips.

Mammal diets

Mammal	Food
Rhinoceros	plants, leaves, grass
Fruit-bat	fruit, flowers, nectar
Gorilla	leaves, plants
Polar bear	seals, fish
Cheetah	antelopes, gazelles
Hedgehog	insects, worms
Tarsier	birds, lizards, insects
Long-tailed macaque	crabs, shell fish, fruit
Panda	bamboo, rats, snakes, flowers

Herbivore (plants)		Carnivore (meat)		Omnivore (both)	

Giant hunger

In spring and summer, a blue whale eats as much as four tonnes of food a day, about twice as much as a well-fed person eats in a year. It swims, mouth wide open, through the sea, sucking in thousands of litres of water which contains krill (tiny shrimp-like creatures). Instead of teeth, the whale has huge bony plates called baleen hanging down inside its mouth. They strain the water, leaving the krill.

DID YOU KNOW?

Elephants eat up to ½ tonne of plant food a day. They have 24 teeth for grinding it. The teeth do not grow all at once, but in fours. As the first set wears down, a second set grows. At the age of 45 an elephant grows its last teeth, each weighing 4 kg (9 lb).

203

Eyes, ears and noses

Super smell

Dogs have an excellent sense of smell. An Alsatian has 44 times more smell cells in its nose than a human being. It can smell things about one million times better than man. Dogs also have superb hearing. They can pick up much higher sounds than human ears are able to hear.

DID YOU KNOW?

In 1925 Sauer, a Dobermann Pinscher, tracked two thieves 160 km (100 miles) across the Great Karroo desert in South Africa just by following their scent.

Wide-eyed

The biggest mammal in the world, the blue whale, has the biggest eyes. They are as big as footballs, quite small for its huge size but over six times wider than a human eye and 150 times wider than a pygmy shrew's eyes.

What big eyes . . .

Animals that feed at night have special ways of finding their way in the dark. Some, such as moles and bats, have tiny eyes but very good hearing and smell. Others, such as bush babies and tarsiers, have huge-fronted eyes. The Eastern tarsier's eyes are 17 mm (0.6 in) across. If a human's eyes were the same size in proportion to its body, they would be as big as grapefruit.

Big ears

An African elephant has huge earflaps. Each is about 1.8 m (6 ft) across and nearly as big as a single bed sheet. Elephants flap their ears to keep cool and a female beats her ears on her back to call her young. An elephant spreads out its ears to make it look more threatening to enemies.

Ear conditioning

Ears get cold quickly especially if the wind is blowing. The jack rabbit from the USA and the fennec fox from the Sahara Desert use their huge ears to keep cool. Air blowing across the ears cools down the blood in the ears. The jack rabbit's ears can be 21 cm (8 in) long, a quarter of the total length of its body.

A duck-billed platypus has a beak similar to a bird's but it is soft. It uses its beak to sift mud for food and has a pair of nostrils near the tip. The beak has lots of very sensitive nerve endings and the platypus finds its food of worms and small fish by touch. Underwater, a platypus can cover its eyes and ears to stop water getting in.

Cats' eyes

At the back of a cat's eye there is a special layer which reflects light. This means that cats can make much better use of light than human beings. They can hunt well at night because they are able to see in very dim light.

Bat radar

Bats navigate and find food in the dark using sound. They make about 50 high squeaking noises a second. The sound hits a solid object and the bat's large sensitive ears pick up the echo. They seem to be able to tell the shape of an object by this echo.

In an experiment, bats used echo-location to fly through wires 30 cm (12 in) apart in total darkness without hitting them. If a bat's mouth is full it cannot squeak so some use their noses. Folds of skin called 'nose-leaves' around their noses direct sound like megaphones.

Star-nosed mole

Moles spend most of their lives underground searching for food. They have very poor eyesight but very sensitive noses. The star-nosed mole of North America has a strange rosette of 22 tentacles surrounding its nose. They help the mole find its way underground by touch.

Big nose

The African elephant has the biggest nose of any mammal. A large male's trunk is about 2.5 m (8 ft) from base to tip. The trunk is used for breathing, smelling and sucking up water. It also acts as an extra hand for picking up food and scratching. Elephants in Kenya's National Park even learnt to turn taps on with their trunks.

Tops and tails

Antlers and horns

Antlers are made of bone. They fall off every autumn and grow back in spring. Each year they get bigger and more branched. Usually only the males have antlers for fighting off rivals in the mating season. Horns are made of keratin which also makes hair. They grow throughout an animal's life.

Travellers' tails

A kangaroo uses its tail for balance. As it bounds along the ground, its body leans forward and its large tail is stretched out behind. In this way, a red kangaroo can leap over 7 m (25 ft) at a time, nearly four times the length of its body. Giant leaps of 12 m (40 ft) have been known.

Longest horns

The longest horns belong to the water buffalo in India. A huge bull shot in 1955 had horns which measured 4.24 m (14 ft) across from tip to tip.

Heavy headgear

The North American elk has the longest antlers of any animal. They can be up to 1.78 m (5.8 ft) long. The moose has the heaviest antlers. They can weigh as much as two heavy suitcases.

Amazing But True

Synthetoceras was a strange mammal which lived about 15 million years ago in North America. It looked like a deer but instead of antlers had two small horns on its forehead and a huge forked horn in the shape of a Y growing on its nose.

Getting the point

The white rhinoceros has a huge front horn. It can be up to 1.58 m (5 ft) long which is about three times as long as a human arm.

Rhinoceroses also have a shorter back horn. If the horns get broken off they will grow back at a rate of about ½ cm (¼ in) a month.

Secret weapon

The skunk's tail hides a very effective secret weapon. When it is threatened, the skunk lifts up its tail and squirts out a vile-smelling liquid from a gland hidden underneath. The terrible smell given off can reach up to ½ km (0.3 miles) away.

Useful tails

Squirrels make good use of their long, bushy tails. If they hibernate in winter they wrap their tails round them like fur coats to keep warm. The ground squirrel in the Kalahari Desert keeps cool by angling its tail over its head like a parasol.

Flying the flag

When ring-tailed lemurs are walking along the ground in search of food, each keeps its striped tail raised high in the air. This shows the others where each lemur is and keeps the group safely together.

Tree-top tails

Some mammals which spend their lives up in the tree-tops have 'prehensile' tails. This means the tail can be used as an extra arm or leg to grasp hold of the branches. Spider monkeys have such strong tails that they can easily support their whole body weight on their tail alone.

DID YOU KNOW?

The Asian elephant has the longest tail of any land mammal. Excluding the tuft of hair on the end, the tail can be up to 1.5 m (5 ft) long.

Mammal tails		
Mammal	Body length	Tail length
Snow leopard	1.75 m	1.13 m
Jerboa	15 cm	30 cm
Red kangaroo	2 m	1.05 m
Giant anteater	1 m	60-90 cm
Long-tailed shrew	5-10 cm	3-8 cm
Spider monkey	40-62 cm	50-90 cm
Palm squirrel	11-18 cm	11-18 cm
Bottle-nosed dolphin	3-4 m	0.75 m (width)
Honey bear	1-1.2 m	5 cm
Hippopotamus	3-3.5 m	25-50 cm

Coats and camouflage

Warm coats

All mammals have some hair. It helps to keep them warm by stopping heat escaping from their bodies and helps protect them from injury. A mammal's coat usually has two sorts of hair – a soft underfur with longer 'guard hairs' on top. The colour of some coats helps hide the mammal from enemies and is also used for making signals.

Longest hair

Mammals that live in cold places have the longest hair. The musk ox in Greenland has hair 60-90 cm (24-35 in) long and can live in temperatures as low as −27°C (−60°F). Without its thick, warm coat it would freeze to death.

Hair flower

The hyrax has a very unusual hair 'flower'. On its back is a gland surrounded by long hairs of a different colour to its coat. When the hyrax is threatened these hairs stand on end so that the flower seems to 'bloom'.

Walrus whiskers

Some mammals have very sensitive whiskers which help them to find their way around in the dark or underwater. A walrus's moustache contains about 700 hairs. It uses these to feel its way around in murky water. The hairs may also be used as forks to hold shellfish in place while the walrus sucks out the soft insides.

DID YOU KNOW?

Until the age of three months a cheetah cub has a thick mane of smoky-grey hair on its back. The mane is about 8 cm (3 in) long and helps hide the cub among dry grasses and bushes. Manes also make an animal look bigger and fiercer than it really is to scare away enemies.

Cunning colours

The patterned coats of mammals such as tapirs, tigers and giraffes help to hide them from enemies or to stalk their prey unnoticed. Their coats blend in with the patches of light and shadow in the jungles and grasslands where they live. The black and white coat of a Malayan tapir disguises it so well that, when it is lying on the forest floor, it looks like a harmless pile of stones.

Thick tufts

The tuft of hair at the end of an elephant's tail is about 20 cm (7½ in) long. Each hair can be up to 3 mm (0.1 in) thick, over 40 times thicker than human hair.

Hairy heirlooms

In the last Ice Age which ended 10,000 years ago, rhinoceroses and mammoths adapted to the freezing conditions by growing long, warm coats. Cave paintings show the woolly rhinoceros with a thick black and reddish coat. Whole mammoths have been found deep-frozen in the ground in Siberia with some of their coats still intact.

Pin cushion

Mammals' quills and prickles are types of hair but may be very hard and sharp. Some porcupines have quills up to 40 cm (16 in) long. A Canadian porcupine has about 30,000 quills each up to 12 cm (5 in) long. Put end to end, they would reach a third of the way up Mount Everest. When attacked, a porcupine charges backwards and sticks its quills into its enemy. As it moves forward again the quills are left behind causing serious wounds.

Amazing But True

A pangolin is covered in very unusual scales because they are actually made from hairs. When a pangolin is born the scales are soft but they soon harden and help to protect the pangolin from predators. Ordinary hair grows between the scales and on the underside of a pangolin's body.

Green hair

The sloth in South America hangs upside-down in trees. Unlike the hair of any other mammmal, a sloth's long hair grows from its stomach down towards its back. Sloths are so dirty that green algae grow on their coats This camouflages the sloth among the trees and is an ideal egg-laying site for some moths. The newly-hatched caterpillars feed on the algae.

Communication

Sights and sounds

Other mammals cannot speak as people do but communicate by smell, sight, sound and touch. Each species has different signals to warn others in the group of danger, mark its territory, call its young or find a mate.

Smelly signals

The tenrec, an insect-eater from Madagascar, spits on a spot it wants to mark, then rubs its hand along its side and on the wet place. It does this to mark its territory with its own strong body smell. Other tenrecs recognise the scent and are warned to stay away.

Tail talk

Dogs use their tails to show their feelings. A happy dog wags its tail. A frightened dog puts its tail between its legs. An angry cat, though, swishes its tail from side to side and holds it upright if it is content.

Baby talk

Baby animals make signals. A baby orang-utan's small size, big eyes, high forehead and jerky movements all give out a special message. They tell the adults in the group that this is a baby who needs to be looked after.

Laughing hyena

Hyenas hunt together in teams and make many different noises for communication. They growl, grunt, whine and yelp but also burst into noisy choruses which sound like hysterical laughter. Only human beings can really laugh.

Body language

Chimpanzees are among the very few mammals which can pull faces to show their feelings. They can show anger, happiness and interest very much like human beings. But if a chimp seems to be grinning, showing its teeth, it is probably frightened, not smiling. Chimps also shake their fists to show anger, and cuddle and touch each other to show affection.

Whale of a song

Whales build up series of sounds into 'songs'. A song may last for about ten minutes but some humpback songs lasting 30 minutes have been recorded. Some are sung over and over again for as long as 24 hours. Whales have very loud voices. Some are even louder than the sound of a jet plane.

Rousing chorus

Howler monkeys live high up in the tree tops in South American forests. To warn off enemies they make one of the loudest mammal sounds. Every morning and evening the monkeys sing in chorus, their throats swelling up like huge balloons. They can be heard about 8 km (5 miles) away.

Amazing But True

Dolphins have a wide vocabulary of over 32 sounds. They use squeals, clicks, barks and whistles to 'talk' to each other. A dolphin uses different sounds to tell others in the group who it is, where it is and to warn them if there is danger. Dolphins also use sound as bats do to navigate and to find their food.

Colour coded

Monkeys have very good eyesight and so can use colour to signal to others in their group or to enemies. Many have brightly-coloured hair and skin which show others which species they belong to and which sex they are.

Mandrill

The male mandrill's scarlet and blue face and bottom warn off rivals.

Uakari

The uakari has a red face which gets brighter if it is angry or excited.

De Brazza's monkey

These are part of a large group of monkeys called guenons. Colour is used

Moustached monkey

by the guenons to tell the difference between the many types.

Instinct and intelligence

Clever monkey

Most animals behave according to their instinct but some animals are also able to learn facts and work out problems. Monkeys and apes are among the most intelligent animals. Johnnie, a rhesus monkey living on a farm in Australia, learned to drive a tractor. He was also able to understand commands such as 'turn left' and 'turn right'.

Sign language

A 13-year old gorilla, called Koko, was taught from an early age to use sign language. She now knows about 1,000 words. Koko is very fond of her cat and describes him as 'Soft good cat cat' and herself as 'Fine animal gorilla'. In an intelligence test taken at the age of seven, Koko proved to be just as clever as a human seven-year old.

Some mammals use twigs or stones as tools. The sea otter floats on its back in the water with a large stone balanced on its stomach. It smashes shellfish against the stone to open them up to eat.

The otter keeps its face turned away to avoid being hit by sharp pieces of broken shell. One otter was seen to open 54 mussels in 86 minutes. It smashed them against a stone over 2,000 times.

Washing up

Macaques are very intelligent monkeys. Scientists studying a group of macaques in Japan, began to feed them with sweet potatoes. A year later they were amazed to see a 3½-year old female, Imo, dip her potato in a pool to wash off the sand. The others followed her lead but soon found that washing the food in the sea gave it a better, salty taste.

Going home

Some animals are able to find their way back home even over very long distances. In 1979 a doctor in the USSR found and looked after an injured hedgehog. She later gave it to her granddaughter who lived in another town. Two months later she found the hedgehog sitting on her doorstep again. It had walked 77 km (48 miles) back home, much further than a hedgehog would usually go.

Which way?

In the autumn mammals such as whales and bats make long journeys to warmer places to feed or breed. This is called migration. These animals seem to find their way there and back each year without getting lost. Scientists think they must have a built-in compass telling them which route to take.

Amazing But True

A young artist, D. James Orang, won first prize in an art contest held in 1971 in Kansas, USA. His paintings sold well and he became quite famous. The judges did not realise that the painter was in fact a six-year old orang-utan, Djakarta Jim, living in Topeka Zoo.

More animal nomads

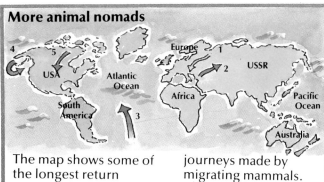

The map shows some of the longest return journeys made by migrating mammals.

↑ **1** Noctule bat
2,300 km

↑ **2** European pipistrelle
1,300 km

↑ **3** Humpback whale
8,000 km

↑ **4** Alaskan fur seal (male)
5,000 km

↑ **5** Caribou
2,250 km

Sea marathon

The longest journey is made by grey whales. In late autumn they leave their feeding grounds in the Bering Sea and travel 9,650 km (6,000 miles) south along the west coast of the USA to Mexico. This is about the same distance as from London to Tokyo. In the spring they return north by the same route. The journey takes about 90 days.

Fast asleep

Instinct tells some mammals to hibernate during cold winters when food is scarce. Their breathing and pulse rates slow right down and their body temperature drops. Some live off fat stored in their bodies; others store food in their dens. Marmots hibernate for the longest time. They sleep for 7-8 months every year, losing about a quarter of their body weight.

Families and herds

Safety in numbers

Many mammals live in families or herds. They work together to defend themselves and search for food. Often the members of a group are closely related. A herd of antelopes may include parents and children, aunts, uncles and cousins. Animal groups often have definite leaders.

Job sharing

Mole rats in Africa have very well-organised family groups. One large female is the queen and has all the babies. The smaller mole rats do the hard work, digging tunnels and finding food. The larger rats are much lazier than this. They look after the nests for the young and sound the alarm if they see an intruder near the burrow.

DID YOU KNOW?

The greatest gathering of any one type of mammal takes place on the Pribilof Islands in the Bering Sea. Each year about 1½ million Alaskan fur seals go there to breed, producing 500,000 pups.

Anti-social sloth

Some mammals live very solitary lives. The three-toed sloth spends 18 hours of its day asleep and the rest feeding, all by itself.

Hunting packs

Wolves hunt in packs, following a set plan of attack. When tracking a moose, wolves set out in single file. Once a moose is sighted they stand very still, then suddenly rush towards it. As soon as it starts to run, the wolves attack. A large pack of about 16 wolves may track up to 12 moose before finally catching one.

Largest herds

Amazing But True

Prairie dogs, or ground squirrels, live in vast systems of burrows called 'towns'. Each town is divided into smaller family units called 'coteries'. A prairie dog town found in Texas, USA in the 19th century contained an

incredible 400 million animals. It covered an area about twice the size of Belgium.

Bat caves

Bats are very sociable animals and live together in huge cave colonies. The largest bat colony in the world is in Bracken Cave, Texas, USA. During the summer the cave is the home of as many as 20 million Mexican free-tailed bats.

The largest herds ever recorded were those of springbok in southern Africa in the 19th century. When food and water became scarce, the springbok would set off in search of new pastures. The last great herd was seen in 1896. It is said to have covered 5,360 sq km (2,070 sq miles), over three times the area of London, England. There were over 10 million animals.

Some animal groups have very unusual names:
A clowder of cats
A leap of leopards
A sloth of bears
A skulk of foxes
A labour of moles
A crash of rhinoceroses
A trip of goats
A shrewdness of apes
A troop of kangaroos
A pride of lions
A pod of dolphins

Jumbo care

Elephants live in herds of 200 or more animals, led by female elephants. During the day the herd splits into smaller groups to feed and find water. The young are looked after by one or two mothers in 'nursery groups'. Females spend all their lives with the herd but single males sometimes leave and are then known as 'rogues' because they can become very fierce. If an elephant dies the herd mourns and stays by the body for several days, covering it with leaves and earth before they go away.

Mammals at home

Home, sweet home

The type of home a mammal has depends on how much protection it needs from predators and the weather, and if it needs a safe place for its young. Many mammals do not have fixed homes. They wander in search of food. Some live in one area, called a territory, which they defend against intruders.

DID YOU KNOW?

Sea mammals have no fixed home in the water but some have special sleeping habits. Florida manatees sleep on the sea bed. They come to the surface every ten minutes or so to breathe. Sea otters sleep floating on the surface. They wind strands of seaweed round their bodies to stop themselves drifting.

Long sleep

Big cats, such as leopards, sleep for between 12-14 hours a day. They lie on the ground or stretch out along tree branches. They do not need shelters as they live in a warm climate and have no natural enemies.

Mouse house

A harvest mouse builds its nest among tall grasses. Large nests are about the size and shape of cricket balls. The mouse splits blades of grass into thin strips with its teeth and weaves them into a framework. The blades are still joined to the stalks so the nest is firmly wedged. The framework is padded out with more grass, feathers and even pieces of string.

Amazing But True

Burrows are the most common type of homes for small mammals. Mole rats are among the best burrowers. The Russian mole rat, digging with its teeth, can shift 50 times its own

weight of soil in about 20 minutes. Moles can dig a 2 m (6½ ft) long tunnel in about 12 minutes. At this rate it would take a mole only four years to dig its way from London to Paris.

Apes asleep

Chimpanzees and orang-utans sleep in flimsy, temporary nests up in the trees. It takes a chimp about five minutes to build a nest. It bends branches across to form a firm base and then weaves smaller twigs into it. If the night is cold, apes wrap themselves up in leaf or grass 'blankets'.

Escape routes

Rabbits dig large tunnel systems underground. The tunnels lead to living and sleeping rooms and nurseries. Above ground the rabbits dig out special 'bolt' holes which they stay close to when they are feeding outside. If there is danger, the rabbits bolt head first down the nearest hole to safety underground.

Houseproud badgers

Badgers live in setts made up of chambers with connecting tunnels. One of the largest setts known had 94 tunnels. The same sett may be used over and over again for as long as 250 years. Badgers are very houseproud. They line their bedrooms with bracken, moss and grass. On dry mornings they drag huge piles of bedding outside to air in the sun.

Master builders

Beavers are ingenious builders. First they build a dam of logs and mud across a river to form a pond. In the pond they build a dome-shaped wooden lodge the size of a large tent. With its strong teeth, a beaver can fell a tree ½ m (20 in) thick in just 15 minutes. Inside the lodge is a living area above water level, reached through underwater tunnels.

Record breaker

Beaver dams are usually about 23 m (75 ft) long. The largest dam ever built is on the Jefferson River, USA. It is 700 m (2,296 ft) long and strong enough to bear the weight of a person riding across it on horseback.

Bear caves

Some bears hibernate in the winter when it is cold and food is scarce. They dig dens in the ground or find caves or hollow trees to live in. A female polar bear digs a den in the snow in October and has her cubs there. They leave the den in the spring.

Mammals at home

Mammal	Home
Badger	Sett or earth
Fox	Earth or kennel
Hare	Form
Bear	Den
Otter	Holt
Rabbit	Burrow or warren
Squirrel	Drey

Runners

Fastest on land

Cheetahs are the fastest land mammals with a top speed of 115 kph (71 mph), as fast as an average car. They can only run fast for short distances though and have to rest after about 500 m (550 yards). Cheetahs have flexible backbones which allow

them to take giant 7 m (23 ft) leaps. They can reach 72 kph (45 mph) from a standstill in just two seconds. In the 1930s cheetahs were raced against greyhounds in London. The cheetahs won.

Let's dance

Sifakas, or white lemurs, of Madagascar spend a lot of their time high up in the tree tops. They can swing easily from tree to tree. Their legs are much longer than their 'arms' so running on all fours along the ground is impossible. Instead, they do a type of dance on their back legs. They bounce from one foot to the other, holding their arms high in the air.

Pronghorn puff

The fastest land mammal over long distances is the pronghorn antelope of the USA. It can keep up a speed of 45-50 kph (28-31 mph) for about 14 minutes and has a top speed of 85 kph (53 mph). A pronghorn can run fast for so long because it has very well-developed lungs and a heart twice as big as that of other animals of a similar size.

DID YOU KNOW?

The sloth is the slowest land mammal in the world with a top speed of only 2 kph (1.3 mph). It would take a sloth travelling at normal speed about 22 minutes to go 100 m (110 yards). The fastest man in the world can run this distance in under 10 seconds.

Top speeds

Cheetah	115 kph
Blackbuck	80 kph
Brown hare	72 kph
Race horse	69 kph
Greyhound	66 kph
Red fox	64 kph
Giraffe	51 kph
African elephant	40 kph
Arabian camel	32 kph
American porcupine	16 kph
House rat	9 kph
Common shrew	4 kph
Sloth	2 kph

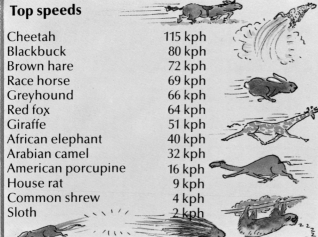

Climbers

Climbing aid

Some mammals have their own special ways of making climbing up tree trunks easier. The slow-moving Canadian porcupine has non-slip pads on the soles of its feet. It also has spines underneath its tail which help it to grip the tree trunk. An African spiny squirrel also has spines on its tail.

Sure-footed

Some mammals have specially adapted feet for climbing. Rocky Mountain goats in the USA are very sure-footed and can climb up nearly vertical slopes and walk safely along narrow ledges. Their hooves have sharp edges which dig into cracks in the rocks to give a secure foothold and their soles have hollows which stick to rocks like suction pads.

Amazing But True

One of the best mountain climbers was a beagle from Switzerland called Tschingel. From 1868-1876 she climbed 53 of the most difficult mountains in the Alps, 11 of which had never been climbed before, and many easier ones. In 1875 she climbed Mont Blanc, the highest mountain in the Alps and was made a member of the exclusive Alpine Club.

Short cut

Most big cats are good climbers but the puma has an easier way of getting up and down trees. It is an excellent jumper. From a standstill it can leap 7 m (23 ft) up into a tree and jump down to the ground from heights of up to 18 m (60 ft).

Speedy climber

The fastest animal mountain climber is the chamois, a mountain goat which lives in the Pyrenees and Alps in Europe. It can climb 1,000 m (3,280 ft) in only 15 minutes. At this rate a chamois could climb to the top of Mount Everest, the highest point on Earth, in just over two hours.

Swinging gibbons

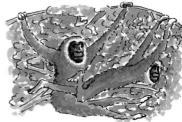

Some mammals do not need to climb well. A gibbon has arms twice as long as its body. The easiest way for it to move through the trees is to swing. Its armspan is about 2.1 m (7ft) and it can swing 12 m (39 ft) from one branch to the next, gripping the branches firmly with its long, curved fingers.

Flying mammals

Air-borne bats

Bats are the only mammals which can fly although some mammals can glide. There are over 900 different species. Bats are the second largest group of mammals, after rodents and make up one fifth of the world's mammals. Bats live all over the world, except in very cold places. There are two main groups – the large fruit bats or flying foxes, and the smaller insect-eaters. Some bats also feed on birds, lizards, fish, nectar and blood.

Nectar eaters

Jamaican flower bats and tube-nosed fruit bats eat nectar. They hover near flowers and stick their long tongues deep down inside to reach the food. Bats help to pollinate flowers. Pollen stuck to their bodies is carried to another flower.

Taking to the air

The Latin word for bats is 'chiroptera' which means 'hand-wings'. About 60 million years ago some insect-eating mammals developed into bats and their bodies became adapted for flight. A bat's wings have formed from its hands and arms. Its fingers are very long and support the skin stretched across them. The thumb is left free. The wing is also attached to the bat's back legs and often to its tail.

DID YOU KNOW?

Vampires are the most dangerous bats as they spread diseases such as rabies. There are many legends about vampires. In Eastern Europe it was thought that vampires were evil people who could turn into bats. To gain control over other people, they sucked their blood. Some ways of scaring away vampires were to show them a crucifix or to wear a necklace of garlic.

Bat ears

Bats have the best hearing of all land mammals. They have very sensitive and often very large ears which some use for locating their prey in the dark. The long-eared bat's body is only 5 cm (2 in) long but its ears are 4 cm (1½ in) long. If the bat was as big as a hare, its ears would be over 44 cm (1½ ft) long.

Bat homes

Bats feed at night and spend the day sleeping in caves or in tree tops. Some caves may be home to thousands of bats. Other bats make temporary shelters. They sleep under banana leaves, in empty burrows or even inside bamboo stems. Some South American bats make tent-like shelters out of palm tree leaves.

Catching fish

The hare-lipped bat in tropical America is an expert fisherman. It flies low over ponds and lakes. Spotting a fish just below the surface, it swoops down, raking the water with its large claws and scoops the fish up into its mouth. Its legs are not attached to the skin of its wings so they are free to act as fish hooks.

Winter warmth

To avoid the cold winter months, some bats migrate to warmer places. Noctule bats travel the furthest, flying 2,300 km (1,430 miles) from Moscow to Bulgaria. Other bats hibernate in caves or in hollow tree trunks. Most hibernating mammals wake up every 10-20 days but brown bats sleep solidly for up to 66 days.

Flying lemurs

A few mammals are very good gliders though they cannot actually fly. Flying lemurs, or colugos, of the Far East are about the size of rabbits. Their front and back legs are joined by folds of furry skin down each side. The colugo spreads these out like wings and glides from tree to tree. It can glide for a distance of 91 m (300 ft) before landing.

Super gliders

Flying phalangers, such as the sugar glider, of Australia, and the flying squirrels of North America can also glide from tree to tree. Flying phalangers are in fact marsupials. They glide with their young in their pouches until the babies are two months old. Flying squirrels are rodents. They can glide as far as 450 m (⅓ mile).

Sea mammals

Sea mammals

There are over 4,000 species of mammals but only about 121 of these are sea mammals. Sea mammals are divided into three groups:

Pinnipedes – seals, sea-lions, walruses
   (32 species)
Sirenians (or sea cows) – manatees, dugongs
   (4 species)
Cetaceans – whales, dolphins, porpoises
   (about 85 species)

Sea unicorn

A narwhal has only two teeth which grow straight forward from its top jaw. The male's left tooth carries on growing in a spiral. It can be up to 2.5 m (9 ft) long. Narwhals are nearly extinct today because they were once hunted for their valuable tusks which were sold as unicorn horns. No one has yet found out what narwhals use their tusks for.

DID YOU KNOW?

The ancestors of sea mammals once lived on land. About 50 million years ago they began to return to the sea for food and their bodies adapted to life in the water. The whale's front legs became flippers, its back legs disappeared

and its nostrils became a blow-hole on top of its head. Sea mammals can hold their breath for a long time. A fin-back whale is able to stay underwater for 40 minutes; a bottle-nosed dolphin for two hours.

Seal tears

Seals lying on rocks out of the water often look as if they are crying. This is because they produce tears to keep their eyes moist. In the sea the tears get washed away but on land they trickle down the seals' cheeks.

Humpback acrobat

The humpback is the most athletic whale. It leaps high into the air and crashes down into the water on its back. It can even turn complete somersaults in the air. A humpback whale's body is often covered in barnacles which may weigh as much as eight people. The whale may leap to try and get rid of the weight.

Power propeller

The killer whale is the fastest sea mammal. It uses its strong tail as a propeller to speed it through the water. Thrashing its tail up and down, it can reach a top speed of about 65 kph (40 mph), eight times faster than the fastest human swimmer.

Whale blubber

Instead of fur, whales have a thick layer of fat, called blubber, round their bodies. Blubber keeps them warm and helps support their large bodies in the water. Some whales have blubber 38 cm (15 in) thick. Whales have long been hunted for the valuable oils in their blubber. A blue whale's blubber can weigh as much as four tractors and may contain over 120 barrels of oil.

Pinnipede records

Largest	Southern elephant seal
Smallest	Ringed seal
Fastest	Californian sea-lion
Deepest-diver	Weddell seal
Most common	Crabeater seal
Rarest	Monk seal

Amazing But True

The mermaid legend is thought to come from the rather ugly dugong. Close to, it is hard to believe that these lumbering creatures could have been mistaken for mermaids but from a distance they do look a little like human forms with fish-like tails.

Walking teeth

In the breeding season huge herds of walruses gather on islands in the Bering Sea. Adults, which can weigh over a tonne, use their tusks to drag themselves over the land. The Latin name for walrus, *Odobenus rosmarus* actually means 'the one who walks with its teeth'.

Dolphin care

Some dolphins travel in family groups called pods, of up to 1,000 animals. If a dolphin is ill or wounded, the others push it to the surface so it can still breathe. A shark may be able to kill a single dolphin but if it attacks a pod, the dolphins ram it with their 'beaks'. They scare the shark off and may even kill it.

Mammals of the cold

Out in the cold

Mammals living in very cold places need special survival skills. Many have thick coats for keeping warm and broad feet for walking on ice and snow. The vicuña, a relation of the camel, lives in the Andes in South America. It has such a warm coat that it can even overheat. But it also has bare patches on its legs. To cool down, it turns so that these are facing the wind.

High home

The highest-living mammal is the wild yak of Tibet and China. It can climb to heights of over 6,000 m (20,000 ft) in search of food. Its long, thick blackish coat protects it from the biting cold. People in Nepal keep domestic yaks for milk, wool and dung for fuel.

Snowshoe rabbit

Snowshoe rabbits in North America get their name from their broad feet. These act like snowshoes and stop the rabbit sinking in the deep snow. Long hairs grow on the sides of the feet and between the toes. They keep the rabbit's feet warm and help them to grip the frozen ground.

DID YOU KNOW?

Macaques living high up in the mountains of northern Japan have to cope with very harsh winters. They keep warm by taking long baths in the hot, volcanic springs nearby.

Cool cats

The rare snow leopard, or ounce, lives in the mountains of Central Asia. It has a thick, smoky-grey coat with black rosette markings. In summer the snow leopard lives nearly 6,000 m (20,000 ft) up in the mountain peaks. In winter it comes down to the lower slopes below 3,000 m (10,000 ft) in search of food.

All change

The Arctic fox, some stoats and the snow hare change colour as the seasons change. They have brown summer coats, moult in autumn and turn white in winter. Throughout the year they blend in with the countryside and are very well hidden from hungry predators.

Mountain mammals

The list shows the maximum heights at which various mammals are found.

By comparison, Mount Everest, the highest point on Earth, is 8,848 m tall.

6,000 m	Tibetan antelope
5,800 m	Woolly hare
5,600 m	Mongolian wolf
5,500 m	Puma
4,700 m	Brown bear
3,600 m	Snow vole
	Red panda

Deep-sea diver

The Weddell seal lives in the Antarctic, further south than any other mammal. It spends most of its time under the pack ice, kept warm by a thick layer of fat under its skin. It chews holes in the ice to reach air to breathe.

Hardy huskies

Husky dogs are among the hardiest animals. They have thick coats and can live in temperatures as low as −45°C (−50°F) without shelter. They are also very strong. A team of 12 can pull a sled weighing half a tonne, as much as eight people and their luggage.

Amazing But True

Polar bears are sometimes seen on land. A teacher at a school near the northerly Kara Sea, USSR, heard the door bell ring and went to answer it. She found that the caller was a huge polar bear leaning on the door bell.

Abominable snowman

Many people claim to have seen yetis in the Himalayas. They are supposed to be ape-like creatures with long, shaggy coats. In 1951 photographs of yeti footprints were published but no one has proved yetis exist. It is thought that yetis are, in fact, large black or brown bears. A more unusual explanation is that they are 'visions' or hallucinations caused by a lack of oxygen at high altitudes.

Ice bear

The largest polar mammal is the polar bear. The heaviest recorded weighed over a tonne. Polar bears live on the pack ice near the North Pole. This is the bear's hunting ground. It waits by an air-hole for a seal to surface and kills it with a blow of its paw. Polar bears are strong swimmers but prefer to use pieces of ice as rafts.

225

Mammals of the desert

Desert life

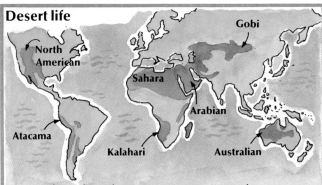

North American, Sahara, Gobi, Arabian, Atacama, Kalahari, Australian

Deserts have less than 25 cm (10 in) of rain a year. They cover about a fifth of the Earth's land surface. Deserts are sandy, rocky or covered in stones and gravel. The Sahara Desert is almost as big as the whole USA. The temperature there may reach 57°C (134°F) during the day and drop well below freezing at night. Many plants and animals live in deserts. They all face the same problem – finding enough water to stay alive.

Plant food

Desert plants provide food and water for many animals. Cacti store water in their leaves and stems. Giant saguaro cacti in the North American deserts can weigh as much as 10 tonnes of which 9 tonnes may be water. Mammals eat the plants and seeds and can get enough water from them to live without drinking.

Underground cool

Most small desert mammals spend the day underground to avoid the heat. Scientists studying gerbil burrows in the Kara-Kum Desert, USSR, found that just 10 cm (4 in) below ground the temperature was 17°C (61°F) cooler than above. Mammals' breathing helps keep the burrows moist. In the day the burrow entrance is blocked to stop moisture escaping.

Sand survivor

The rare addax, a type of antelope, lives among the sanddunes in the southern Sahara. It is one of the few large mammals that can survive such harsh conditions. The addax never needs to drink. It gets all its moisture from the plants it eats.

DID YOU KNOW?

About 5,000 years ago the Sahara Desert was covered in rich grassland and trees. Paintings found in caves in Tassili, Algeria, which date from about that time, show giraffe, hippopotamus and lions, people hunting and cattle grazing.

Living in the desert

Here are some of the ways mammals have of coping with the desert heat and lack of water:

1 Hunt only during cooler night
2 Sweat very little so lose little water
3 Get water from the plants and seeds they eat
4 Concentrated urine so body loses less water
5 Large ears which give off excess heat
6 Small mammals spend day in cool burrows

Little leaper

Kangaroo rats are an important part of desert life. They are often eaten by other animals for the water in their bodies. The rats can hop very fast to avoid their enemies, covering 6 m (20 ft) in one second. They use their long tails as rudders when jumping and can even change their course in mid-air.

Kit fox

The kit fox hunts for food at night, well hidden by its greyish-black coat. It has excellent hearing for detecting its prey in the dark. It also loses heat through its large ears to keep cool and they are lined with thick hair to keep out dust and sand.

Spit and polish

Desert wallabies and kangaroos in Australia have an unusual way of keeping cool. When it gets very hot they pant and make a lot of saliva. They lick the saliva over their bodies and rub their faces with their wet paws.

Sleepy squirrel

The Mojave squirrel in the USA survives long droughts by sleeping for whole days at a time in its underground burrow. Sleeping through hot, dry weather is called aestivation. The squirrel saves energy and is out of the heat.

Ships of the desert

There are two types of camel – the one-humped Arabian camel and the two-humped Bactrian camel. Both are well equipped for desert life. A camel's hump can weigh up to 13.5 kg (30 lb) and contains fat which can be used when there is no food. Camels can survive for many days without food and water. After a drought they will drink up to 114 litres (25 gallons) of water in one go.

Worlds apart

Australia's animals

Because Australia has been cut off from the rest of the world for over 60 million years, it has very unusual animals. Almost all its mammals are marsupials (mammals with pouches). There are over 150 kinds of Australian marsupials from tiny marsupial mice and moles to marsupial cats. Outside Australia marsupials are only found in South America with just one species in North America.

Honey possum

A honey possum, or noolbenger, of Western Australia, is about the size of a mouse. It has a special way of eating nectar and pollen. Its long tongue is covered in bristles with a tip like a tiny brush. Pollen sticks to the brush as it feeds.

Some unusual marsupials

Boodie

Member of the rat kangaroo family.

Numbat

Also called a banded anteater.

Quoll

A marsupial cat.

Bandicoot

Pouch opens to rear. Latin name means 'badger with a pouch'.

Amazing But True

The biggest collection of marsupial fossils was found in the Naracoorte Caves, Australia, in 1969. They showed giant marsupials including a creature the size of a rhinoceros. It probably died out about 40,000 years ago.

Wombat digger

Wombats are about the same size and shape as badgers. They are expert diggers and live in huge underground burrows surrounded by a maze of tunnels. A wombat's pouch opens backwards so that the baby being carried inside is not showered with earth as the wombat digs.

Marsupial records

Biggest	Red kangaroo	Up to 2.13 m tall
Smallest	Ingram's planigale	9 cm long
Fastest	Red kangaroo	48 kph
Rarest	Marsupial wolf	Last known died 1933.
Most common	Kangaroo	Over 50 species
Longest-lived	Common wombat	26 years

Madagascar

Madagascar is a huge island off the east coast of Africa. It is bigger than France. About 30 million years ago it became separated from Africa. Nine-tenths of the island's animals and plants are found nowhere else in the world. Its most famous mammals are lemurs which are related to monkeys and apes.

DID YOU KNOW?

The sportive lemur gets its name because, if attacked, it raises its fists like a boxer and punches its enemy. It feeds on Somy tree flowers. The tree is covered in sharp spikes but the lemur does not seem to hurt itself as it leaps from stem to stem.

Rousing chorus

The indri, the largest of the lemurs, lives mostly high up in the tree tops. It uses sound to scare away enemies and call its young. Every morning and evening, families of indris break into wailing songs. Each indri joins in at a different time so the strange chorus may last for many minutes.

Sun worship

Sifakas, or white lemurs, start off each day by lying in the sun for an hour or so. They climb to a tree top and face the sun with their arms outstretched. They do this to warm themselves up after a cool night but local people believed that the lemurs were worshipping the sun.

Fat store

Dwarf lemurs are amongst the smallest of the lemurs. The fat-tailed dwarf lemur eats insects, leaves and sap. During the rainy season it builds up a fat store under its skin and in its tail. It lives off this supply in the dry season when food is scarce.

Tenrecs

Another group of mammals found only in Madagascar are tenrecs. There are about 20 species of these small insect-eaters. Some have bristly coats like hedgehogs, others have fur. The common tenrec is the largest insect-eater in Madagascar. It may be as much as 40 cm (16 in) long, about the same size as a cat.

Mammals in danger

Under threat

Over 550 species of mammals are in danger of dying out for ever. When an animal species dies out, it is said to be extinct. If it is likely to die out unless it is protected, it is said to be endangered or threatened.

Why in danger

Many mammals become endangered because their homes are destroyed by farmers or foresters or they are hunted for their meat or fur. The South American rain forests contain about half of the world's plant and animal species. As they are destroyed to make room for farms or buildings, thousands of species are lost. It is thought that a piece of rain forest the size of Switzerland is cut down each year.

Run, rhino, run

All five species of rhinoceros are listed as endangered. Rhinos have long been hunted for their horns. A powder made from horn was thought to cure fevers and headaches. In 1978 there were about 140,000 rhino in the wild. Ten years later this number had been reduced to 14,000.

Giant panda

Giant pandas once lived all over China but are now only found in the south-west. Pandas live mainly on bamboo. If this dies or is cut down, they may starve. In 1981 the World Wildlife Fund and the Chinese Government started the project 'Save the Panda' to protect them.

DID YOU KNOW?

In 1700 there were some 60 million buffalo in North America. Millions were killed for their meat and because their grazing land was needed for farming. By 1880 there were only a few hundred left. Today the buffalo are making a slow comeback. There are now about 10,000 in the wild.

Operation tiger

Many of the big cats, including the Asian lion, the leopard and the tiger, are endangered. In 1945 there were over 100,000 tigers in India; by 1970 probably about 4,000 were left. Tigers were hunted for their fur and for sport. Today there are special tiger reserves in India and tigers are now strictly protected by law.

Monkeys and apes

The golden lion tamarin is one of the world's rarest monkeys. Only about 200 still survive in patches of forest in Brazil. Much of the monkey's forest home has been cleared to make way for sugar cane and coffee plantations and for building. One fifth of all the species of monkeys and apes in the world are endangered, including proboscis monkeys, black gibbons, chimpanzees and orang-utans.

Some endangered mammals

Mountain gorilla (Africa)	Less than 400 left in the wild.
Arabian oryx	Last seen in the wild in 1972. Now being re-introduced.
Indian lion	Hunted and forest home destroyed.
African elephant	Over 50,000 killed a year for the ivory from their tusks.
Grey whale (North Pacific)	Migration routes and breeding grounds destroyed by ships.
Baiji dolphin (China)	Less than 400 left; the most threatened whale species.
Sea otter (North Pacific)	Hunted for valuable fur; hunting now banned.

How to help

Unless human beings stop destroying habitats and polluting water, mammals such as blue whales and polar bears could become extinct by the beginning of the next century. The World Wildlife Fund was set up in 1961 to help protect the world's animals. It now has over 4,000 conservation projects in over 135 countries round the world. Groups like this and laws banning hunting or poaching have helped save some of the mammals most at risk.

Unsafe seas

As the seas become more polluted, many sea mammals are in danger of dying out. Chemical waste, sewage and oil spilt from tankers kill the mammals' food supplies. Seals and whales are also hunted for their meat and skins. Today they are protected but some are still killed. It is thought that there are now only 500 Mediterranean monk seals left and that the Caribbean monk seal may be extinct.

The smallest mammals

Smallest on land

The smallest land mammal is the tiny Savi's pygmy shrew which lives in southern Europe and Africa. It is 3.8 cm (1½ in) long with a tail which measures 2.5 cm (1 in). A fully-grown shrew weighs only about as much as a table tennis ball.

Smallest meat eater

The dwarf or least weasel which lives in Siberia is the smallest carnivore. An adult measures 17-20 cm (6.6-7.8 in) in length. It weighs about as much as ten lumps of sugar.

Pencil legs

The royal antelope which lives in West Africa is the smallest antelope in the world. Adults are only 25-30 cm (10-12 in) tall and weigh about 3-3.6 kg (7-8 lb). A royal antelope living in the London Zoo was said to have had legs thinner than pencils. Its hooves were so tiny that it was able to stand in a teaspoon with room to spare.

DID YOU KNOW?

The very rare bumblebee bat from Thailand is the smallest flying mammal. Adults have a wingspan of about 160 mm (6.3 in), about the same as that of a large butterfly. They weigh about as much as five drawing pins.

Smallest at sea

The smallest mammal in the seas is the Commerson's dolphin. An adult weighs 25-35 kg (55-77 lb), 3,500 times lighter than a blue whale, the largest sea mammal.

Miniature monkeys

The world's smallest primate is the lesser mouse lemur which lives on the island of Madagascar. When it is fully grown, it is about 11 cm (4.3 in) long, with a 15 cm (6 in) long tail. It

weighs only 50 g (1.7 oz). The tiny pygmy marmoset which lives in South America comes a close second. It weighs up to 75 g (2.6 oz), about as much as a hen's egg.

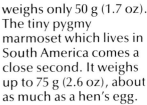

More small fry

Group	Smallest	Average weight (adult male)
Cat family	Rusty-spotted cat	1.35 kg
Seals	Ringed seal	127 kg
Deer	Northern pudu	7-8 g
Rodents	Northern pygmy mouse	7-8 kg
Domestic cat	Singapura	1.8 kg
Freshwater mammal	Southern water shrew	7.5-16 g
Bears	Malay bear	25-40 kg

Pocket sized

The very rare Ingram's planigale, a type of pouched mouse found only in north-west Australia, is the smallest marsupial in the world. Its body and head are 45 mm (1.7 in) long, its tail the same length again and it weighs only a little more than an airmail envelope.

The smallest dogs

The smallest breed of dogs is the chihuahua but the smallest dog ever known was a Yorkshire terrier. It died in 1945 aged two years. It was 6.3 cm (2½ in) tall at the shoulder, only 9.5 cm (3¾ in) from its nose to its tail and weighed an incredible 113 g (4 oz), about the same size as a hamster.

Amazing But True

The closest relation to the African elephant, the world's largest living land mammal, is said to be the comparatively tiny hyrax. Hyraxes are about the size of rabbits but in prehistoric times they were almost as large as cows. Elephants and hyraxes are thought to have come from the same group of mammals, millions of years ago.

Mini horse

The smallest breed of horse is the Falabella from Argentina. Adults are less than 76 cm (30 in) tall. The smallest horse ever known was a tiny stallion called Little Pumpkin from the USA. Fully grown, it was only about the size of a small dog.

The biggest mammals

Sea giant

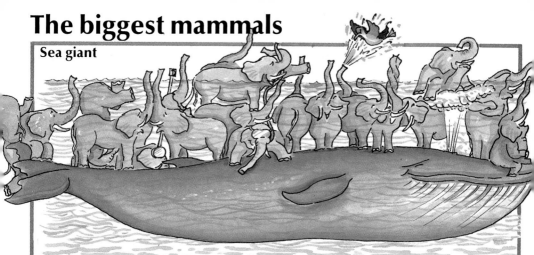

The biggest mammal that has ever lived is the gigantic blue whale. A female caught in the South Atlantic in 1922 was over 33 m (110 ft) long, nearly 1½ times as long as an Olympic swimming pool. Blue whales are also the heaviest mammals in the world. A single whale can weigh as much as 130 tonnes, over 20 times heavier than a bull (male) African elephant and almost as heavy as 2,000 men.

Amazing But True

A blue whale calf is the biggest mammal baby. When it is born, a calf can be over 7 m (25 ft) long and weigh nearly 2 tonnes. By drinking up to 600 litres (132 gallons) of its mother's rich milk a day it can double its weight in just a week. By the time it is seven months old, a calf may weigh as much as 23 tonnes.

Largest on land

The biggest land mammal in the world is the African elephant. An adult bull (male) is usually about 3 m (10½ ft) tall and weighs some 5½ tonnes. The largest African elephant ever recorded was about 4 m (13 ft) tall and weighed over 12 tonnes, as much as 16 average-sized cars.

Skyscraper

With its long neck and legs, the giraffe is the tallest mammal on Earth. An adult Masai giraffe bull can be over 5 m (17 ft) tall. A tall man would only come up to the top of its leg. The tallest giraffe ever recorded in the world was 5.87 m (19 ft 3 in) tall.

Gentle giant

The largest ape is the mountain gorilla in Africa. An average male stands 1.75 m (5 ft 9 in) tall and weighs about 195 kg (430 lb), with a massive chest of 1.5 m (5 ft). Gorillas are very gentle but very strong. Scientists have worked out that a two-year old gorilla's arms are about three times stronger than a two-year old child's.

Wonder wings

The largest flying mammal is the Bismarck flying fox, a bat from New Guinea. Its head and body are only 45 cm (18 in) long, but it can measure 1.6 m (5½ ft) across its outstretched wings, 2½ times the wingspan of a pigeon.

DID YOU KNOW?

The sperm whale has the heaviest mammal brain. Its brain weighs up to 9 kg (20 lb), six times heavier than a human brain. The whale has a very large head, about a third of its body length, so there is plenty of room for its big brain.

Biggest rodent

The capybara in South America is the world's largest rodent. It is about the size of a sheep, weighing up to 113 kg (250 lb). A harvest mouse, one of the smallest rodents in the world, is over 18,000 times lighter than its heavyweight relation.

Heavyweights

Group	Mammal	Heaviest ever
Bear	Kodiak bear	751 kg
Seal	Elephant seal	4-5 tonnes
Antelope	Giant eland	898 kg
Deer	Alaskan moose	816 kg
Marsupial	Red kangaroo	91 kg
Cat	Siberian tiger	384 kg
Horse	Belgian stallion	1.44 tonnes
Dog	St Bernard	140.6 kg

235

Habitat map

The type of place a mammal lives in is called its habitat. The larger map shows six main habitats and some of the animals found in them.

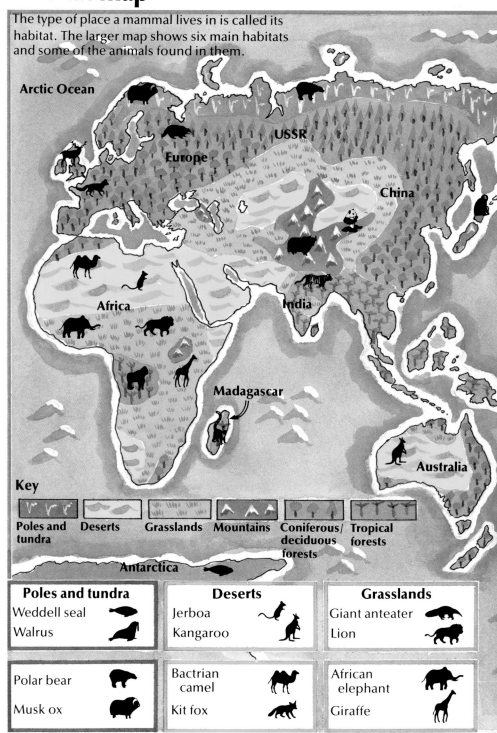

Arctic Ocean

Europe

USSR

China

Africa

India

Madagascar

Australia

Antarctica

Key

Poles and tundra	Deserts	Grasslands	Mountains	Coniferous/ deciduous forests	Tropical forests

Poles and tundra
Weddell seal

Walrus

Polar bear

Musk ox

Deserts
Jerboa

Kangaroo

Bactrian camel

Kit fox

Grasslands
Giant anteater

Lion

African elephant

Giraffe

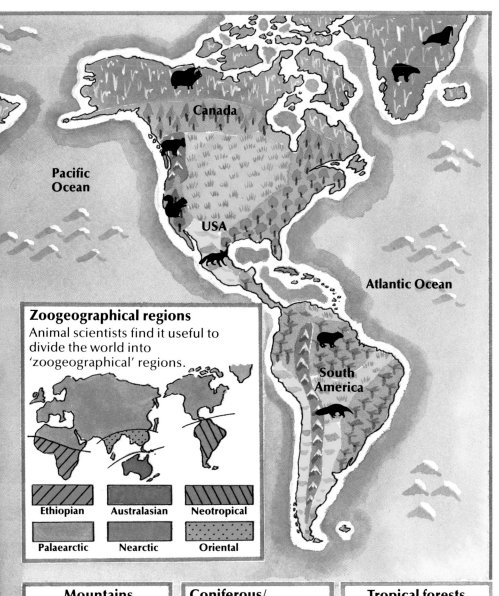

Pacific
Ocean

Canada

USA

Atlantic Ocean

South
America

Zoogeographical regions

Animal scientists find it useful to divide the world into 'zoogeographical' regions.

Ethiopian	Australasian	Neotropical
Palaearctic	Nearctic	Oriental

Mountains
Yak

Giant panda

Japanese macaque

Mountain goat

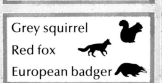

Coniferous/ deciduous forests
Red deer

Grey squirrel

Red fox

European badger

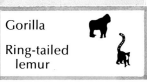

Tropical forests
Indian tiger

Capybara

Gorilla

Ring-tailed lemur

Glossary

Adaptation Special characteristics to help animals survive. For example, Arctic mammals have very thick, warm fur to protect them from the cold.

Aestivation A time of inactivity or deep sleep to save energy and keep cool during very hot and dry weather.

Camouflage Some mammals have special colouring or markings which help disguise them and hide them from their enemies.

Carnivore An animal that only or mainly eats meat.

Conservation Protecting rare animals from becoming extinct.

Endangered Animals in danger of becoming extinct or dying out.

Evolution Animals gradually change over a very long time to become better suited to the way in which they live (depending on food supplies, habitat and climate).

Extinct Animals that no longer exist. They become officially extinct if there have been no certain records of them for 50 years.

Gestation The length of time of a mammal's pregnancy.

Habitat The type of place an animal lives in, for example, desert, jungle, mountain, grassland.

Herbivore An animal such as an elephant that mostly or only eats plants.

Hibernation A deep sleep or time of inactivity to save energy during the cold, winter months.

Marsupial Mammals with pouches. Their young are born tiny and ill-formed. They feed and grow further inside their mother's pouch.

Migration A return journey made by some mammals every year to a place for feeding or breeding.

Monotreme A mammal which lays eggs such as the duck-billed platypus and spiny anteater. The most primitive group of mammals.

Nocturnal Animals such as bats that are active at night when they hunt for food and rest during the day.

Omnivore Animals that eat both plants and meat.

Placental mammal The young develop fully inside the mother's body before they are born.

Predator A hunting animal that kills other animals for food.

Primates The group of mammals that includes monkeys, apes and man. Their special features include a large brain, and fingers (and sometimes toes) designed for grasping.

Territory An area which an animal or group of animals 'owns' and defends against other animals.

Vertebrate An animal with a backbone and an internal skeleton. Fish, amphibians, reptiles, birds and mammals are all vertebrates.

Warm-blooded Animals that can control their own body temperature so it stays the same whatever the weather outside, allowing them to be active in the heat or cold.

Index

BIRD FACTS

Bridget Gibbs

CONTENTS

Illustrated by Tony Gibson and Stephen Lings

Designed by Tony Gibson

Consultant: Rob Hume
Editor of BIRDS magazine, published by
The Royal Society for the Protection of Birds

What is a bird?

How many birds?

There are about 8,600 different kinds, or species, of birds in the world. These are split into 28 groups called orders. More than half of all living birds are in the songbirds group.

Marathon fliers

Many birds can quickly travel vast distances to take advantage of the seasons and the best supplies of food. This movement is called migration. The champion migrant is the Arctic tern. It covers a round trip of 40,000km (25,000 miles) from the Arctic to the Antarctic and back. Terns can live for more than 20 years.

Featuring feathers

Birds are the only animals with feathers. When you look at a perched bird, most of the feathers you see are small ones that give its body a warm, smooth covering. When flying, birds show the larger, stiffer wing feathers used for flight.

DID YOU KNOW?

Wheatears living in Greenland are larger than those found further south. Being larger helps the birds to survive cold and longer migration flights to central Africa. The farther north a bird lives, the larger it tends to be.

Waterproof birds

Ducks, swans and most sea birds spend months on water and many birds dive underwater in search of food, but they never get wet through to the skin. They coat their feathers with oil from a special gland and constantly preen to keep feathers overlapping like tiles on a roof.

Running scared

Features of birds

All birds have:
Feathers
Wings (though a few, such as ostriches, cannot fly)
Hollow bones (except for some flightless and diving birds)
Beaks
All birds lay eggs

Some birds run rather than fly from danger. The wild turkey, hoopoe lark and red-legged partridge all fly quite well, but prefer to sprint short distances to get away from people or predators.

Lightest and least

Birds are the only animals with hollow bones. This makes their skeletons the lightest for their size of any animal. They have fewer bones than mammals, but they have more neck bones. Nearly all mammals, even giraffes, have seven bones in their necks. Herons have about 16 and swans have as many as 25.

The orders* of living birds

	Number of species
Runners and walkers	
Ostrich	1
Rheas	2
Cassowaries, emus	4
Kiwis	5
Fliers	
Tinamous	about 50
Penguins**	18
Divers	4
Grebes	about 20
Albatrosses, petrels	90
Pelicans, gannets, cormorants	about 59
Herons, storks, ibises, flamingos	118
Ducks, geese, swans	149
Vultures, hawks, eagles, falcons	287
Pheasants, grouse, megapodes	about 265
Cranes, rails, bustards	176
Oystercatchers, plovers, sandpipers, gulls, terns	320
Pigeons	271
Cockatoos, parrots	330
Cuckoos	128
Turacos	22
Owls	146
Nightjars	95
Swifts, hummingbirds	about 400
Mousebirds	6
Trogons	about 35
Kingfishers, bee-eaters, hoopoes	196
Woodpeckers, toucans, barbets	about 400
Songbirds and perching birds (from warblers to crows)	4,800

*An order is a group. (See top of previous page.)
**Penguins have become flightless. They use their wings to swim.

Birds of the past

The bird pioneer

The earliest known bird-like creature is Archaeopteryx, which lived about 150 million years ago. Fossils show that it had feathers, a wishbone and wings like a bird, but that it also had teeth, claws on its wings and a long, bony tail like a reptile.

What a water carrier

Ancient shells of elephant bird eggs were at one time used to carry water by people in Madagascar. The giant, emu-like bird produced the largest eggs ever known, equivalent in size to 180 hen's eggs.

Dinosaur descendants?

The existence of Archaeopteryx and other creatures, with their combination of bird and reptile features, has shown that birds may be the living descendants of dinosaurs.

The largest bird ever to fly was *Argentavis magnificens* with a vast, 7.6m (25ft) wingspan. It probably did not flap its wings to fly but soared like a glider, much as South American condors do today.

Where eagles dared

The Haast eagle of New Zealand was a giant eagle with a wingspan of up to 3m (10ft). It preyed on other giants, the flightless moas. The biggest of these stood about 3m (10ft) high. The last Haast eagle died more than 500 years ago, but there may still have been some moas living in the 1800s.

Bird heavyweight

The heaviest bird of all time was *Dromornis stirtoni*. It weighed an amazing 500kg (over half a ton). This is nearly four times heavier than an ostrich, which is the largest living bird. It lived in Australia about 10 million years ago, but survived until about 25,000 years ago. Not surprisingly, Dromornis was a flightless bird.

The dawning of birds

Some of the earliest true birds were sea birds. One of these, Hesperornis, was nearly 2m (6ft) long. Its wings seem to have been almost non-existent, but its very strong legs must have made it a powerful swimmer. Unlike modern birds it had teeth.

The passenger pigeon made the most rapid disappearance ever known. In the 1800s it was so common in the USA that flocks of over 2,000 million birds were estimated. By 1900 there were none left in the wild, and the last one died in a zoo in 1914.

Too tasty by half

The great auk was a big sea bird with tiny wings and quite incapable of flight. Sadly, man's greed caused it to become extinct by 1844. Both its single egg and its flesh were regarded as excellent food. Its oil was used as lamp fuel and even its feathers were valued.

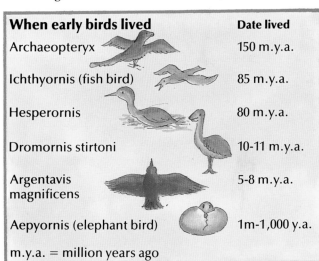

When early birds lived	Date lived
Archaeopteryx	150 m.y.a.
Ichthyornis (fish bird)	85 m.y.a.
Hesperornis	80 m.y.a.
Dromornis stirtoni	10-11 m.y.a.
Argentavis magnificens	5-8 m.y.a.
Aepyornis (elephant bird)	1m-1,000 y.a.

m.y.a. = million years ago

Feather care and flight

Zippy feathers

The parts of a feather (called vanes) either side of the central shaft, are kept in shape by a system of hooks. Each vane is made up of barbs. These are held together by tiny hooks. When ruffled, a feather has only to be drawn through the bird's beak to zip the barbs together again.

How many feathers?

Feathers make up about one sixth of a bird's weight. Hummingbirds have fewest feathers, some having less than 1,000. Some swans have more than 25,000. But hummingbirds have more feathers per square centimetre than swans.

Moulting

Feathers become worn with use and are usually replaced every year. In most birds, the shedding of feathers, called moulting, is gradual, so they are still able to fly reasonably well. Ducks and geese moult all their wing feathers at once in the autumn and are unable to fly for two to four weeks.

Herons have special feathers that break up into powder. They rub this into feathers that are sticky with slime from feeding on eels. The resulting sticky balls are then removed with tiny comb-like teeth on the middle claw of each foot.

Flight patterns

Birds have different ways of flying. Large birds soar in spirals, small birds often have bouncing flight, and others fly fast and straight.

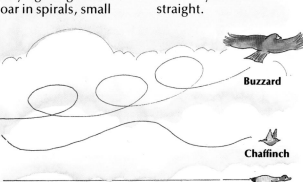

Buzzard

Chaffinch

Mallard

Fastest fliers

The fastest level flight so far reliably timed is that of the eider duck at 76kph (42mph). But the peregrine, a falcon that dives on to its prey in mid-air from a great height, can reach speeds of at least 180kph (112mph) in a dive.

Featherless freeze

Penguins seem unable to move at all when they are moulting. The emperor penguin stands on the ice for three to five weeks while its old feathers fall out in big patches. During this time, it does not eat.

Amazing But True

In 1973 a Ruppell's griffon vulture collided with an aeroplane flying at 11,270m (37,000ft) over the coast of western Africa. This is the highest altitude at which any bird has been identified. The usual height for this vulture is up to 1,500m (5,000ft).

Flying speeds
Level flight in calm air

Bewick's swan	72kph
Mallard	65kph
Pheasant	54kph
Cedar waxwing	46kph
Grey heron	43kph
Swift	40kph
Starling	35kph
House sparrow	30kph

Fishy business

Baby grebes are fed on fish, but their parents also feed them feathers from their own bodies. The feathers may prevent fish bones injuring the baby grebes' stomachs.

Drying out?

Cormorants often stand on sandbanks or breakwaters with their wings held out. They do not have completely waterproof plumage and may do this to dry out.

Plumage

Camouflage

The plumage of many birds blends with their background and helps to hide them from enemies.

Tawny frogmouth looks like a tree stump.

Bitterns pose like this to blend in with reeds.

Ringed plover is hard to spot on a pebbly beach.

Changing colour

Plumage may change colour from wear and tear. In autumn, the plumage of the male black lark of Asia is mottled. During the year the pale tips of the black feathers crumble away, so by spring the bird's plumage is black.

Seasonal switch

Ptarmigans live in the Arctic and on high mountains. To provide year-round camouflage, their plumage changes colour with the seasons. In spring it is mottled brown to blend with plants, in autumn it is grey to look like rocks and in winter it is white to match the snow.

DID YOU KNOW?

The pink colouring of flamingos depends on the food they eat. In the wild, they filter shrimps and algae from water. In captivity, they are often fed on carrot juice to prevent their feathers fading to dull grey.

Take terns

The colour of a bird's plumage can play a part in its search for food. Terns and many other fish-eating sea birds have white underparts. Unsuspecting fish cannot see them against the bright sky.

Noisy tails

Male snipes have a noisy way of showing a mate that they have found a nesting place. They fly over the site, then dive down with their stiff outer tail feathers spread out each side. These special feathers vibrate in the air, making a loud, whirring noise known as drumming.

Longest and shortest

The resplendent quetzal of Central America has magnificent, emerald green tail feathers. Over 60cm (24in) long, they are more than twice its body length. At the other extreme, birds such as kiwis and emus look tailless, having no special tail feathers.

Amazing But True

The highly ornamental phoenix fowl is bred for shows in Japan. Its fantastically long tail coverts* grow for about six years without a moult. The longest ever recorded were 10.59m (34.75ft), which is about as long as a bus.

Bouncing bishops

The red bishop of African plains is pale brown for most of the year. To find a mate, his plumage changes to black and red, and he fluffs out his feathers making him look like a brilliantly coloured ball. He then "bounces" over the grassland in a strange, bounding flight.

Follow their leader

Brent geese migrate in flocks from Siberia to Europe. To make sure they keep together and do not lose sight of one another, the birds have a white rump that is easily seen from behind in flight.

Tail length compared to total length

	Total length	Tail length
Crested argus pheasant	240cm	173cm
Peacock	225cm	160cm
Lady Amherst's pheasant	150cm	100cm
Pheasant	80cm	35cm
Red kite	60cm	25cm
Red-billed blue magpie	40cm	23cm
Paradise whydah	38cm	26cm
Malachite sunbird	25cm	14cm
Grey wagtail	19cm	8cm
Long-tailed tit	14cm	7.5cm

*The coverts are feathers which cover the bases of the wing and tail feathers.

Beaks and feet

Unique beak

The wrybill, a New Zealand plover, is the only bird in the world with a beak that curves sideways. It uses this odd beak to probe for insects under stones on beaches, but no-one knows why it is curved.

Upside-down feeder

The flamingo holds its unusual curved beak upside down for feeding. It sweeps it through shallow water, stirring up mud. Water is sucked into the beak and then pumped out through its sieve-like edges, leaving behind tiny shrimps and algae.

Getting a good grip

Birds never fall off branches when they go to sleep. They naturally grip any branch they land on, as their feet automatically lock into position with the toes clamped around the branch. To move, birds use their toe muscles to release their grip.

Record runner

The flightless ostrich has feet with only two toes, which are the most highly adapted for running of all birds. It can easily run at about 48kph (30mph) for 15-20 minutes, and over 70kph (43mph) in short bursts.

Types of toes

Most birds have four toes, but some have three and the ostrich has only two. Perching birds have feet to grasp branches, swimmers have webbed or lobed feet, and birds of prey have large, sharp talons.

Webbed foot
Canada goose

Sharp talons
Golden eagle

Lobed toes
Red-necked grebe

Perching foot
Greenfinch

Beak facts

Longest	Australian pelican	34-47cm
Longest for its size	Sword-billed hummingbird	10cm (Total length: 20cm)
Shortest	Glossy swiftlet	3mm
Broadest	Shoebill	about 12cm
Largest for its size	Toco toucan	23cm (Total length: 66cm)

Seed-eaters

Finches, buntings, parrots and other birds that eat seeds have stout, strong beaks, often with a hooked tip. These powerful beaks are used to open tough seed casings. Crossbills have the most extreme adaptation. They use their awkward-looking beaks to force open the cones of conifer trees.

Puffins are the only birds to moult their beaks. In other birds, beaks constantly grow and wear down throughout their lives. Puffins have brightly coloured beaks for the mating season. The outer layer is then shed, leaving them with smaller, dull beaks for the rest of the year.

Lily-trotter

Jacanas have the longest toes of any bird. Those of the African jacana are up to 8cm (3in) long including the very long claws. The toes spread the bird's weight so that it can walk across floating waterweeds and lily pads in search of food without sinking.

Sensitive probes

Birds with long beaks used for probing for buried food can actually feel with their beaks. Snipes rely on their sensitive beaks when probing deep into wet mud in search of worms. Their beaks are also so flexible that the tip can be opened to grasp worms underground.

Amazing But True

Pelicans have beaks with giant pouches of soft, elastic skin, which they use to scoop up fish from water. The pouch is so massive that it can hold several times more food than the pelican's stomach. Fully stretched underwater, it can hold about 13 litres (three gallons) of water, as much as a large bucket.

Fantastic fit

The snail kite of North and South America has a long, curved beak that fits exactly inside the shell of the apple snail on which it feeds. Its beak can cut through the muscle holding the snail in its shell.

251

Food and feeding

Feasting or starving

The smaller a bird is, the more time it needs to spend feeding. Big eagles can starve for several days without ill effect, but the tiny goldcrest of Europe needs to eat all day long in winter just to have enough energy to survive the nights.

Heavy hoatzin

The odd-looking hoatzin of the Amazon forests eats leaves and fruit. Its food is stored and also partly digested in an enormous crop, which weighs about one-third of its body weight. The hoatzin is a poor flier and when its huge crop is full it even has difficulty jumping from branch to branch in the trees where it lives.

Cuckoo's caterpillars

Hairy caterpillars have a mild poison in their hairs which brings people out in a rash and makes most birds that might eat them sick. But the cuckoo is able to eat this tasty treat. Every so often, the inside of the cuckoo's stomach, including the caterpillar hairs, peels away and the cuckoo coughs it up in a ball.

Vampire bird

The sharp-beaked ground finch of the Galapagos Islands is a seed-eater, but it is also known to behave like a vampire. Using its sharp beak, it pecks holes in the wings of nesting masked boobies and drinks their blood. The boobies do not seem to mind and the finches get a nourishing drink.

Feeding in flight

Swifts are remarkable for spending virtually their whole lives in the air. They sleep, feed and drink on the wing. To feed, they open their wide mouths and catch flying insects. As a result, the swift's beak has become reduced to little more than a rim around its mouth.

How much food?

Bird	Average food per day	Equivalent to
Pelican	1.8kg fish	Half its body weight
Eagle	up to 1kg meat	Quarter of its weight
Giant hummingbird	15g nectar or insects	Over half its weight
Waxwing	210g berries	Three times its weight

Not a fussy feeder

The bird with the widest variety of diet ever recorded is the North American ruffed grouse. Its food is known to have included at least 518 kinds of animals and 414 different plants.

Woodpecker weapons

Woodpeckers have strong, pointed beaks to chisel into wood and sensitive, long tongues to probe for insects and grubs. The tongue may be sticky, as in the green woodpecker, or barbed and harpoon-like as in the great spotted woodpecker. A special mechanism allows it to extend over 10cm (4in) beyond the beak tip.

Hummingbirds

Hummingbirds feed on nectar, sucking it up with their long tubular tongues while they hover in front of flowers. Although they appear to be still while hovering, their wings beat at incredible speed with the tips tracing a figure of eight. Up to 80 wing beats per second have been recorded.

Gulls and golf balls

Gulls will pick up unopened shellfish and drop them from a height in an attempt to get at the tasty contents. Herring gulls have been known mistakenly to try this out on golf balls.

Buzz, buzz, buzzard

Although it is a very large bird, the honey buzzard feeds on wasps and bees. It follows them to their nests and then digs out the grubs and honeycomb wax. The buzzard has dense feathers on its face to protect it from stings.

Amazing But True

Bullfinches raid fruit orchards, eating flower buds on the fruit trees. No-one knows why, but they are very choosy. They will strip all the flowers off Conference pear trees but not touch some other varieties.

253

Biggest and smallest

Almighty ostrich

The African ostrich is the largest living bird. Males are larger than females and can be 2.7m (9ft) tall. They weigh up to 156kg (345lb), which is about 90,000 times heavier than the smallest hummingbird.

Walking on stilts

The black-winged stilt of southern Europe, Asia and central Africa has the longest legs compared to its body of any bird. In terms of size, it is rather like a slim starling walking on stilts. The stilt's legs allow it to wade in water too deep for many other birds, in search of food.

Group	Biggest	Weight
Swans	Mute swan	8-12kg
Herons	Goliath heron	4.3kg
Owls	Eagle owl	4kg
Crows	Raven	1.7kg
Hummingbirds	Giant hummingbird	20g

Biggest birds

Big babies

Some birds are at their heaviest when they are very young. A wandering albatross nestling weighs up to about 16kg (35lb). It loses a lot of this when it starts to exercise its wings and is about one third lighter by the time it is able to fly properly.

Amazing But True

When ostriches are bounding along on the run, each stride they take carries them about 3.5m (11ft) forwards. Their powerful legs are by far the biggest of any bird and can be over 1.2m (4ft) long.

Heaviest flier

The world's heaviest flying birds are the kori bustards of eastern South Africa. Huge males weigh up to 18.1kg (40lb), which is about the same as a full-size television. They have a wingspan of 2.5m (8ft).

Whopper wingspan

The strong winds that blow over the world's southern oceans help keep giant albatrosses aloft for days on end, soaring around like gliders. The wandering albatross is the biggest with a huge wingspan of more than 3.5m (11ft). A recent study showed it could fly up to 960km (600 miles) a day.

Smallest birds		
Group	**Smallest**	**Weight**
Hummingbirds	Bee hummingbird	1.6g
Crows	Hume's ground jay	25g
Owls	Least pygmy owl	30g
Herons	Least bittern	50g
Swans	Black-necked swan	4.5kg

Record nests

The largest nest ever recorded was built by bald eagles in Florida, USA. It measured 2.9m (9.5ft) wide and 6m (20ft) deep. It was estimated to weigh more than two tonnes, which is about the same as two army jeeps.

DID YOU KNOW?

The smallest bird in the world is the bee hummingbird of Cuba. It measures 5.7cm (2.25in) long, of which nearly half is its beak. It is smaller than many of the butterflies in the rain forest where it lives.

Egg extremes

Ostriches lay the largest eggs of any living bird. They measure about 15-20cm (6-8in) in length and weigh around 1.7kg (3.7lb). The shell is so strong that it can support the weight of a 127kg (20st) man. The smallest eggs are those laid by the vervain hummingbird. They are about 1cm (0.4in) long.

The smallest nests are built by hummingbirds. The bee hummingbird's is thimble-sized and the vervain hummingbird's is about the size of half a walnut shell.

Flightless midget

The Inaccessible Island rail, which lives on a remote island in the Atlantic, is the world's smallest flightless bird. It weighs only 34.7g (1.2oz), about the size of a newly hatched domestic chick, and has similar fluffy feathers.

Food facts

Type of bird food	Biggest bird that mainly eats that food
Seeds	Ostrich
Leaves and grass	Mute swan
Fruit	Emu
Fish	Wandering albatross
Birds	Sea eagle
Meat	Andean condor
Insects (locusts)	White stork
Worms	Curlew

Attracting a mate

Centre stage

In many grouse species males perform courtship displays at special sites called leks. Each male claims a territory there, with the most mature and strongest commanding positions in the centre where they will attract the most females. Usually about 10-15 males gather at a lek but visiting females will choose to mate only with the one or two most dominant or attractive.

Feet first

Looking rather like soldiers, blue-footed boobies display by strutting in front of each other with heads held high. The male and female both have bright blue feet which they display prominently during their courtship.

Fancy frigatebird

Some male birds have pouches on their chest or throat which they puff out in colourful displays to attract a mate. The most showy of all belongs to the male frigatebird, whose throat pouch inflates to an enormous bright red balloon.

Dancing cranes

Pairs of cranes perform a spectacular courtship dance before mating. In Australia, the high leaps and deep bows of the athletic brolga cranes have inspired many Aboriginal dances.

Building a bower

In Australia and New Guinea the males of some species of bowerbirds build and decorate an elaborate bower to attract a mate. The satin bowerbird builds a corridor-shaped bower of twigs about 10cm (4in) wide and decorates it with blue objects such as flowers, feathers, butterfly wings and shells. It even paints the inside of the bower with blue juice from berries, using a piece of bark.

Courting grebes

Western grebes have an extraordinary and lengthy courtship dance. A pair start by facing each other on the water, then dive and reappear side by side. Rearing up on their tails with their necks held high but their heads tilted forward, they then race across the water as if on a skateboard. The courtship continues with the pair diving and surfacing with weed in their beaks. They hold this while performing a delicate dance together.

Paradise plumage

Male birds of paradise have the most fabulous feathers in brilliant colours. Some have head or tail feathers 70cm (28in) long. Others have thin tail plumes like long, curled wires. Count Raggi's bird of paradise has brilliant red, feathery plumes on his back. He hangs upside down in a tree to show himself off to best effect. Up to ten males may display in one tree.

Preening and feeding

Many birds preen each other and rub their beaks together when courting. Others use gifts of food. The male common tern is one of many birds that offers its partner food.

Courting couples

Male and female court and pair for life	Mute swan, crow, bullfinch, owls
Male and female pair up each year to breed	Storks, herons, grebes, finches
Male courts many females. Each female nests and rears her young alone	Prairie chicken, ruff, blue bird of paradise
Female courts male and lays eggs. Male is left to hatch eggs and rear young alone	Phalaropes, African jacana, dotterel

Birds' nests

Woven nests

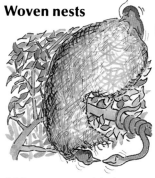

African weaver birds make some of the most intricate nests of all. The spectacled weaver weaves a nest of strips of leaves and grass, hanging from a branch. Starting with a ring of grass, the nest is built into a ball shape, with a long, sock-like, tubular entrance hanging from one side to keep out snakes. Some weavers build entrance tunnels as long as 60cm (2ft).

DID YOU KNOW?

Birds' nest soup is made from the nests of cave swiftlets in Asia. Huge colonies of these little birds live in vast caves, making nests of saliva stuck to the roofs and walls. It takes the edible-nest swiftlet about 30 to 40 days to build its nest. Two nests are used to make one bowl of soup.

Holed-in hornbill

The red-billed hornbills of Africa make their nest in a hollow tree. They use a tactic unique to hornbills to stop snakes and monkeys stealing their eggs and chicks. With the male's help, and using mud and droppings, the female seals herself inside the nest hole. The male feeds the female through a tiny opening.

Made to measure

The European long-tailed tit makes a beautiful, dome-shaped nest of moss and lichen, lined with feathers. Up to 2,000 feathers are used in the lining. The nest is coated with lichens for camouflage and bound up with cobwebs so that it can stretch as the young birds grow inside it.

Mallee fowl mound

Mallee fowl of Australia lay their eggs in huge mounds of earth and rotting leaves built by the males. The eggs are covered over with sandy soil and kept warm by heat from the rotting vegetation, and by the sun. The male constantly tests the temperature of the mound with his beak. If it gets too hot or cold, he opens it up or piles on more leaves and soil. These compost-heap nest mounds may be up to 4.6m (15ft) in height and 10.6m (35ft) across.

Mud oven nest

Rufous ovenbirds of South America are about the size of a thrush but build a huge, round nest, about twice the size of a soccer ball. The cement-like nest is made of mud mixed with grass and hair, and may weigh up to 10kg (22lb). It has an arched entrance from which a tunnel leads to an egg chamber.
Perched on a support such as a tree stump or fence post, it looks like a native mud oven, which is how the birds got their name.

Fostering and stealing

Some birds lay their eggs in other birds' nests. Some, such as the European cuckoo, use the other, often much smaller bird as a foster parent to hatch their eggs and raise their chicks. Others, such as the American bay-winged cowbird, simply steal nests. They throw out the eggs in them, then lay their own and rear their chicks.

Nest materials

Bird	Nest usually made of
Swallow	mud, saliva
Toucan	wood chips, regurgitated seeds
Hummingbird	cobwebs, moss, leaves, petals
Chaffinch	moss, lichen, feathers, hair
American robin	twigs, grass, fibre, mud
Shag	twigs, seaweed
Flamingo	mud
Waxwing	twigs, grass, pine needles, lichen
American wigeon	grass, down feathers
Kingfisher	fish bones
Mute swan	reeds, bulrushes
Eared grebe	waterweeds
Penduline tit	pussy willow down, grass
Golden palm weaver	coconut palm leaf fibres

Amazing But True

Pied wagtails built a nest behind the radiator grille of the Royal Society for the Protection of Birds' van at Sandy, England. The van continued to be used while eggs were laid and incubated. Four young were hatched and successfully fledged.

Nesting under a roof

The nest colonies of the sociable weaver in southern Africa look like huge growths in the tops of trees. Up to 300 nest chambers may be built in one colony. The birds first lay straws across a large branch to make a roof. Straw nests are then built under it, with the straws' sharp ends facing down the entrance tunnels, making it hard for baboons to reach in or small animals to enter.

Eggs and young

Keeping eggs cool

Most eggs must be kept warm, at about 35°C, in order to hatch them. But the grey gull, which nests in the hot deserts of Chile, has to cool its eggs to keep them at the right temperature. Instead of sitting on the eggs as most birds do, it stands over them, keeping them cool in the shade of its body.

Criss cross bill

Timing it right

Blue tits lay about 12 eggs in spring. They feed their chicks on small caterpillars which hatch out to feed on new leaves just when the blue tits' eggs hatch. Because of this precise timing, blue tits have only one chance to rear chicks each year.

Little and often

Blackbirds feed their chicks on worms, which they can find all year round. They lay only four eggs, compared to the blue tit's 12, but raise an average of three broods in a season. So blackbirds can have up to 12 young, the same as blue tits, but spread them out through the summer.

Busy parent birds

Baby birds in the nest constantly demand food. A pair of great tits carried food to their chicks 10,685 times in 14 days. A female wren fed her young 1,217 times in 16 hours.

Newly hatched crossbill chicks have small, straight beaks so that their parents can feed them. After about two weeks, the upper part of the beak starts to grow and by about six weeks it bends over the lower part, forming the typical crossed bill.

Egg and chick facts

Bird	Eggs laid	Hatched after	Chicks cared for
Mallee fowl	5-35	63 days	no parent care
Mute swan	5-7	34-40 days	87 days
Emu	7-16	59-61 days	3-6 months
Wandering albatross	1	75-82 days	9-12 months
Ptarmigan	3-12	25 days	10 days
Emperor penguin	1	62-64 days	5 months
Crossbill	3-5	12-13 days	24 days
Golden-winged warbler	4-6	10-11 days	10 days

One nest of the North American redhead, a species of duck, was found to have 87 eggs. This enormous number was created by several ducks making use of the same nest, instead of each building their own. Nests where such an unmanageable number of eggs has been laid are nearly always abandoned.

Liquid diet

Newly hatched flamingo chicks have an unusual diet. They are fed on liquid produced by their parents, rather like mammals feed their young on milk. The nourishing liquid comes from the parent's crop and dribbles out of the beak as a dark, reddish colour.

Spot the chicks

Gouldian finches of tropical Australia lay their eggs in a dome-shaped, grass nest with a side entrance. Their chicks are hatched with luminous or reflective marks inside their mouths, which glow in the dark. This makes sure the parents can see them in the darkness of the nest to feed them.

Too fat to fly

Young gannets are fed so much fish that they become too fat to fly. Their parents give up feeding them when they can eat no more. They then scramble to the cliff edge and drop into the sea, where they swim off, heading south for the winter. They starve for a week or two until they are light enough to get airborne and fly the rest of their journey.

Egg recognition

No birds' eggs ever look identical. Even those in a single clutch laid by one bird will all be slightly different in colour or markings.

Guillemots lay the most varied eggs of all. They may be white, yellowish, blue or blue-green with dark lines, spots or blotches. Huge numbers lay eggs side by side on bare cliff ledges. The enormous variety helps each bird to spot its own egg when returning from a fishing trip.

DID YOU KNOW?

Baby birds have an "egg tooth" to help them break out of the shell. This is a tiny knob at the tip of the beak. Most chicks take about 30 minutes to an hour to hatch out, but chicks of large albatrosses may need six days to get out of their tough eggshell.

Sea birds

Colour-coded chicks

Kittiwakes vigorously defend their nests high up on narrow cliff ledges, chasing off any strange adult that has appeared in their absence. To make sure youngsters are not attacked by mistake, they have black on the back of their heads, which contrasts with the adults' white heads.

Porpoising penguins

Penguins are excellent swimmers. Using their wings as flippers to propel themselves along, they swim up and down through the surface of the sea like dolphins. Their top speed is about 9kph (5.5mph). They can shoot out of the water on to land or ice in one leap of up to 2m (6ft).

Foul fulmars

Fulmars belong to the group of sea birds called tube-noses, with tube-shaped nostrils on their beaks. The name fulmar may come from the word "foul", as the birds defend their nests by spitting foul-smelling oil from their stomachs at intruders.

Amazing But True

In 1979 an Aleutian tern took the wrong route and was found in England when it should have been 8,000km (5,000 miles) away in Alaska, USA. Instead of flying north to Alaska after wintering in the northern Pacific Ocean, it flew east and crossed the Atlantic Ocean.

Breeding in millions

Many sea birds find safety in numbers at breeding time. Colonies of penguins in the southern oceans contain millions of birds. Biggest of all is a colony of ten million chinstrap penguins in the South Sandwich Islands. This colony covers an area the size of 1,000 soccer pitches.

Taking the plunge

Gannets plunge-dive into the sea from heights of up to 30m (100ft) to catch fish. To help them survive the impact of the water on their bodies, they have spongy bone around the head and beak, and air sacs under the skin around the throat and breast.

Pattering petrels

Storm petrels fly low, fluttering over the sea in search of shrimps and plankton. The Wilson's storm petrel flies so close to the water its webbed feet patter along on the surface, so that it appears to be hopping or skipping along.

Penguin profiles

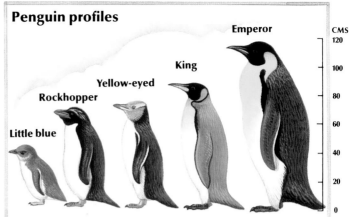

There are 18 species of penguins. All live south of the Equator, but only six live in Antarctica.

Pirates in the air

Skuas steal food from other ocean birds. The arctic skua catches fish and small birds, but is more likely to use its speed and flying skill to chase kittiwakes and terns, making them drop or cough up their food.

DID YOU KNOW?

Emperor penguins dive down to depths of 265m (870ft), staying under for up to nine minutes, occasionally even twice as long. Between dives, they comb their feathers to trap air in them, which helps to keep them warm in the cold water.

Swoop and scoop

Frigatebirds fly over the sea, often far from land, but never swim. They spend almost their whole lives in the air, using their enormously long wings and long, forked tail to fly with great agility. Like skuas, frigatebirds are pirates. They harass birds such as boobies, scooping up dropped food in the air with a swift downward swoop.

Gull facts

Largest	Great black-backed gull
Smallest	Little gull
Most common	Kittiwake
Rarest	Relict gull (in Siberia)
Hardiest	Ivory gull (lives in Arctic)
Longest-lived	Herring gull (44 years)
Largest colonies	Kittiwake

Water birds

Waders

There are about 200 species of wading birds, most of which feed in soft mud and sand at the water's edge. Different species can feed in the same place without competition as their beaks are adapted for finding different foods. Those with short beaks pick food from on or just below the surface. Those with longer beaks mainly probe deeper for worms and shellfish.

Beaks less than 5cm long – ringed plover, knot, sanderling, turnstone, dunlin
Beaks 5-10cm long – redshank, black-tailed godwit, oystercatcher, snipe, avocet
Beaks over 10cm long – curlew

Stained cranes

The adult sandhill crane of North America has grey plumage. But the feathers of its back, neck and breast often become coloured with rusty brown stains. Living by or near to marshes, it preens itself with a muddy beak in which there may be traces of iron, which causes brown staining.

Snake bird

The anhinga, or snake bird, gets its name from its long, snake-like neck and head, often the only part seen when it is swimming. It uses its sharp, pointed beak to spear fish, then tosses them into the air with a violent shake of its head, so it can catch and swallow them. Just like a snake swallowing food, its neck bulges as large fish pass down.

Skimming the water

Skimmers look as if they have upside-down beaks, as the lower part is longer than the upper. They fish in shallow water, flying with the lower part of the beak slicing through the water like a knife. When it touches a fish, the skimmer nods its head down and snaps its beak shut to catch it.

Amazing But True

Bright blue swans were seen on a river in the city of Norwich near the east coast of Britain in April 1990. A chemical is thought to have polluted the water but, luckily, the swans did not seem to suffer.

Whirlpool water bird

Phalaropes often spin around in circles while swimming. This creates a whirlpool, which stirs up the small animals on which they feed.

Diving from danger

Moorhens swim on ponds and lakes with their heads nodding vigorously. But if danger threatens, they dive underwater. They stay under by gripping weed with their feet and poke the tip of the beak above water to breathe.

Heron umbrella

To catch fish, the black heron crouches in water and holds its wings like an umbrella, shading the surface from the bright African sun. It may do this to see the fish more clearly, or the fish might be attracted to swim into the shade.

Sawbills

Red-breasted mergansers are sawbill ducks. They have narrow beaks with edges toothed like the blade of a saw. This gives them a firm grip on slippery fish.

DID YOU KNOW?

Bewick's swans have black and yellow faces but each one has a unique pattern. Hundreds of them arrive to winter in England from Siberia each year. Many have been given names and can be easily identified without having to be caught.

Diving dipper

The dipper is the only songbird that dives underwater to feed. It stands on rocks in streams, bobbing up and down, dipping its head into the water to look for insects, worms and snails. It uses its wings to swim underwater and can even run along on the bottom.

How ducks feed

Grazers graze on grasses and other plants on salt marshes and grassy banks.	Wigeon, American wigeon
Dabblers feed on or just under the water. They can up-end, or tip up, to reach down further.	Gadwall, pintail, mallard, shoveler, teal, black duck
Divers can dive down to the water bed. They can stay under for half a minute or more.	Pochard, goldeneye, tufted duck, eider, ring-necked duck, merganser

Birds of prey

Hunters in the sky

Birds of prey are hunters, feeding on mammals, other birds, fish, insects and snakes. Owls alone hunt by night; all the others belong to a group called raptors and hunt by day. The main features of raptors are:

Excellent eyesight
Strong, hooked beaks for tearing flesh
Large feet for holding and carrying prey
Strong, sharp, hooked claws or talons for grasping prey and killing it
Powerful wings

Fire followers

Insect-eating birds of prey such as kites follow grassland fires for an easy food supply. They feed on insects that take to the air to escape from the burning grass.

Eagle eyes

Birds of prey have the best eyesight of all birds. Golden eagles, which have eyes of a similar size to ours, can see a hare from a distance of 3.2km (2 miles) in good light against a contrasting background.

Vegetarian vulture

The palm nut vulture of West Africa is the only vegetarian bird of prey. Its main food is the fruit of the oil palm tree, which it plucks from among the dense palm fronds. It also eats shellfish and fish.

DID YOU KNOW?

Like many raptors, female sparrowhawks are much bigger than males. Males catch small birds like finches and tits, while females prey on larger birds such as thrushes and pigeons. This may help them to avoid competing for food, so larger numbers can live in one area.

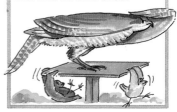

Raptor records

Biggest	Andean condor	12kg (3.1m wingspan)
Smallest	Philippine falconet	35g (150mm long)
Fastest	Peregrine falcon	about 100kph (level flight)
Rarest	Madagascar serpent eagle	probably less than 10 birds
Longest-lived	Andean condor	20-30 years average lifespan

Bone-breaker

One of the biggest vultures with a wingspan up to 3m (10ft) is the bearded vulture or lammergeier, also called the bone-breaker. It carries large bones from dead animals up to 80m (260ft), dropping them on to rocks to break them. It then eats the marrow and shattered bone. Lammergeiers also eat tortoises, using the same method to crack open their shells.

Ferociously fast

When hawks and falcons spot prey, they dive at great speed and hit it hard with outstretched talons, often killing it instantly. The peregrine falcon is one of the fastest, making spectacular, steep dives on to prey in mid-air at speeds of at least 180kph (112mph).

Big birds of prey		
Group	Biggest bird	Wingspan
Vultures	Andean condor	3.1m
Eagles	Wedge-tailed eagle	2.84m
Owls	Eagle owl	2m
Buzzards	Upland buzzard	1.9m
Kites	Red kite	1.8m
Harriers	Marsh harrier	1.6m
Falcons	Gyrfalcon	1.6m
Hawks	Northern goshawk	1.5m

Late start

Eleonora's falcons breed on Mediterranean islands in the autumn, long after most birds have reared their young. The chicks are hatched to coincide with the southbound migration of millions of small birds, which make easy prey for the falcon to feed to its hungry brood.

Flexible approach

The harrier hawk has double-jointed legs, which it uses in its search for eggs or chicks in tree hole nests. It clings on to the edge of a tree hole with one foot, bending its leg backwards so it can reach its other foot down into the nest.

No monkeying around

The huge harpy eagle of the South American rain forests causes terror in the treetops. It flies skilfully among the trees at up to 80kph (50mph), snatching up monkeys and sloths.

267

Tropical forest birds

Parrot power

Most parrots live in pairs or noisy flocks in tropical forests. They have strong, hooked beaks, which they often use in climbing. Macaws can even hang from branches by their beaks. Parrots' feet are also powerful tools and are unique in being used like hands to hold food.

Pitta patter

Pittas are colourful, plump birds with short tails and long, strong legs. Although quite able to fly, they run around on the forest floor and fly only when necessary.

Antbirds

Swarms of soldier ants marching across the forest floors in Panama are often accompanied by antbirds. The birds rarely eat the ants, but prey on the insects that are disturbed by them.

Bee my guide

The greater honeyguide of Africa is so-called because it guides honey badgers to bees' nests. The bird will call to a honey badger, or even a human, to make it follow to where it has found a bees' nest. It waits while the badger breaks open the nest to get the honey. It can then eat the grubs and beeswax.

Amazing But True

Hummingbirds drink eight times their weight in water each day. This is about a cup of water for the 20g (0.7oz) giant hummingbird. To equal this, an average-sized man would need to drink a small bath of water.

Hanging about

Sparrow-sized hanging parrots have an unusual form of camouflage. They hang upside down from a branch, bent double, and look just like leaves. They roost in this position and may even feed like this.

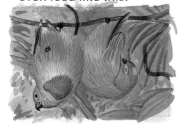

Parrot facts

Largest	Hyacinth macaw	100cm long
Smallest	Buff-faced pygmy parrot	8.4cm long
Rarest	Spix's macaw	under 10
Most widespread	Rose-ringed parakeet	Africa and India
Longest-lived	Sulphur-crested cockatoo	82 years (in captivity)
Country with most species	Australia	52 species

Top heavy toucan

Being 50cm (20in) long, the keel-billed toucan is a large bird, but much of this length is taken up by its huge, colourful beak. Although toucans' beaks look top heavy, they are actually hollow and very light. They are used to reach fruit from branches too small to bear the birds' weight, but why they are so huge and remarkably colourful is a mystery.

Aerial acrobats

No other bird beats the hummingbirds for aerial skills. As well as being able to hover in mid-air while they suck nectar from flowers, they can fly sideways, backwards, and even upside down. Their wings make a humming noise as they fly, which is how they got their name.

Birds to be wary of

Cassowaries are large, flightless birds of the rain forests of northern Australia and New Guinea. On their heads they have a horny casque, like a helmet, up to 15cm (6in) high. This protects them as they push through dense undergrowth. They defend themselves with powerful kicks, and are known to have killed humans with their dagger-like claws.

Preparing for paradise

The preparation made for courtship display by male birds of paradise is as elaborate as the display itself. In the forests of New Guinea, the magnificent bird of paradise clears an area about 6m (20ft) wide, even pulling leaves off trees to make sure of enough sunlight in which to show off his plumage.

Diet with a difference

Scarlet macaws in the mountain forests of South America gather on river banks and other earth cliffs to eat soil. They get vital minerals from the soil, which their diet of fruit and seeds lacks.

DID YOU KNOW?

Almost half the world's bird species are found in the tropical forests of South America. They are either breeding there or have travelled to escape the North American winter. But an area of rain forest about the size of six soccer pitches is being destroyed every minute. At this rate, most of the forests and their bird life will be gone in ten years' time.

Birds of grasslands . . .

Rich pickings

Vultures glide high over the African savanna for hours on end. They rarely kill prey, but fly thousands of kilometres in search of fresh carcasses. As many as 200-300 vultures may gather at a large carcass, as the birds use their keen eyesight to spot when others far away fly down to feed.

Secretary bird

The secretary bird of African grasslands is a unique bird of prey which hunts on foot. Striding about on very long legs, it hunts for small animals, including deadly poisonous snakes, which it kills by stamping on them.

Burrowing owl

The burrowing owl lives in deserted prairie dog burrows on the American plains. It hunts at night, but often stands at its burrow entrance during the day. When alarmed, it can frighten enemies by making a sound exactly like a rattlesnake.

DID YOU KNOW?

The huge flightless emus of Australia's scrubland may roam hundreds of kilometres in a year in search of food and water. In 1932, both farmers and the Royal Australian Artillery waged war as many of the 20,000 emus on the move attacked crops. Eventually, a barrier fence 1,000km (620 miles) long was put up to protect the farms.

Amazing But True

The estimated population of the red-billed quelea of southern Africa is 100,000 million, making it the world's most numerous bird. It is also the world's worst bird pest, as flocks of at least 10,000, and sometimes millions, feed together, destroying entire crops like a swarm of locusts.

Dry grassland birds

Typical birds of dry grasslands are:
Europe – Stone-curlew
Asia – Pallas's sandgrouse
Australia – Emu
N. America – Meadowlark
S. America – Rhea
Africa (southern) – Kori bustard
(northern) – Temminck's courser

and deserts

Thirsty work

Sandgrouse live in deserts and fly up to 80km (50 miles) to a waterhole to drink every day. Young chicks cannot fly to reach water, so parents take it to them. They ruffle their belly feathers and soak them in water, then fly back to the nest with the water held in their feathers like a sponge which the chicks can suck. Sandgrouse may carry water like this for 30km (20 miles).

Cool colours

In deserts, colour is important for camouflage and keeping cool. The most common colouring is cream, sandy or white to blend with sand or rock. Light colours reflect heat, whereas dark ones absorb it, so pale plumage also helps birds to stay cool.

Living with little water

Deserts have less than 25cm (10in) of rain a year. Birds can live where there is so little water because they lose so little from their bodies. Their urine is much more concentrated than that of mammals and they have a higher body temperature, so they lose less water by evaporation to keep cool. In some desert birds, water loss is reduced even further by their body temperature rising during the day.

Desert fortresses

Cacti are home for some desert birds. The sharp spines keep out enemies. In America, elf owls roost and nest in holes in saguaro cacti and cactus wrens build nests in among spines of the cholla cactus.

Roadrunner

The roadrunner lives in the deserts of Texas and Mexico. Although it can fly, it usually dashes around on foot, grabbing lizards and small snakes with its beak for food.

Keeping cool

Birds have various ways of coping with high desert temperatures. Some keep cool by panting, some stand with their backs to the wind to catch cooling breezes and some go

underground in abandoned burrows or stay in the shade of rocks. Long legs help birds to keep cool, as more heat is lost from bare legs than feathered bodies. The turkey vulture even squirts excrement on to its legs and feet to cool itself.

Nocturnal birds

Batty bird

The oilbird lives in dark caves in South America. It spends its whole life in darkness, only leaving the caves at night to feed on the fruits of forest trees. Amazingly, it finds its way around in the caves by echo-location, like a bat. It makes tiny, clicking sounds and uses their echoes to tell how far it is from the walls or other oilbirds.

DID YOU KNOW?

Storm petrels spend their lives far out at sea, but have to come to land to nest. They are so weak and easy for predators to catch that they only come ashore on dark nights. Each bird finds its way to its burrow by listening to the calls of its mate and by using its very good sense of smell.

Flexi-necks

Owls have such huge eyes that there is no room to move them in their sockets. Instead, they turn their whole heads to look sideways. They have very flexible necks and can turn their heads right round to look backwards and even upside down.

Green for go

The American black skimmer sometimes feeds at night. It flies over water dragging its long beak through the surface and this stirs up luminous plankton which glow green along the skimmer's trail. Fish are attracted to the green colour, and the skimmer flies back along the same line to snatch them up.

Ear, here!

Owls' hearing is superb. Many have feathery tufts that look like ears, but in fact, their ears are large openings hidden just behind the flat discs of feathers around their eyes. The discs probably help to direct sounds into their ears. In many owls one ear is bigger than the other and one is often higher than the other. This difference makes it easier for an owl to judge exactly where a sound is coming from and so pinpoint its prey even in pitch darkness.

Sense of smell

Kiwis are unique in having nostrils at the tip of their long beaks. Most birds have nostrils at the base of the beak and use hearing and sight rather than smell to find food. But kiwis are nocturnal birds and use their sense of smell to find earthworms and insects in the dark.

Night activity

The main reasons for nocturnal activity are:
Less competition for food
Access to food not available in the day
Safety from predators for feeding or breeding

Amazing But True

The little blue or fairy penguin of southern Australia is shy at sea and nocturnal on land. But despite this, it has accustomed itself to the glare of publicity and floodlights on Phillip Island near Melbourne, the one place where it can be seen close to. Here, after dark in the breeding season, crowds gather to watch the evening parade of fairy penguins waddling hurriedly ashore to their nest burrows.

Nocturnal gull

The distinctive looking swallow-tailed gull of the Galapagos Islands is the only known nocturnal gull. Its huge eyes, for seeing squid which it catches at night, are made even more striking by crimson eyelids.

Silent flight

Unlike most other birds of prey, many owls hunt at night. To help keep their movements quiet as they swoop on to prey, their wing feathers have soft, fringed edges and they have feathers on their legs and feet.

Owl facts

Biggest	Eagle owl	71cm long (wingspan 1.5m)
Smallest	Elf owl, least pygmy owl, long -whiskered owlet	all 130cm long
Rarest	Laughing owl	probably under 10
Most widespread	Barn owl	
Strangest food	Blakiston's fish owl	crayfish
Noisiest	Pel's fishing owl	voice carries 3km
Longest-lived	Eagle owl	72 years (in captivity)

Bird voices

Variety of voices

Birds use their voices to communicate in calls and songs. Calls are simple notes, often not musical, used for a warning and to keep contact within a group. Songs are used to attract a mate and to advertise the ownership of territory. Some birds' voices have been given special names:

Bittern	boom
Diver	wail
Grebe	whinny
Oystercatcher	pipe
Nightjar	churr
Mallard (duck)	quack
Goose	honk
Owl	hoot
Dove	coo
Swift	screech

Many birds are named after their calls. The chiffchaff, cuckoo, curlew, kittiwake, chickadee and towhee all call their name. Some American nightjars make sounds like their names: the whip-poor-will, the poor-will and the chuck-wills-widow.

Blooming booming

In New Zealand, male kakapos make a loud booming noise to attract females, but many years they do not boom and the birds do not breed. They start to boom and nest when there is a sudden abundance of pollen on the plants that produce their favourite fruits. This tells them that there will be plenty of fruit on which to feed their chicks.

Two tunes together

A few birds, including the reed warbler, can sing two notes at the same time and so sing two tunes at once. The North American brown thrasher even manages to sing four different notes together at one point in its song. The colourful gouldian finch of Australia is equally amazing. It makes a droning sound like bagpipes while singing two songs at once.

Different dialects

Young chaffinches can sing a basic song. But they only learn a proper chaffinch song as they grow up and hear other chaffinches singing. Because they copy each other, chaffinches in any one part of Europe all sound the same, but if birds from different areas are compared, dialects or variations can be detected.

274

My word!

The African grey parrot is one of the most talkative cagebirds. A female called Prudle won the "Best talking parrot-like bird" title at the National Cage and Aviary Bird Show in London for 12 years from 1965-76. She could say almost 800 words, and retired unbeaten.

Copycat birds

Marsh warblers nest in Europe but winter in Africa. They are superb mimics and can copy 60 or more bird voices. Scientists know where the birds have spent the winter because they can recognize the sounds of African birds in the marsh warblers' songs.

Barbet duet

Black-collared barbets in Africa make very loud, distinctive calls. But what sounds like a simple song is actually a duet. The first part of the call, "to", is made by one bird and the second part, "puddely", is made by its mate.

DID YOU KNOW?

The familiar call of the cuckoo in Europe is made only by the male bird. Although paintings of cuckoos often show them with beaks wide open, they sing "cu-coo" with the beak closed.

Record voices

The Indian peacock has one of the loudest, most far-carrying calls which echoes for kilometres. In contrast, the notes of treecreepers are so high and hiss-like that we can hardly hear them.

Amazing But True

Birds do most of their singing at dawn and dusk, but the red-eyed vireo, a small American bird like a warbler, sings all day long throughout the summer. One individual was once counted singing 22,197 times in ten hours.

Contact calls

Migrating geese make loud, honking noises, called contact calls, to help them stay together.

A flock of long-tailed tits feeding in a wood constantly twitter to each other to keep in contact.

Instinct and learning

Bird brain or computer

Birds have very small brains compared to humans, so their ability to learn is limited. But they are born with an inbuilt ability to do many things, rather like a computer that has been programmed. This inbuilt behaviour is what we call instinct.

Nesting instinct

African weaver birds do not learn from one another how to build their intricate ball or sock-shaped nests, they instinctively know how. Scientists reared four generations of weavers in captivity without giving them any nest materials. They then gave materials to great-great-grandchildren of the original weavers and the birds built a perfect nest despite never having seen one.

Doorstep diet

Blue tits were first recorded pecking at the tops of bottles of milk on doorsteps about 70 years ago. From being inquisitive, tits learned that this was an easy source of food. The behaviour soon spread. Chaffinches, robins and song thrushes are among birds that have learnt to copy this habit.

Starlings on course

In an experiment on migration, starlings were caught as they flew across the Netherlands. They were ringed and released in Switzerland. southern France, Spain and Portugal. They had instinctively flown south-west, making no allowance for having started further south

Of those recaptured later, most adults were found at their usual winter quarters near the English Channel, but the young were found in than normal. Incredibly, after returning to their breeding grounds, when autumn came again they flew back to south-west Europe for the winter.

Migration mystery

Many birds migrate over vast distances, returning to the same sites year after year. Birds are known to navigate by recognizing landmarks and by using smell and sound. They also instinctively use the sun or stars as a compass. Several species are known to have a sort of compass in their heads. But exactly how all this is used to find their way is a mystery.

Telling the time

Like many other animals, birds have an accurate sense of time. If food is put out on a bird table at the same time each day, birds quickly learn to appear at that time. This sense of time tells them when to breed and when to migrate.

Sophisticated fishing

Just like fishermen, the American green heron has learnt to use bait to catch fish. It picks an insect up and drops it into the water. If the bait starts to float away without luring a fish, the heron will retrieve it and even take it to a different place to try again.

Using tools

More than 30 species of birds use tools to help them get food or build nests. The woodpecker finch of the Galapagos Islands uses a cactus spine to probe into holes in wood and hook out grubs. It may use a broken spine or snap one off a cactus. It may even trim a spine to a more manageable length.

Relationships

Pecking order

Most birds live fairly solitary lives, perhaps joining up in groups to breed or to roost at night. Other birds live in a permanent flock. They have a strict "pecking order" and are ranked according to their aggressiveness. This establishes the birds' relationships to one another, so they do not fight constantly.

Easy pickings

Some birds use animals or larger birds to help them find food. African carmine bee-eaters perch on kori bustards to catch flies that flit up out of the way of the bustards' feet. North American cowbirds run among cattle to catch insects that are flushed out as the cattle graze.

Peregrine protection

Red-breasted geese nest close to peregrines in the Arctic. This strange attraction to the fierce falcons helps to protect their young. Goslings are easy prey for arctic foxes, but when the peregrines are about, the foxes stay away.

DID YOU KNOW?

Many parent birds use other birds without young to help feed their chicks. The helper may be unrelated, but is often a brother or sister of the parent, or older offspring of the pair. Red-throated bee-eaters often use helpers, which gives the young 80 per cent more chance of being reared. If helpers nest the next year, they may in turn be helped by the young they looked after.

Roosting

Birds gather for the night in huge roosts. A roost keeps them warmer, gives protection from predators, although those at the edges are vulnerable, and may help in finding food the next day. Starling roosts can contain a million or more birds, which split into much smaller flocks for feeding. A flock that has not found much to eat one day may follow one that fed well when they set out from the roost next morning.

Hoping for hornweed

Gadwalls are surface-feeding ducks. They like to eat American hornweed but cannot dive to get it. Instead they wait for coots to bring up beakfuls and then steal some or pick up dropped scraps.

Feeding together

Some birds get food by working in groups. Up to 40 white pelicans close in on a shoal of fish by forming a horseshoe around it, then dip their heads underwater together for an easy catch. Some cormorants swim in groups called rafts, diving together to catch fish in shoals.

Biggest flocks

Passenger pigeon (extinct)	2,230,272,000
Brambling	70,000,000
Red-billed quelea	32,000,000
Sooty tern	20,000,000
Adélie penguin	2,000,000
Starling	2,000,000
Red-winged blackbird	1,000,000
Budgerigar	1,000,000
Lesser flamingo	1,000,000

Less of a look-out

Birds feeding in flocks spend less time on the look-out for predators and so have more time to feed. An ostrich feeding alone spends 35 per cent of its time looking around, but if two feed together, each wastes only 21 per cent of its time and so can spend more time feeding. Four ostriches in a group feed for 85 per cent of their time.

Amazing But True

A male pied flycatcher will often try to pair with two females, but keeps them up to 2km (1.2 miles) apart so neither finds out about the other. If both the females lay eggs and hatch them out, the male deserts one and only feeds the chicks of the other.

It takes two

The turkey vulture uses its good sense of smell to detect dead animals as it flies over rain forest. But its beak is too weak to rip tough hide. The king vulture cannot smell a carcass, but has a strong beak. It follows the turkey vulture, rips the hide and both get a meal.

Chicks in a crèche

Some birds use crèches to protect chicks from predators. When eider ducklings hatch, they gather in huge crèches of 100 or more and are guarded by unrelated "aunty" eiders. This gives them much greater protection from gulls.

Birds in danger

Harming our habitats

In the past ten years, the number of threatened bird species in the world has risen sharply from 290 to 1,029. A threatened species is one in danger of dying out, or becoming extinct. Much of the increase is the result of our misuse of our environment, poisoning and destroying birds' habitats and food.

Water catastrophe

The Coto Doñana National Park in Spain is home to 125,000 geese, 10,000 flamingos and thousands of other water birds that rely on its marshland. Tourist hotels and golf courses built beside the marsh use four billion litres (880 million gallons) of water a year. Now, new developments threaten to take more than twice as much water again – a catastrophe for the birds.

Amazing But True

In 1979, the Chatham Island black robin was almost extinct, with only five birds left. A unique experiment by the New Zealand Wildlife Service, using local tom tits to foster chicks, brought the numbers over 100 in under ten years. Incredibly, every living bird is descended from a single female who lived to about 14, more than twice the normal age.

Birds as prey

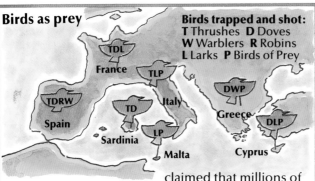

Birds trapped and shot:
T Thrushes D Doves
W Warblers R Robins
L Larks P Birds of Prey

France — TDL, TLP
Spain — TDRW
Italy — TD
Sardinia — LP
Malta
Greece — DWP
Cyprus — DLP

Threatened birds are usually protected by law. Sadly, this does not always help them. A report in 1990 by the British-based Royal Society for the Protection of Birds claimed that millions of protected birds are being killed in Europe. Buzzards, goshawks, falcons and other birds of prey are being shot. Many other species are being trapped to sell as cagebirds or for food.

Captive breeding

Many species survive because they are bred in captivity and released back into the wild. Zoos are being asked to breed birds such as the snowy white Bali starling, which poachers have reduced to a population of 30 in its natural habitat in Indonesia.

Rare parrot

The New Zealand kakapo is a huge nocturnal parrot, too heavy to fly. Sadly, it proved easy prey for cats and rats introduced from Europe. Now, with only 43 birds left, efforts are being made to get some to breed on a cat-free island. Kakapos breed slowly, about every four years, but in 1990 one laid an egg, giving biologists hope.

Saltmarsh sparrow

Until May 1987, when the last one known died, the dusky seaside sparrow was the world's rarest bird. Its only habitat seems to have been saltmarsh in Florida, USA. Work on reclaiming part of the coast changed this marshland and contributed to the sparrow's extinction.

Some endangered birds

Imperial woodpecker	Mexico	extinct?
Paradise parrot	Australia	extinct?
Ivory-billed woodpecker	Cuba	under 10?
Bachman's warbler	Cuba	under 10?
Echo parakeet	Mauritius	under 20
Eskimo curlew	N. America	under 30?
Mauritius kestrel	Mauritius	under 30
Japanese crested ibis	China	about 40
California condor	N. America	40
Slender-billed curlew	Asia	under 100?

DID YOU KNOW?

The widespread house sparrow was at one time protected by law. It was deliberately introduced to other continents from Europe. But its spread was too successful. It bred so rapidly that by the time the law was withdrawn it had already become a pest.

Walls of death

Hundreds of thousands of birds are killed every year by fishing fleets. In the Pacific, nets up to 80km (50 miles) long, called "walls of death", are used to catch fish. They also kill shearwaters and albatrosses, which dive for food and get entangled. Similar nets in the Barents Sea kill 800,000 birds a year.

Oil pollution

Oil pollution kills huge numbers of sea birds, especially guillemots. Laws exist to stop ships deliberately pouring oil into the sea, but accidents still happen. In 1989, a huge spill from the Exxon Valdez tanker oiled 1,600km (1,000 miles) of Alaskan coast. Over 300,000 sea birds died, a record for an oil spill. 144 bald eagles and 1,016 sea otters were also killed.

Bird lifespans
Larger for longer

The larger a bird is, the longer it may live. But most birds in the wild do not die of old age, they fall victim to natural or man-made hazards. Lifespans of birds in the wild are difficult to study, but records are being built up by ringing birds. One of the problems is knowing a bird's age when it is first ringed.

Albatross ages

Albatrosses are thought to be the longest-lived birds and the wandering albatross may live for about 80 years. A female royal albatross at Otago, New Zealand has been known for over 58 years and was already an adult when first ringed. As it takes 319 days to raise a single albatross chick and few survive long enough to breed, albatrosses need to live a very long time to make sure that enough chicks survive to replace them when they die.

Cocky cockatoo

The oldest known captive bird was a greater sulphur-crested cockatoo called Cocky, which died at London Zoo in October 1982. He was known to be over 80 years old and probably at least 82.

DID YOU KNOW?

About 75 per cent of all wild birds die before they are six months old. Millions are killed by cats and a similar number by cars. Many more die from disease, starvation, bad weather and other predators such as rats, foxes and birds of prey.

Condor in captivity

Kuzya, a male Andean condor in Moscow Zoo, was at least 77 when he died in 1964. He had lived outside in an aviary at the zoo ever since being taken there as an adult in 1892.

Short and sweet

Small birds generally have very short average lifespans because most die when they are still only fledglings. Once they reach adulthood, they have a better chance of survival.

Breeding balance

Most birds produce huge numbers of young, which offset the losses they suffer. Each year, about seven million pairs of blackbirds breed in Britain and between them hatch about 70 million eggs. That would make a possible total of 84 million blackbirds by the end of the year. In reality, about 70 million fledglings and adults die and the population stays about the same.

Robins' range

European robins are short-lived, with an average life expectancy of just six months. So "the robin" that seems to appear regularly in a garden year after year is almost certainly a succession of different birds. The greatest age so far recorded for a robin in the wild is 12 years and 11 months, but this is exceptional.

Bird strikes

Some birds meet an early death when they are in collision with aeroplanes. Such accidents, known as bird strikes, cause major damage and expense to airlines and have also caused human deaths. Gulls are most often involved in bird strikes but pigeons, starlings, lapwings, cowbirds, swallows, martins, swifts and swans have all been identified.

Bird lifespans

	Average	Maximum known
Blue tit	1 year	12 years
Starling	Up to 1½ years	21 years
House sparrow	1½ years	12 years
Robin	1½ years	12 years
Great tit	1½ years	9½ years
Bee hummingbird	Up to 2 years	?
Kestrel	2 years	15 years
Woodpigeon	2½ years	16 years
Blackbird	2½ years	14½ years
Little owl	2½ years	10 years
Mute swan	3 years	21 years
Tawny owl	3¼ years	20½ years
Swift	8 years	16 years
Kiwi	10 years?	?
Emperor penguin	20 years	?
Common crane	?	50 years
Ostrich	30-40 years	68 years

Migration map

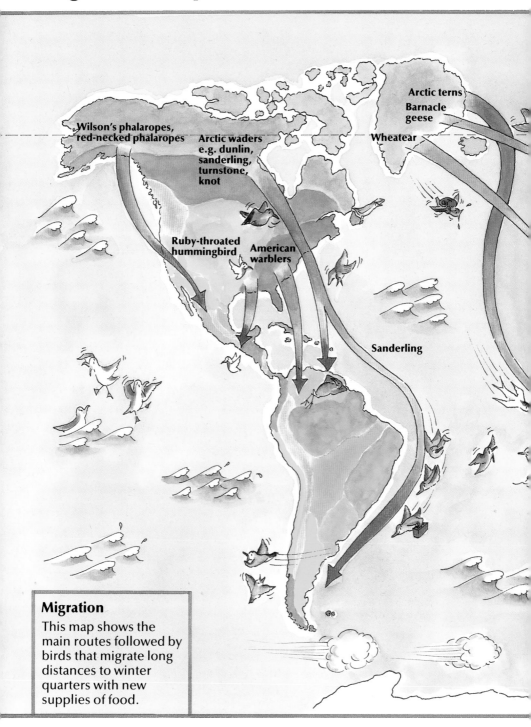

Arctic terns
Barnacle geese

Wilson's phalaropes, red-necked phalaropes

Arctic waders e.g. dunlin, sanderling, turnstone, knot

Wheatear

Ruby-throated hummingbird

American warblers

Sanderling

Migration

This map shows the main routes followed by birds that migrate long distances to winter quarters with new supplies of food.

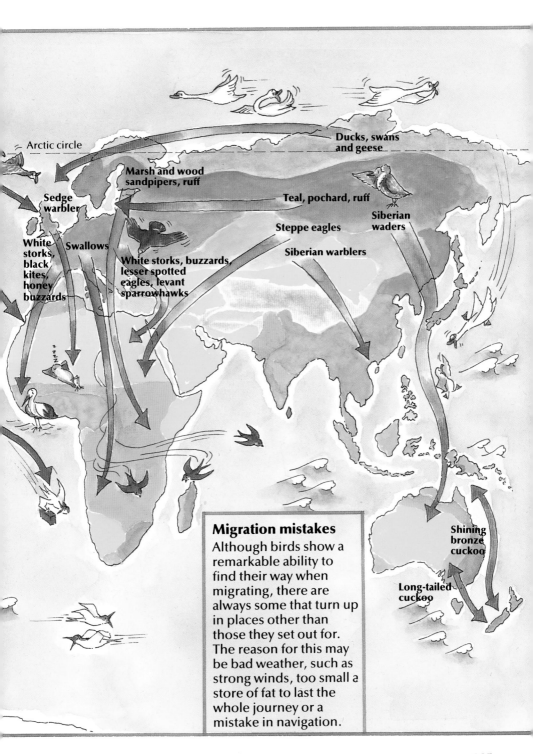

Arctic circle

Ducks, swans
and geese

Marsh and wood
sandpipers, ruff

Sedge
warbler

Teal, pochard, ruff

Siberian
waders

Steppe eagles

White
storks,
black
kites,
honey
buzzards

Swallows

White storks, buzzards,
lesser spotted
eagles, levant
sparrowhawks

Siberian warblers

Shining
bronze
cuckoo

Long-tailed
cuckoo

Migration mistakes

Although birds show a
remarkable ability to
find their way when
migrating, there are
always some that turn up
in places other than
those they set out for.
The reason for this may
be bad weather, such as
strong winds, too small a
store of fat to last the
whole journey or a
mistake in navigation.

Glossary

Bill Another word for beak.

Breeding plumage The plumage during the courtship and nesting season. In most species, only males develop specially coloured or shaped breeding plumage to attract a mate.

Breeding season The time of year, usually spring, when birds find a mate, build a nest and rear young.

Camouflage Plumage colours and patterns that blend with a bird's background and hide it from enemies.

Clutch The number of eggs a bird lays at one time.

Colony A group of birds of the same species nesting close together.

Courtship display Special behaviour to attract a mate. It may involve showing off breeding plumage or brightly coloured skin, special calls or dances.

Coverts The feathers covering the bases of the wing and tail feathers. The tail coverts grow long and showy in the breeding plumage of some birds.

Crepuscular birds Birds such as woodcock that are most active at dawn and dusk, when they hunt for food.

Crop A pouch-like part of the gullet of many birds in which food is stored and may be partly digested.

Diurnal birds Birds that are active during the day and sleep at night.

Fledgling A young bird that has just started to fly.

Flock A large group of birds moving around together.

Glide To fly with wings kept still and stretched out.

Incubate To keep an egg at the right temperature, usually about 35°C, for the chick to develop inside, until it is able to hatch out of the shell. Most birds sit on eggs to keep them warm.

Lek An area where male birds gather to display to females in the breeding season.

Length Birds are measured from the tip of the beak to the tip of the tail, as if laid out flat.

Migration Long-distance journeys made by some birds, according to the seasons, usually between their nesting area and wintering area.

Moulting The shedding of feathers, usually once or twice a year. In most birds, feathers drop out singly as new ones grow underneath.

Nestling A young chick in the nest, unable to fly or feed itself.

Nocturnal birds Birds such as most owls that are active at night, hunting for food.

Plumage A bird's covering of feathers.

Predator A bird or other animal that hunts and kills birds or animals for food.

Roost Sleep. The place where birds sleep is also called a roost. Some birds such as waders may gather in roosts numbering tens of thousands of birds.

Wingspan The measurement from one wing tip to the other when the wings are fully spread.

Index

OCEAN FACTS

Anita Ganeri

CONTENTS

Illustrated by Tony Gibson and Isabel Bowring

Designed by Tony Gibson

**Consultant: Dr David Billet,
Institute of Oceanographic Sciences, Surrey, England**

The salty seas

Watery Earth

Over two thirds of the Earth is covered in sea water. This lies in the Pacific, Atlantic, Indian Arctic and Southern Oceans. Together they form a continuous stretch of water which covers an area nine times bigger than the Moon's surface. The oceans contain 97 per cent of all the water on the Earth.

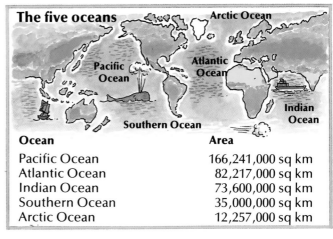

The five oceans

Arctic Ocean

Pacific Ocean

Atlantic Ocean

Southern Ocean

Indian Ocean

Ocean	Area
Pacific Ocean	166,241,000 sq km
Atlantic Ocean	82,217,000 sq km
Indian Ocean	73,600,000 sq km
Southern Ocean	35,000,000 sq km
Arctic Ocean	12,257,000 sq km

Why is the sea blue?

On sunny days the sea looks blue because it reflects the blue light rays from the Sun. The Yellow Sea near China gets its colour from yellow clay washed down by rivers. The Black Sea is coloured by mud blackened by hydrogen sulphide gas. The White Sea gets its name from the ice which covers it for 200 days each year.

DID YOU KNOW?

The Earth formed some 4,600 million years ago. Soon afterwards, the early oceans began to fill with water. Water vapour gas rose from volcanoes and hot rocks on the new Earth's surface. As it cooled, it formed storm clouds and soon the first rain fell to form the seas. The first seas were as acidic as lemon juice and only a few degrees below boiling point.

Sea water soup

Sea water contains about three per cent of sodium chloride, or common salt. This is the same as putting two cupfuls of salt in a bucket of water. It also contains many other chemicals, including magnesium, calcium and even traces of arsenic and gold. Some of the salt comes from undersea volcanoes. Most comes from the land. As rain falls, it dissolves salt in the rocks, and rivers carry it into the sea.

Oceans and seas

Ocean	Largest sea	Area in sq km
Pacific Ocean	South China Sea	2,974,600
Atlantic Ocean	Mediterranean Sea	2,505,000
Indian Ocean	Arabian Sea	7,456,000
Southern Ocean	Weddell Sea	8,000,000
Arctic Ocean	Barents Sea	1,300,000

Ocean or sea?

In some places the oceans are divided into different areas, called seas. Some seas are parts of the open ocean, such as the Sargasso Sea in the Atlantic Ocean. Other seas are partly enclosed by land, such as the South China Sea. This sea covers an area bigger than Argentina.

Amazing But True

Without sea plants, there would have been no animal life on Earth. Sea plants appeared 3,500 million years ago. They were tiny blue-green algae which gave off oxygen as they made their food. Over several million years enough oxygen collected in the atmosphere to support the first animals. Today algae produce over half of the world's oxygen.

The salty sea

The amount of salt in sea water is called its salinity. This is measured as the number of parts of salt in one thousand parts of water. It is written as ‰. In most places the salinity of the oceans is about 35‰. There is enough salt contained in the sea to cover the land with a layer 153m (520ft) thick.

Sea and sound

Sound travels through sea water about 4.5 times faster than it does through air. The sound of an undersea explosion off Australia reached Bermuda, half way round the world, just 144 minutes later.

Water supply

Oceans play a vital part in the world's weather. As the Sun shines on the sea, millions of litres of water rise into the air as invisible water vapour. It cools to form clouds and falls back to the Earth as rain or snow. Rivers and streams carry the water back to the sea and the water cycle starts again. Little new water is ever made on Earth. The same supply is used over and over again.

Restless oceans

Changing oceans

The Earth's hard crust is split into seven large pieces and many smaller ones, called plates. These lie like giant rafts on the layer of softer rock beneath the crust. As the plates drift apart or collide, they change the shape and size of the world's oceans.

Ancient oceans

About 170 million years ago all the continents formed one landmass called Pangaea. Around it lay a vast ocean, Panthalassa.

As Pangaea split into today's continents, the Indian, Atlantic and Southern Oceans were created. Panthalassa shrank to half its original size and became the Pacific Ocean.

Cracking up

New crust is constantly being made under the sea. As underwater plates move apart, liquid rock, called magma, rises to plug the gap. It cools and forms huge mountain ranges called spreading ridges. The ocean floor grows by about 4cm (1.5in) a year. When Christopher Columbus sailed across the Atlantic in 1492, the ocean was 20m (66ft) narrower than it is today.

Sliding under

When underwater plates collide, one plate is often pushed under the other and melts back into the Earth. These are called subduction zones. They form long, narrow trenches in the sea bed, over 10km (6 miles) deep. Without subduction zones, the Earth would have grown about a third bigger in the last 200 million years because of all the new crust made.

Amazing But True

Fossil sea shells and slivers of ocean crust found high up on Mount Everest show that the Himalayas were once part of the sea floor. Today they are 500km (310 miles) from the sea. They formed 40 million years ago when India drifted north and crashed into Asia. This collision pushed seabed rocks 8km (5 miles) into the air.

Rock ages

Compared to the continents, the sea bed is very young indeed. The oldest continental rocks are about 3,800 million years old. The oldest pieces of ocean crust are only 180-200 million years old. They formed at the time of the early dinosaurs.

Island birth

Volcanoes are common along ocean ridges. In November 1963 an underwater volcano erupted near Iceland and formed a new island called Surtsey. Four days later Surtsey was 61m (200ft) high and 610m (2,000ft) long. Within just 18 months the first leafy green plant was growing on the island. Five years later there were 23 bird species and 22 insect species living on Surtsey.

Salt lake

About 6.5 million years ago the Mediterranean Sea became cut off from the oceans. In about 1,000 years the water dried up, leaving the sea bottom caked in a layer of salt 1km (0.6 miles) thick. Then the sea level rose in the Atlantic and water flowed back into the sea over the Straits of Gibraltar in the biggest waterfall ever. The sea took about 100 years to refill.

Sea quakes

There are about one million earthquakes a year. Many happen underwater in the "Ring of Fire" around the Pacific Ocean. The deepest seaquakes occur beneath ocean trenches, up to 750km (470 miles) below sea level. Most are never felt but in 1947 a seaquake off the Mexican coast shook a ship so violently that its cargo of heavy steel shifted 15cm (6in) along the deck.

Flood warning

Today about a tenth of the Earth is covered in ice. Scientists are worried that burning coal, oil and wood is making the Earth warmer. A rise of 4°C (7°F) would melt all the ice and raise sea level by about 70m (230ft). Coastal cities, such as Sydney, Tokyo and New York would be drowned.

Under the sea

Seascape

Under the sea, the landscape is as varied as on land. Scientists divide the sea up into different "zones", depending on the depth of the water. This profile shows the average depth of the water in each zone.

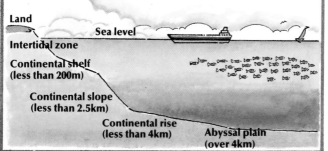

Land
Sea level
Intertidal zone
Continental shelf (less than 200m)
Continental slope (less than 2.5km)
Continental rise (less than 4km)
Abyssal plain (over 4km)

Land margins

The continental shelf, slope and rise form the continental margin around the land. The width of the continental shelf varies from about 1km (0.6 miles) on the Pacific coast of South America to 1,200km (745 miles) around northern Siberia. Most of the fish we eat come from the waters over the continental shelves.

Mountain maze

There are underwater mountains in all the oceans. Some are so huge they rise above the surface. Others, called seamounts, are volcanoes which never grow above sea level. There are about 10,000 seamounts on the ocean floor, all over 1km (0.6 miles) high. Great Meteor seamount in the Atlantic is over 100km (62 miles) wide at its base and 4km (2.5 miles) high.

DID YOU KNOW?

Mauna Kea

The highest mountain on Earth is not Mount Everest, but Mauna Kea in the Pacific Ocean. This volcano rises 10,203m (33,476ft) from the sea floor to form one of the Hawaiian islands. Mount Everest is the highest mountain on land, at 8,848m (29,029ft).

Under pressure

The deeper you go under the sea, the greater the pressure of the water pushing down on you. For every 10m (33ft) you go down, the pressure increases by 1.1kg per sq cm (15lb per sq in). In the deepest ocean, the pressure is equivalent to the weight of an elephant balanced on a postage stamp.

Rolling plains

Abyssal plains cover nearly half the sea floor. They are over 4km (2.5 miles) below sea level and are the flattest places on Earth. Even on their steepest slopes, you would have to walk 2km (1.2 miles) to climb just 2m (6ft).

Cold and dark

The sea gets darker and colder the deeper you go. Most sunlight is absorbed in the top 10m (33ft) of water. No light at all reaches below 1,000m (3,280ft), even on the sunniest day. The surface water may be over 21°C (70°F), but 1,500m (4,920ft) down it is as cold as the inside of a fridge.

Amazing But True

The deepest point on Earth is the Marianas Trench in the Pacific. It is 11,034m (36,200ft) deep. If a 1kg (2.2lb) steel ball were dropped into the trench, it would take over an hour to reach the bottom.

Ocean depths

Ocean	Average depth	Deepest point
Pacific	4,200m	11,034m
Atlantic	3,300m	9,560m
Indian	3,900m	9,000m
Southern	3,730m	8,264m
Arctic	1,300m	5,450m

Black smokers

Hot water seeps up through cracks in the Pacific sea floor at temperatures of over 350°C (662°F). As it reacts with minerals in the rocks the water turns black. The minerals themselves form chimney stacks as tall as houses around the cracks. The water gushes out of the chimney like black smoke.

Deep sea carpet

About three-quarters of the deep ocean floor is covered in a thick, smooth ooze. This is made up of the bodies of countless animals and plants which have

Avalanche

Underwater earthquakes can trigger off great avalanches of mud and sand which cascade down the continental slope. These are called turbidity currents. They can cover areas of the sea bed the size of France with a layer of mud over 1m (3ft) thick. In 1929 a huge turbidity current 100km (62 miles) wide snapped apart 13 undersea telephone cables near to Newfoundland, Canada.

drifted down from the surface, mixed with mud. The ooze collects at just 6m (20ft) every million years. It is usually 300m (948ft) thick but can be up to 10km (6.2 miles) thick.

Oceans in motion

On the move

Ocean water is always on the move. The wind drives huge bands of water, called currents, around the world. The West Wind Drift current flows round Antarctica. It carries over 2,000 times more water than the Amazon, the largest river on Earth.

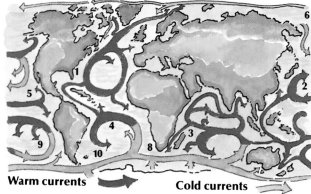

The world's main currents

Warm currents may be as hot as 30°C, while cold currents may be as chilly as –2°C.

Warm currents

1 Gulf Stream
2 Kuroshio
3 Agulhas
4 South Equatorial
5 Equatorial counter

Cold currents

6 Oyashio
7 Labrador
8 Benguela
9 Humboldt (Peru)
10 West Wind Drift

DID YOU KNOW?

Currents affect the Earth's climate by driving warm water from the Equator and cold water from the Poles around the Earth. The warm Gulf Stream brings milder winter weather to Bergen, Norway than to New York, much further to the south. It keeps the Norwegian coast an incredible 24°C (43°F) warmer than other places equally far north.

Welling up

Off the coast of Peru, cold water rises up from the depths. It is very rich in nourishment and produces food for millions of fish and birds. In a single year fishermen may catch 10 million tonnes of anchovies alone. Every two to ten years, this food supply is destroyed by a warm current called El Niño.

Horse latitudes

On either side of the Equator there are calm belts of ocean with very little wind. These are called the horse latitudes because sailing ships carrying horses were often stuck in them for days. The sailors had to throw the horses overboard as they ran out of food for them.

Water attraction

Twice a day, tides make the sea level rise and fall. Tides are caused by the Moon and Sun pulling the water into giant bulges on either side of the Earth.

When the Moon and Sun pull in a straight line, they cause very high tides and very low tides. These are called spring tides.

When the Moon and Sun pull at right angles, they cause lower high tides and higher low tides. These are called neap tides. Spring and neap tides happen twice a month.

Extreme tides

The greatest tides happen in the Bay of Fundy, Canada. They can rise over 15m (50ft), high enough to drown a five-storey building.

Amazing But True

The ground under our feet also rises and falls twice a day, just as the oceans do. When the Moon is directly overhead, it rises by 50cm (18in), three times the width of this book.

Tsunami terrors

Tsunamis are giant waves caused by earthquakes or volcanic eruptions under the sea. They speed along as fast as jet planes. As they near land they rear up to great heights and can drown whole islands. The largest tsunami known rushed past Ishigaki Island, Japan in 1971. It was an incredible 85m (278ft) high. It caused no damage but tossed a 750-tonne block of coral 2.5km (1.5 miles).

Making waves

Waves are caused by the wind blowing across the surface of the sea. The stronger the wind and the longer it blows, the bigger the waves are. Waves only disturb the surface of the water. Submarines only have to dive to about 100m (328 ft) to avoid being battered by even the severest storms.

Giant waves

The highest recorded natural wave was 34m (112ft) high. It was seen by *USS Ramapo* in 1933. Some of the biggest waves happen along the south-east coast of Africa. In June 1968, the tanker *World Glory* was broken in two by a series of waves about 30m (98ft) high.

Along the shore

Coast to coast

If all the coastlines were straightened out, they would reach to the Moon and half way back again. These are the top ten coastlines:

Country	Length
Canada	90,908km
Indonesia	54,716km
USSR	46,670km
Greenland	44,087km
Australia	25,760km
Philippines	22,540km
USA	19,924km
New Zealand	15,134km
China	14,500km
Greece	13,676km

Sticky customer

Animals living along the shore have to survive being battered by the waves. A limpet clings to its rocky perch so firmly that it would take a force 2,000 times the limpet's own weight to prise it off. Limpets feed on seaweed, using a rasping tongue with over 2,000 tiny teeth.

Taking a beating

Along the coastline, the land is constantly being worn away by the force of the waves. This is called erosion. The waves carve out cliffs, caves and high arches along the shore. At Martha's Vineyard, Massachusetts, USA, the cliffs are being eaten away by 1.7m (5.5ft) a year. The lighthouse has been moved three times to prevent it slipping into the sea.

DID YOU KNOW?

The world's highest sea cliffs are on the north coast of Moloka'i, Hawaii. They are 1,005m (3,300ft) high, over three times as tall as the Eiffel Tower, Paris.

Slimy seaweed

Another problem faced by life on the shore is the danger of drying up when the tide goes out. Seaweeds keep moist by covering themselves with slimy mucus. The longest seaweed in the world is the Pacific giant kelp. It grows 60m (196ft) long, at an amazing 45cm (18in) a day.

Sand colours

Sand forms when wind and rain wear down rocks into tiny pieces. Yellow sand also contains minute pieces of quartz. Pink or white sand contains coral, and green sand contains the gem, olivine. Black sand contains volcanic rock or coal.

Prickly character

Sea urchins sometimes disguise themselves from enemies by draping scraps of seaweed over their spines. Most sea urchins are fist-sized but some grow to 36cm (14in) across. Using their spines and sharp teeth, sea urchins burrow into sand and rock. A Californian sea urchin drilled 10mm (0.39in) into a solid steel girder. This took 20 years.

Hitching a lift

Hermit crabs borrow discarded sea-shells to protect their soft bodies. As they grow, they find a bigger house to move into. Sea anemones hitch lifts on the crab's shell and share its food. In return, they protect the crab from enemies with their stinging tentacles.

Mud and mangroves

Mangrove trees grow in huge muddy swamps where tropical rivers flow into the sea. The trees may be 40m (131ft) tall. Their long, tangled roots anchor them in the shifting mud. Saltwater can kill plants so mangroves eject waste salt through their leaves or store it in old leaves which they then shed.

Amazing But True

Mudskippers are odd fish which spend much of their time out of water in mangrove swamps. They take in oxygen through their skin. The Malayan mudskipper's fins form suckers so it can climb easily up the mangrove trees.

Riding the surf

The plough snail lives in southern Africa. When the tide is out, the snail burrows into the sand. As the tide comes in, it comes to the surface and sucks water into its foot. Using its foot like a surf-board, it lets the water sweep it high up the shore to find food.

Seashore molluscs

Molluscs are a huge group of animals found on land and in water. They range from octopus and squid to tiny seashells. These are some of the molluscs found along the shore:

Bivalves (Double shell)
Mussel
Oyster
Scallop
Razor shell

Univalves (Single shell)
Limpet
Winkle
Whelk
Cowrie

Coral

Coral builders

Huge coral reefs are built by tiny animals called polyps. They use chemicals from sea water to build hard skeletons around their soft bodies. The polyps are helped by tiny plants living inside them. Millions of polyps live in vast colonies. When they die, layers of hard coral skeletons are left. Coral grows at about the same rate as fingernails.

Longest reef

The Great Barrier Reef is the longest coral reef and the biggest structure ever built by any living creature. It stretches for 2,028km (1,260 miles) off the north-east coast of Queensland, Australia, covering an area the size of Iceland. The reef has taken at least 15 million years to grow to its great size. It is so vast that it can even be seen from the Moon.

Clamming up

Coral reefs are home to thousands of creatures. The giant clam has the largest shell in the world. It can be 1.2m (4ft) wide and weigh over 0.25 tonnes. The two halves of the shell fit together so tightly that they can grip a piece of thin wire.

Good shot

Pistol shrimps are only about 5cm (2in) long but possess deadly weapons. When a fish passes, the shrimp snaps its large right claw making a sound like a pistol shot. This sends shock waves through the water, stunning fish up to 1.8m (6ft) away. The shrimp then has time to close in for the kill.

DID YOU KNOW?

Every day coral grows a new band of limestone on its skeleton. Its rate of growth is affected by the seasons, Moon and tides. Scientists studying coral fossils have worked out that 400 million years ago, the year was 400 days long. Since then, days have been getting one second shorter every 132 years.

Sea pens

Sea pens are soft corals, related to the stony reef builders. They are named after old-fashioned quill pens because they look like feathers sticking up from the sea floor. Some would reach a person's waist, others are just a few centimetres tall. At night they glow with ripples of purple light if they are touched.

Sensitive coral

Reef-building coral is very sensitive and grows best in water with the following features:

1. **Temperature** – warm water, between 25-29°C.
2. **Depth** – water less than 25m deep.
3. **Saltiness** – water no saltier than 30-40 parts of salt to a thousand parts of water.
4. **Purity** – water must be clear and unpolluted.

Crown of thorns

Large chunks of the Great Barrier Reef are being eaten away by "crown of thorns" starfish. These strange creatures have up to 23 arms and are covered in thick, red spines.

Home, sweet home

Pencil-thin pearlfish live in the bodies of some sea cucumbers. The fish are about 15cm (6in) long. As many as three pearlfish spend the day sleeping inside one sea cucumber, with their heads sticking out of its tail end.

Amazing But True

Small cleaner wrasse run beauty parlours on the coral reef. Larger fish queue up to have dead skin and parasites picked off their bodies. Even moray eels, which can grow 3m (10ft) long, stay quite still while the wrasse clean bits of leftover food from their sharp teeth.

To eat a piece of coral, the starfish grips it with its arms. Then it pushes its stomach out of its body to cover the coral and takes about three hours to digest a large piece. As few as 15 of these starfish can eat an area of coral the size of a football pitch in just 2.5 years.

Sweet dreams

Parrot fish have a most ingenious way of keeping safe while they sleep. At night, they secrete a jelly-like bubble around their bodies. This sleeping bag takes about half an hour to build and to break out of.

Coral islands

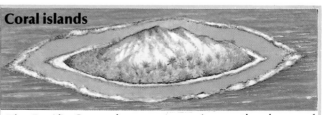

The Pacific Ocean has thousands of horseshoe-shaped coral islands, called atolls. These began thousands of years ago as coral reefs growing on the slopes of volcanic islands. As the volcano sank, the coral kept growing to form a low-lying atoll around a deep, blue lagoon.

Small fry

Billions of tiny plants, called phytoplankton, drift near the surface of the sea. They use sunlight and minerals from the water to make their own food. Phytoplankton start the ocean food chain. Without them, little could live in the sea. They are eaten by small sea animals which in turn are eaten by fish. Over 2 million million tonnes of plant plankton grow each year in the oceans. This is about ten times the weight of the world's population.

Seahorse slowcoach

Despite its strange shape, the seahorse is a tiny fish. Dwarf seahorses live in the Gulf Stream current, south of Bermuda. They are just 40mm (1.5in) long. Seahorses are the slowest moving fish. They hover in the water, propelling themselves along with their back fins. Even at top speed, it would take a seahorse about 2.5 days to travel 1km (0.6 miles).

Amazing But True

The staple diet of the huge blue whale are tiny shrimp-like animals called krill. Krill are only about 6cm (2.4in) long but they live in vast shoals which may be 5m (16ft) deep. A blue whale eats 4 tonnes of krill a day, sieving it from the sea water.

Part-time plankton

Sea slugs start life as animal plankton floating near the sea surface. They grow up without having to compete with adults for food and space. Some adult sea slugs are about the size of grains of sand. Others weigh over 1kg (2.2lb).

Smallest fish

The smallest known sea fish is the dwarf goby from the Indian Ocean. Adults are only about 8.9mm (0.35in) long and could easily fit on a fingernail. Another dwarf goby from Samoa is the world's lightest fish. It would take 500 adults to weigh just 1g (14,175 to 1 oz).

Blowing bubbles

The *Janthina* snail lives on the sea surface. To stay afloat it blows bubbles at the rate of one per minute and joins them together to make a raft from which it hangs upside down.

Red alert

In spring, many types of plant plankton breed quickly because of the warm weather. If a type of plankton called a dinoflagellate is involved, this growth can cause disaster.

These plants are very poisonous. They colour the sea blood red, with as many as 6,000 plants in one drop of water. They kill millions of fish and shellfish.

Long-distance travel

Sea fleas travel great distances every day. In the evening, they swim up to the surface to feed. At dawn they return to the deep sea for safety. Sea fleas are only slightly bigger than pinheads. Their 400m (1,312ft) journey is equivalent to a human being swimming 644km (400 miles) a day.

DID YOU KNOW?

Pea crabs are the smallest crabs in the world. They live and feed inside the shells of oysters, scallops and mussels. Some of these crabs have shells only 6.3mm (0.25in) long, about the size of a pea.

Shrinking shark

The world's smallest known shark is the spined pygmy shark from the Pacific Ocean. Adults measure just 15cm (6in) long. This is 120 times shorter than the whale shark, the world's largest shark.

More small fry

Group	Animal	Average size
Sea urchin	Sea biscuit	5.5mm wide
Starfish	Cushion star	9mm wide
Lobster	Cape lobster	10cm long
Shell	*Ammonicera rota*	0.5mm long
Squid	*Parateuthis tunicata*	12.7mm long
Octopus	*Octopus arborescens*	50mm wide
Turtle	Atlantic ridley	70cm long

Attack and defence

Man eater

The great white shark has huge jaws filled with rows of triangular, razor-sharp teeth. Each tooth may be over 7.5cm (3in) long. As the front teeth wear out, the next row moves forward to replace them. Great white sharks sometimes eat people, mistaking them for large fish. Other objects found in their stomachs include coats, a full bottle of wine and a porcupine.

Deadly tentacles

The Portuguese man-of-war paralyses its prey with its long, stinging tentacles. These trail for over 30m (100ft) from its floating body. Once they have trapped some food, the tentacles can shrink to 15cm (6in) long in just a few seconds so the food can be passed to the mouth.

Puffer surprise

The death puffer fish is one of the world's most dangerous animals. Its gut, skin, liver and blood contain a poison strong enough to kill a person in just two hours. In Japan, its flesh is eaten as a great delicacy but chefs have to train for three years before they are allowed to serve it. Despite all their careful cooking, about 20 people a year still die after eating these very risky meals.

Electric shock

Some fish use electric shocks to kill prey and defend themselves. The most powerful electric sea fish is the black torpedo ray. It makes enough electricity to power a television set.

Amazing But True

A starfish can escape from an attacker by leaving some of its arms behind. All starfish can grow new arms and some species grow a whole new body from a tiny piece of arm. The process can go wrong. A starfish may end up with as many as nine arms instead of the usual five.

Super smell

Many fish use their excellent sense of smell to guide them to food. Sharks can smell blood from injured prey nearly 500m (1,640ft) away. A hammerhead shark's nostrils are on the ends of its hammer-shaped head. If it smells food, it swings its head from side to side to find out which direction it should swim in.

Hired defences

Soft-bodied Mexican dancer sea slugs combine self-defence with a good meal. They eat sea anemones, complete with their stinging cells. These cells travel through the sea slug's body and rest just under its skin. If the sea slug is touched, the borrowed stinging cells shoot into its enemy.

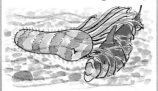

DID YOU KNOW?

Sea cucumbers look harmless but they have a dramatic way of fending off enemies. If a hungry fish comes too close, the sea cucumber shoots out streams of sticky threads which look like spaghetti. These entangle the attacker, giving the sea cucumber time to make a getaway.

Sinister stones

Ugly stonefish have double protection from enemies. They are well camouflaged on the sea floor, looking just like weed-covered rocks. They also have 13 sharp spines on their backs. These can pierce a rubber shoe and are deadly poisonous.

Smokescreen

Cuttlefish squirt out thick clouds of brown ink to confuse their enemies. This gives the cuttlefish time to escape. Cuttlefish ink is called sepia and was once used as artists' ink and in photography.

Sailing by

The fastest ocean hunter is the sailfish. When chasing prey, it can speed along at 109kph (68mph). This is faster than a cheetah, the fastest land animal. At high speed, the fish's sail-like back fin slots down into a groove on its back and its other fins are pressed close to its body. This makes it superbly streamlined and able to cut cleanly through the water.

More speedy sea hunters

These are the top speeds recorded for various types of fish over short distances.

Fish	Top speed
Bluefin tuna	100kph
Swordfish	90kph
Marlin	80kph
Wahoo	77kph
Yellowfin tuna	74kph
Blue shark	69kph
Flying fish	56kph
Barracuda	43kph
Mackerel	33kph

Life in the depths

Going down

Deep down in the oceans, the water is pitch black and very cold. Despite this, thousands of fish and invertebrates (animals without backbones) live in the depths there.

0 – 200m
Sunlit zone
Most sea creatures live in the top 150m where it is warm and sunny.

Sargassum weed

200 – 1,000m
Twilight zone
No plants can live below about 150m.

Below 1,000m
Deep sea zone

Mackerel

Jellyfish

Hatchet fish

Lantern fish

Viper fish

Tripod fish

Rat tail

Black swallower

Big mouth

Gulper eels live some 7.5km (4.5 miles) down in the Atlantic Ocean. They can grow over 1m (3ft) long. Some feed on dead animals drifting down from the surface. A tiny shrimp may take a week to fall 3km (1.8 miles) so the eels make the most of any food they find. They have huge mouths and stretchy stomachs for swallowing prey much larger than themselves.

Flashlight fish

Over half of deep-sea fish make their own lights so they can find their way in the dark. Flashlight fish have two light organs under their eyes. These are made up of billions of tiny, glowing bacteria. If danger threatens, the fish can switch its lights off by covering them with a curtain of skin.

Angling for food

Deep-sea angler fish use their lights to trap food. A long, thin fin like a fishing rod grows over the angler's head. It has a bulb of glowing bacteria dangling on the end, which acts like bait. Small fish mistake the light for a tasty meal and swim straight into the angler's mouth.

DID YOU KNOW?

Deep-sea prawns are often bright red for camouflage. The colour red is difficult to see in deep water and many deep-sea fish are colour blind and cannot see red. One fish, though, has eyes that can pick up red. It also shines its own red light to hunt for the prawns.

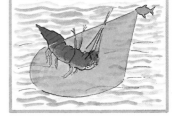

Deepest fish

The deepest fish so far discovered may have been a flatfish like a sole. The fish was about 30cm (1ft) long and was seen 10,911m (35,800ft) down in the Pacific.

Finding a mate

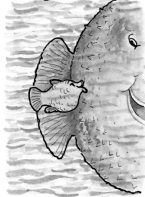

Finding a mate is difficult in the dark depths. When two angler fish meet, they make sure they stay in touch. The male weighs about half a million times less than the female. He attaches himself to her with his teeth and their bodies merge together. All that is left of the male is a small pouch on the female's side which fertilizes her eggs.

Hatchet fish

The hatchet fish's upturned eyes act like binoculars to scan the water above for food. It sees small fish as dark silhouettes against the light coming from above. Its mouth is also turned up to catch food as it drifts down. The hatchet fish's body is flattened from side to side. This prevents it making a silhouette which might attract hungry predators from deeper down.

Deep-sea records

The depths below are the maximum at which each creature has so far been found. The deepest scuba dive by a human being is only 133m (436ft).

Animal	Greatest depth known
Prawn	6,373m
Sea urchin	7,340m
Sea spider	7,370m
Barnacle	7,880m
Sponge	9,990m
Sea star	9,990m
Sea snail	10,687m
Sea anemone	10,730m
Sea cucumber	10,730m

Ocean mammals

Life in the sea

Until about 65 million years ago, the ancestors of whales and dolphins lived on land. They returned to the sea to find food. Here are some of the ways they adapted to the water:

1 Bodies became streamlined for swimming.
2 Front legs became flippers.
3 Back legs disappeared altogether.
4 Nostrils became a blow-hole on top of the head.
5 Hair was replaced by a thick, warm layer of fat, called blubber, under the skin.

Snow white

Pure white beluga whales live in the Arctic Ocean. New-born belugas are reddish brown. They turn grey and finally white when they are five years old. Belugas are nicknamed "sea canaries" because they often make loud chirping noises.

Baby blue

Blue whales have the biggest babies of any animal. A new-born whale can weigh over 5 tonnes, some 1,000 times heavier than a new-born human baby. It drinks 600 litres (132 gallons) of its mother's milk a day and by the age of seven months weighs 23 tonnes. In this time its mother loses 30 tonnes.

Humpback trap

A humpback whale may trap its food by blowing bubbles. A whale circles a shoal of fish and blows a great net of bubbles around them. This confuses and traps the fish. Then the whale swims up through the bubbles, mouth open, gulping the fish down.

Amazing But True

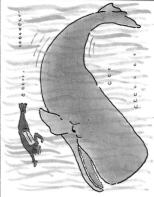

Sperm whales can hold their breath for almost two hours when they dive for food. One whale was found with two deep sea sharks in its stomach. It must have dived 3,000m (10,000ft) down to catch them.

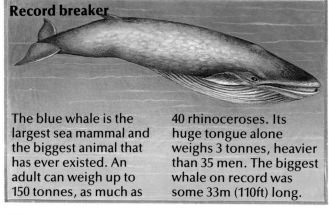
Record breaker

The blue whale is the largest sea mammal and the biggest animal that has ever existed. An adult can weigh up to 150 tonnes, as much as 40 rhinoceroses. Its huge tongue alone weighs 3 tonnes, heavier than 35 men. The biggest whale on record was some 33m (110ft) long.

Sea mammal diets

Mammal	Food	Daily amount
Blue whale	Krill, shrimps	4 tonnes
Sperm whale	Squid, sharks	1 tonne
Elephant seal	Squid, fish	200kg
Killer whale	Seals, birds, sharks	45kg
Bottlenose dolphin	Fish, eels, hermit crabs	8-15kg

Dolphin detection

Dolphins use sound to navigate and find food underwater. They give out high pitched clicks, about 14 times higher than human ears can hear. If the sounds hit solid objects in the water, they send back echoes. From these, the dolphin can tell where and what an object is.

Sea elephant

Seals, sea-lions and walruses belong to a group of sea mammals called pinnipedes. The biggest pinnipede is the huge southern elephant seal. The largest on record was 6.5m (21ft 4in) long and weighed 4 tonnes. It could have towered up to 3m (10ft) in height.

DID YOU KNOW?

A walrus has about 700 hairs on its snout. Each hair is about 3mm (0.1in) thick, some 40 times thicker than human hair. The walrus uses its whiskers to feel its way underwater and find shellfish to eat. It eats these by sucking them out of their shells.

Mermaid myth

Dugongs, or sea cows, may have started the mermaid legend. The largest dugongs were Stellar's sea cows. They were discovered in 1741 but sailors ate so many that the sea cows became extinct just 27 years later.

Speedy seals

The fastest seal is the Californian sea-lion. It can speed through the water at 40kph (25mph). Leopard seals are also very fast swimmers when chasing penguins to eat. To get on to land, they build up speed and shoot 2m (6ft) out of the water to land with a thump on the ice.

309

Birds of the sea

Sea birds

There are about 300 species of sea birds. They are divided into three groups, depending on where they find their food:

Coast birds – pelican, cormorant, gull
Offshore birds – penguin, diving petrel, frigate bird, gannet, tern, puffin, guillemot
Open ocean birds – albatross, shearwater, petrel, fulmar, skua, kittiwake

Walking on water

The sparrow-sized Wilson's storm petrel is one of the smallest sea birds. As it flutters above the sea looking for plankton to eat, it pats the surface of the water with its feet. This makes it look as if it is walking on the water.

Head over heels

Sea eagles perform very unusual courtship displays. In the air, the male dives down towards the female. She turns upside-down and the two birds lock their talons together. They then drop down towards the sea or land, turning cartwheels in mid-air.

Salt hazard

Sea birds take in large amounts of salty sea water as they feed. Too much salt kills birds so they have to get rid of some of it. Special glands in their heads extract salt from the water. It trickles out of the birds' nostrils back into the sea.

Record journey

Many sea birds make long journeys between their feeding and breeding grounds. The Arctic tern makes the longest trip of all. Each year it flies from the Arctic to the Antarctic and back again. This is a round trip of over 40,200km (25,000 miles). In its lifetime, a tern flies the same distance as a return trip to the Moon.

Spitting with rage

To drive intruders away from their nests, fulmars spit at them. The spit is made inside the birds' bodies from the plankton they eat. It is oily and smelly. Fulmars can spit very accurately and hit targets up to a metre away.

Amazing But True

Sea birds such as skuas and gulls have a special way of protecting their eyes from the glare of the sea and sky. Their small eyes contain tiny droplets of reddish oil. These work just like sunglasses to block out the harsh sunlight.

Sea wanderer

The wandering albatross has the longest wings of any living bird. They can measure over 3.5m (11.5ft) from one wing tip to the other. The albatross glides on air currents across the Southern Ocean. If the winds are right, an albatross may fly 900km (1,450 miles) in a day.

Express post

The magnificent frigate bird is the fastest sea bird. It can fly at the same speed as a fast car, over 150kph (93mph). On some South Sea islands, people have trained frigate birds to carry messages to other islands. The birds then return to special posts set up on the beaches.

DID YOU KNOW?

Guillemots live in huge, crowded colonies of over 140,000 birds. They do not build nests but lay their eggs on narrow cliff ledges. The eggs are perfectly designed so they do not fall off. They are long and pear-shaped with pointed ends. If the eggs are knocked, they roll in a circle and stay put.

Baby sitting

Despite temperatures of −62°C (−80°F) emperor penguins nest on the Antarctic ice in the middle of winter. The female lays a single egg, then swims off. The male is left behind to look after the egg. He balances it on his feet and spends about nine weeks without moving or eating. The female returns to feed the chick when it hatches.

Penguin facts

Largest	Emperor penguin	115cm tall
Smallest	Little blue	40cm tall
Fastest swimmer	Gentoo	36kph
Deepest diver	Emperor penguin	265m
Most common	Macaroni penguin	over 16 million
Most northerly	Galapagos penguin	Galapagos Islands

Ocean giants

Super fish

The huge whale shark is the biggest fish in the world. It grows over 18m (59ft) long and weighs 20 tonnes, as much as five rhinos. The whale shark also has the thickest skin of any animal. It is like tough rubber, 10cm (4in) thick. Despite its size, this giant fish only eats tiny sea animals and is quite harmless.

Longest bony fish

Sharks and rays have skeletons of gristly cartilage, rather than bone. Other fish have bony skeletons. The oarfish is the longest bony fish of all. It can grow over 15m (50ft) in length, longer than five table tennis tables laid end to end.

Squid records

Giant squid are the world's largest known invertebrates. The heaviest giant squid on record was found in Thimble Tickle Bay, Canada, in 1878. It weighed 2 tonnes and was about 15m (50ft) long. Giant squid have the biggest eyes of any animal. The Thimble Tickle squid had eyes 40cm (15.5in) across, nearly 17 times wider than human eyes.

Amazing But True

The ocean sunfish is the biggest bony fish. An adult is about the size of a small truck, over 3m (10ft) long and weighing over 2 tonnes. This enormous fish starts life as a tiny egg the size of a pinhead. A new-born ocean sunfish has to grow 1,200 times longer to reach the size of an adult.

The biggest crab

Crabs, lobsters and shrimps belong to a group of animals called crustaceans. Japanese spider crabs are the largest crustaceans known. The biggest spider crab ever found measured 3.7m (12ft 1.5in) across its front claws. A hippo would fit between them.

Mighty manta

Diamond-shaped manta rays are the largest type of ray. They can weigh over 2 tonnes and measure 8m (26ft) from the tip of one wing-like fin to the tip of the other. The rays swim through the water by flapping their wings. They can also jump out of the water, leaping 2m (6ft) into the air.

DID YOU KNOW?

The Portuguese man-of-war belongs to a group of jelly-like animals called siphonophores. Its tentacles can trail for over 30m (98ft). This giant is made up of as many as 100,000 tiny individual animals stuck together. Each has its own special job. Some sting or catch food. Others make the siphonophore float or pull it through the water.

Prize pearl

Clams and oysters sometimes get irritating parasites inside their shells. They cover them with layers of the chemical, calcium carbonate, to form pearls. The biggest pearl ever found came from a giant clam in the Philippines and is called the Pearl of Lao-tze. It weighs over 6kg (14lb) and is shaped like a human brain.

More ocean giants

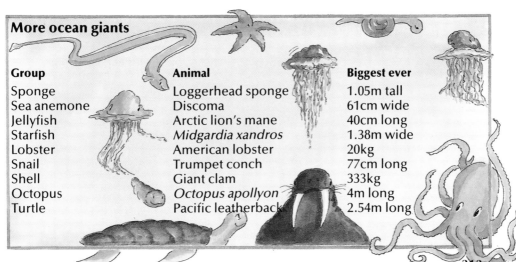

Group	Animal	Biggest ever
Sponge	Loggerhead sponge	1.05m tall
Sea anemone	Discoma	61cm wide
Jellyfish	Arctic lion's mane	40cm long
Starfish	Midgardia xandros	1.38m wide
Lobster	American lobster	20kg
Snail	Trumpet conch	77cm long
Shell	Giant clam	333kg
Octopus	Octopus apollyon	4m long
Turtle	Pacific leatherback	2.54m long

The Pacific Ocean

Vital statistics

Area: 166,241,000 sq km
Widest point: 17,700km
Length: 11,000km
Average depth: 4,200m
Maximum depth:
  11,524m
Volume:
  723,700,000 cu km

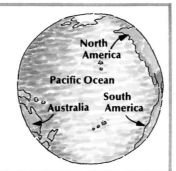

North America
Pacific Ocean
Australia
South America

Record breaker

The Pacific is the largest ocean, covering about one third of the Earth. It is over seven times bigger than the USSR, the world's largest country. At its widest point between Panama and Malaysia, the Pacific stretches nearly halfway round the world.

Epic voyages

The first people to explore the Pacific were Polynesian sailors over 2,000 years ago. They were expert sailors, navigating by the wind, waves, Sun and stars. They used stick charts to teach young sailors how to find islands by understanding the wave patterns around them.

DID YOU KNOW?

Grey whales spend the summer feeding in the Arctic. Then they swim south along the Pacific coast to breed near Mexico, returning north in the spring. This is a round trip of 20,000km (12,500 miles), about the same distance as from London, England to Auckland, New Zealand.

Land bridge

The Bering Strait separates the USA and USSR by just 85km (53 miles). This is the narrowest part of the Pacific Ocean. During the last Ice Age, the sea level was lower than it is today and the Bering Strait was dry land. The first people to live in North America crossed over this land bridge from Asia about 30,000 years ago.

Sound asleep

Sea otters live on the Pacific coast of North America, among the beds of giant seaweed. They spend most of their lives at sea and even sleep in the water, lying on their backs. They wind strands of seaweed round their bodies to stop them drifting away and sometimes cover their eyes with their front paws.

Mountain maker

In the deep ocean trenches at the edges of the Pacific, the sea bed is being dragged back into the Earth. Along the coast of Chile, the Pacific Ocean floor is being forced down under the land. This process formed the Andes mountains about 80 million years ago.

Tropical islands

The Pacific is dotted with islands. Over 100 ancient volcanoes make up the Hawaiian islands, forming a chain 2,800km (1,740 miles) long. Hawaii itself is made up of two huge volcanoes – Mauna Loa and Mauna Kea. Mauna Loa is the world's largest active volcano. It once erupted non stop for 18 months.

Sea serpents

There are about 50 species of sea snake, ranging from 1m (3ft) to 3m (10ft) in length. All of them use poison to kill fish for food. One drop of sea snake venom can kill three adult people. The marine cobra of the Pacific is one of the world's most poisonous snakes. Its venom is about 50 times stronger than that of a king cobra, the world's largest poisonous snake.

Amazing But True

About 2,400m (8,000ft) down in the Pacific, hot water gushes up through cracks, or vents, in the sea bed. The water is heated to 350°C (660°F) yet the vents are home to some incredible animals. Clumps of giant tube worms, each 3m (10ft) long, huge crabs and shrimps live on the vent walls. They eat bacteria which feed on chemicals dissolved in the water.

Galapagos giants

The Galapagos Islands lie about 1,000km (650 miles) west of Ecuador. They are famous for their unusual animals, including large marine iguanas, the only lizards that live mainly in the sea. The islands are also home to giant tortoises which can live for 200 years, longer than any other animal.

The Atlantic Ocean

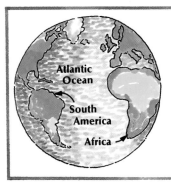

Vital statistics
Area: 82,217,000 sq km
Widest point: 9,600km
Average depth: 3,300m
Maximum depth:
 9,560m
Volume:
 321,930,000 cu km
Age: about 150 million
 years

Still growing

The Atlantic is the second largest ocean, covering about one fifth of the Earth. Each year, the Atlantic grows about 4cm (1.5in) wider, pushing Europe and North America further apart. In a million years' time, the ocean will be about 40km (25 miles) wider than it is today.

Single file

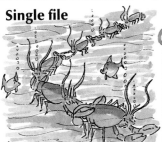

Each year thousands of American spiny lobsters migrate over 100km (62 miles) along the Atlantic coast of Florida. Groups of about 50 lobsters march in single file, hooking their front claws round the lobster in front. The lobsters scuttle over the sea bed as fast as a human being can swim.

DID YOU KNOW?

Bouvet Island in the South Atlantic is the world's most isolated island. It is 1,700km (1,050 miles) away from the east coast of Antarctica. The most remote, inhabited island is Tristan da Cunha in the South Atlantic. The islanders' closest neighbours live on St Helena, some 2,120km (1,320 miles) away.

Living fossil

Horseshoe crabs live along the Atlantic coast of North America. They are not real crabs but are related to spiders and scorpions. Every spring at full moon, thousands of horseshoe crabs come ashore to lay their eggs. The eggs hatch into young crabs just in time to be carried out to sea by high tides at the next full moon.

Mountain high

Mid-Atlantic Ridge is over 11,265km (7,000 miles) long and 1,600km (1,000 miles) wide at its widest point. These mountains lie about 2.5km (1.5 miles) underwater and rise up to 4km (2.5 miles) from the sea bed.

The largest mountain range in the world runs down the middle of the Atlantic Ocean. The

Unsalty sea

For 180km (112 miles) off the coast of Brazil the water in the Atlantic Ocean is hardly salty at all. This is because of the huge amount of water poured into the ocean by the mighty Amazon River. It carries over half of all the fresh water on Earth.

Waterspouts

Waterspouts are common in the Gulf of Mexico. They form when tornadoes or whirlwinds pass from land out to sea. Winds blowing at up to 965kph (600mph) whip the sea into clouds of spray. Waterspouts may be 10m (30ft) thick and 120m (394ft) high. They look like solid water but are mainly water vapour.

Amazing But True

Each year both European and North American eels swim from their river homes to the Sargasso Sea to breed. Then the adults die and the young eels begin an incredible journey home. European eels are only about 8cm (3in) long but they swim 6,000km (3,730 miles) to the rivers. The journey takes about three years.

Methane mussels

Scientists in the Gulf of Mexico have found huge beds of mussels which live on a gas called methane. The gas bubbles out of oily sediment some 3,000m (10,000ft) down in the water. It is turned into energy for the mussels by bacteria living inside their bodies. In some places the mussel blankets are 1.8m (6ft) wide and 7m (22ft) long.

Still waters

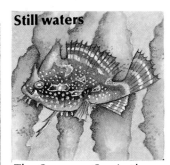

The Sargasso Sea in the North Atlantic is an area of calm water larger than India. Huge rafts of seaweed float on the surface, sheltering some unique animals. The Sargassum fish looks like a piece of the yellowy-green weed. It grips the weed with its front fins as it searches for prey.

Turtle tour

Atlantic green turtles leave their feeding grounds in Brazil and swim 2,000km (1,240 miles) to lay their eggs on Ascension Island. No one knows how they find this tiny island in the middle of the huge Atlantic. They may navigate by the stars or by smell. On the return journey the turtles and their babies hitch a lift on a current running past the island on its way from Africa.

The Indian Ocean

Vital statistics

Area: 73,600,000 sq km
Widest point: 9,600km
Average depth: 3,900m
Maximum depth:
   9,000m
Volume:
   292,131,000 cu km

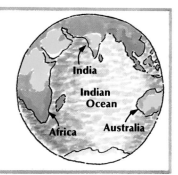

India

Indian
Ocean

Africa   Australia

In third place

The Indian Ocean is the third largest ocean. Its seas hold the record for the warmest and saltiest water. In the Persian Gulf the sea surface temperature reaches an amazing 35.6°C (96°F) in summer. The Red Sea has the saltiest sea water in the world. It is the equivalent to two level teaspoons of salt dissolved in 0.5 litres (1 pint) of water.

DID YOU KNOW?

At night the surface of the Indian Ocean sparkles with light. The light is made by tiny sea plants called dinoflagellates. Large numbers of the plants give off enough light to read by. The lights sometimes form a wheel shape which may be up to 1.5km (1 mile) wide.

Shell shocked

The Indian Ocean is home to the world's most dangerous mollusc. The cone shell is equipped with a deadly weapon. The snail inside has a trunk-like tube loaded with poison which it injects into its victim. The snail uses poison to kill its prey of worms and fish. It can also kill humans.

Hot brines

The Red Sea floor is covered in pools of hot, heavy, very salty water called brine. These form when water trickles through cracks in the sea floor, dissolving salt and metals from the rocks. The water is heated deep inside the Earth and forced up again as brine. As it cools, the brine deposits its metal load on the sea bed.

Pearly nautilus

The pearly nautilus lives deep down in the Indian Ocean. Its shell is 25cm (10in) wide and is divided into about 40 chambers. The animal itself lives in the largest, newest chamber. By regulating the amount of fluid and gas in the other chambers, the nautilus can make itself float or sink and swim along.

Flying fish

To escape from enemies, flying fish shoot out of the water at speeds of up to 32kph (20mph). Then they glide over the surface using their tails as propellers and their fins as wings. After about 40m (130ft) they bounce back on to the surface to give them extra lift. The fish can glide for 400m (1,300ft).

Amazing But True

In 1938 scientists caught an odd-looking fish near the Comoro Islands off Madagascar. To their amazement it was a coelacanth, thought to have become extinct 70 million years ago. They later found that the local fishermen had been catching these fish for many years and using their strong, rough scales as sandpaper.

Big bang

In 1883 a huge eruption blew up two thirds of the volcanic island of Krakatoa in the eastern Indian Ocean. The sound was the loudest ever recorded. It could be heard in Australia over 4,800km (3,000 miles) away. The shock of the eruption was felt 14,500km (9,000 miles) away and caused a huge tidal wave to sweep over Java and Sumatra. The wave killed 36,000 people and carried boats 3km (2 miles) inland, leaving them stranded on top of a hill.

Deep sea fans

The Ganges and Indus carry more sediment (mud and rocks) into the sea than any other rivers. As their water pours into the Indian Ocean, the sediment sinks to the bottom and forms layers hundreds of metres thick. Undersea avalanches carry the sediment downhill where it spreads into a fan shape. The Bengal Fan is so large that it stretches halfway down the Indian Ocean.

Current changes

Most ocean currents flow in one direction all the time. In the northern Indian Ocean, though, they change direction twice a year, driven by the monsoon winds. From November to March the currents are blown towards Africa by the cool, dry north-east monsoon winds. In May the winds blow in the opposite direction, driving the water towards India.

The Polar Oceans

Arctic statistics
Area: 12,257,000 sq km
Area of ice:
  10,000,000 sq km
Average depth: 1,300m
Maximum depth:
  5,450m
**Average thickness of
  ice:** 3-3.5m
Volume:
  13,702,000 cu km

The frozen ocean
The Arctic Ocean is the smallest and shallowest ocean. It is almost entirely surrounded by land. The Arctic Ocean is frozen over for most of the year with the North Pole at the centre of a massive, floating raft of ice. In places, the ice is over 1.5km (1 mile) thick in winter.

Iced water

Fresh water freezes at 0°C (32°F) but sea water freezes at about –2°C (28.4°F) because of the salt in it. When sea water freezes, though, the ice contains very little salt because only the water part freezes. It can be melted down to use as drinking water.

Drifting off
The Arctic gets its name from the Greek word *arktos*, meaning "bear". It is home to huge polar bears which can weigh over a tonne and stand 2.4m (7.75ft) high, twice as big as a tiger. Some bears drift for hundreds of kilometres out to sea on ice rafts. Some never step on land in their whole lives.

DID YOU KNOW?

There are no penguins in the Arctic. Penguins are only found south of the equator. The two species living in Antarctica are well suited to the cold. Their feathers form windproof, waterproof coats which are so warm that the penguins can get too hot. Then they ruffle their feathers and hold out their flippers to cool down.

Whale horn

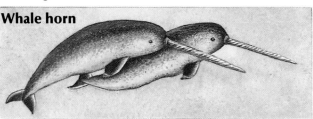

Narwhals in the Arctic Ocean belong to the whale family but have a special feature which none of their relations share. They have only two teeth, growing from their upper lip. In male narwhals, one tooth grows in a spiral, up to 2.5m (9ft) long. At mating time, males may joust with their tusks to fight off rivals.

The Southern Ocean

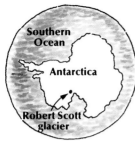

The Southern Ocean is made up of the seas around Antarctica. In winter an area of ocean twice the size of Canada is completely covered in ice. The most southerly part of the ocean is just 490km (305 miles) from the South Pole itself, at the end of the Robert Scott glacier.

Seal survival

The Weddell seal lives in the frozen Southern Ocean, further south than any other mammal. It has to dive over 300m (1,000ft) under the ice in search of food. The seal can stay underwater for up to 15 minutes but it has to surface regularly to breathe. Then it gnaws air holes in the ice with its large front teeth.

Midnight Sun

In June and July the North Pole has constant daylight. At the same time the South Pole has 24-hour darkness. In December and January it is the South Pole's turn for the "midnight Sun" and the North Pole is freezing and dark. This happens because the Poles take turns to face the Sun as the Earth travels round it.

Amazing But True

Some cod-like Antarctic fish have a special way of surviving in the icy seas. Their blood contains a chemical which acts as a natural anti-freeze. Cold can kill fish by freezing their blood or causing ice to form in their cells. The anti-freeze chemical keeps the fish's blood liquid even if the water is several degrees below freezing point.

Iced soup

Despite the cold, the Southern Ocean teems with life. In summer the water nourishes a huge amount of plant plankton which is eaten by small animals, such as krill. In turn the krill is eaten by seals, whales and birds. Krill form swarms so vast they can be seen from satellites. The largest swarm was thought to weigh about 10 million tonnes.

Ice mountains

The Arctic and Southern Oceans are littered with icebergs. These break off the ends of glaciers or ice sheets. Up to 15,000 new icebergs appear each year in the Arctic Ocean alone. The largest iceberg ever was was seen off the coast of Antarctica in 1956. It measured 31,000 sq km (12,000 sq miles), an area larger than Belgium.

Exploring the seas

Studying the sea

The study of the oceans is called oceanography. It is a mixture of biology, chemistry, physics, geology and also meteorology. In 1872 *HMS Challenger* set out on the first scientific voyage round the world. The expedition lasted for just over three years and discovered over 4,000 new species of ocean plants and animals.

Some instruments for measuring the sea

Instrument	Measurement
Echo sounder	Depth of water
Nansen bottle	Collecting water samples
Salinometer	Saltiness of sea
Current meter	Speed and direction of currents
Corer	Collecting samples of deep sea floor
Submersible	Collecting animals; doing experiments on sea floor
Satellite	Wave patterns; temperature

DID YOU KNOW?

If divers surface too quickly after a dive, they may suffer from the "bends". Their air supply contains nitrogen gas which dissolves in the blood. If divers rise too fast, the nitrogen forms bubbles in their blood, causing very sharp pains and even death. The bends may not happen until as many as 18 days after a dive.

Diving suits

Some modern diving suits have their own built-in air supply which can last up to three days. One type, called WASP, has metal hands which are agile enough to do a jig-saw puzzle. In the past divers wore suits weighted down with lead, lead boots and copper helmets. Air was pumped from a ship.

Sea floor maps

Until very recently, scientists had little idea what the deep sea floor looked like. Today they have instruments which use sound to make maps of deep sea features, such as trenches and mountains. The instruments are towed above the sea bed, charting areas of floor 60km (32 miles) wide.

Diving records

Type of dive	Greatest depth
Breath held	105m
Scuba (breathing air)	134m
Helmeted dive	166m
Scuba (breathing gas mixture)	520m
Submersible	10,916m

Record breakers

In 1958 the American nuclear submarine, *Nautilus*, travelled under the ice across the Arctic Ocean, a distance of 2,945km (1,830 miles). It was the first vessel ever to reach the North Pole. In 1960 the nuclear submarine, *Triton*, became the first vessel to travel round the world underwater.

Ocean expeditions

From the 15th to 18th centuries, many great explorers set out to discover new routes across the oceans. The map shows some of the most famous voyages of that time.

→ Columbus (1492-1493)

→ Vasco da Gama (1497-1499)

→ Ferdinand Magellan (1519-1522)

→ Francis Drake (1577-1580)

→ William Barents (1594-1596)

→ James Cook (1768-1780)

Amazing But True

On 23 January 1960 the bathyscaphe, *Trieste*, dived 10,916m (35,813ft), almost to the bottom of the Marianas Trench in the Pacific Ocean. The descent took 4 hours and 48 minutes. The crew travelled in a steel ball with walls nearly 13cm (5in) thick. This was to stop them being crushed by the huge pressure of the water.

Discovering Asia?

When Columbus landed in America in 1492, he thought he was in Asia. At that time people thought the Earth was a third smaller than it really is. No one could convince Columbus that he was wrong. On his second voyage in 1494 he even made his crew swear that the coast of Cuba was Asia.

Viking voyagers

The Vikings may have been the first Europeans to discover America. In about 986 AD, Eric the Red led an expedition to Greenland and founded a settlement there. About four years later his son, Leif the Lucky, is thought to have sailed from Greenland across the Atlantic to land in North America.

Ocean transport

The first boats

The first boats were made by hollowing out tree trunks with fire or a sharp tool. This is why they are called "dug outs". The earliest surviving boat is a dug-out pine canoe. It was found in Holland and is about 8,500 years old.

Sailing ships

The Ancient Egyptians were the first people to use sails 5,000 years ago. These first sails were square and made of reeds. In 1980 a new type of sailing ship was launched. The *Shin Aitoku Maru* has two square, metal sails. A computer works out when to unfurl the sails to catch the wind.

Giant ships

Modern oil tankers are the largest ships ever built. The *Seawise Giant* is one of the biggest tankers of all. Fully loaded it weighs an amazing 574,000 tonnes and is as long as 15 tennis courts laid end to end. A ship this big takes over 6km (4 miles) to stop at sea.

DID YOU KNOW?

The first successful submarine was built in the 1620s by a Dutch inventor, Cornelius van Drebbel. It had a wooden frame covered in greased leather and was rowed along with 12 oars. The biggest submarines today are Russian nuclear submarines. Larger than passenger liners, they can stay under for two years without refuelling.

Raft journey

In 1947 the explorer, Thor Heyerdahl, set out in his balsa-wood raft, *Kon-tiki,* to sail from Peru to the Pacific Islands. He wanted to prove that Inca people could have made this journey 1,500 years ago. The crew lived on fish and rainwater, as the Incas had done. Less than four months later they reached the Pacific island of Raroia.

Speed at sea

The speed of a ship is measured in knots. One knot is the speed of one nautical mile (1.85km or 1.15 land miles) per hour. In the past sailors trailed a knotted rope in the water to see how fast the ship was going. The knots were evenly spaced. By counting the number of knots let out over a set time of 28 seconds, a sailor could measure how fast the ship was going.

Some famous shipwrecks

Ship	Date sank	Cargo recovered
Kyrenia ship (Greece)	4th century BC	400 wine amphoras; 10,000 almonds
Mary Rose (England)	1545	Sundials; arrows; shoes; surgeon's knife
La Trinidad Valencera (Spain)	1588	Bronze cannons weighing 2.5 tonnes each
Wasa (Sweden)	1628	Sails; bronze guns; bodies with clothes on
Vergulde Draeck (Holland)	1656	8 chests of silver
HMS Edinburgh (Great Britain)	1942	5.5 tonnes of gold bars, worth £45 million

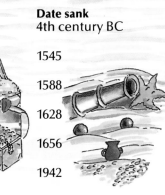

Amazing But True

In 1836 the wooden paddle-steamer, *Royal Tar,* was destroyed by fire and sank. Most of its unusual cargo was lost. The ship had been carrying a collection of snakes and birds, an elephant, two lions, a tiger, two camels, some horses and a group of circus performers, including a brass band.

Iceberg ahoy

Icebergs are a hidden danger to ships because only about one eighth of the ice shows above the water. The *Titanic* was one of the biggest ships ever built. On her first voyage in 1912 she hit an iceberg in the north Atlantic and sank 4,000m (13,000ft) under the sea. Over 1,500 of the ship's passengers died.

Finding the way

For many years sailors navigated by the Sun, Moon and stars. They used instruments called sextants to plot the ship's position by measuring the height of the Sun or Moon above the horizon at a certain time of day. Radio, radar and satellites have now made navigation much more accurate.

Ocean resources

Sea harvest

Each year some 70 to 75 million tonnes of fish are caught in the oceans. Over half comes from the Pacific. The largest single catch ever was made by a Norwegian boat in 1986. It contained over 120 million fish, enough for each Norwegian to have 30 fish each.

The top six most caught fish

Fish	Tonnes per year
Alaska pollack	6.7 million
Japanese pilchard	5.3 million
South American pilchard	4.7 million
Chilean Jack Mackerel	2.7 million
Peruvian anchovy	2.1 million
Atlantic cod	2.1 million

Fish farming

Many countries breed fish and shellfish in underwater farms. On fish farms, plaice grow to adult size in about 18-24 months, about half the time they would take in the wild. They are also easier to catch than in the open sea.

DID YOU KNOW?

About 6 million tonnes of salt are taken from the sea each year. This is enough to build a salt version of the Great Pyramid in Egypt. In hot countries, people use a very simple method to collect salt from the sea. Huge, shallow pans are arranged along the coast. These fill up with sea water as the tide comes in. The water dries up in the hot Sun, leaving the salt behind.

Seaweed sandwich

Seaweed is full of vitamins and calcium. In China and Japan huge amounts are harvested and eaten. In Ireland it is spread over the fields as fertilizer. Seaweed is also used to thicken ice cream and to make shampoo, toothpaste and even explosives.

Gold mine

Sea water contains about 100 times more gold than people own in the world. Sea gold has already been mined on the coasts of Alaska. If all the sea gold could be mined, there would be enough for each person on Earth to have a piece weighing 1kg (2.2lb).

Ocean oil

The top offshore crude oil producers	
(Thousands of barrels a day)	
UK	2,237
Mexico	1,700
USA	1,257
Saudi Arabia	1,107
Venezuela	900

Over a fifth of the world's oil comes from the sea bed. Oil formed millions of years ago from the bodies of tiny sea animals and plants which drifted to the sea bed and were covered in layers of mud and sand. A single North Sea oil rig produces enough oil in one day to fill 70,000 cars with petrol.

Rich droppings

Cormorant droppings, or guano, are the world's most valuable natural fertilizer, about 30 times richer than farmyard manure. About 50 years ago, 5.5 million cormorants nested off the coasts of Peru. In places on the cliffs their guano was an amazing 164ft (50m) thick.

Amazing But True

Some scientists think that Antarctic icebergs could provide desert areas with fresh water. Tugs could tow large icebergs across the Southern Ocean at a rate of 40km (25 miles) a day to Australia and Chile. The journey would take about four months but only half the ice would melt on the way.

Deep-sea nodules

A quarter of the sea floor deep under the Pacific is covered in millions of black, potato-sized lumps, or nodules. These contain valuable metals, such as manganese, iron, copper and nickel. Over millions of years the nodules grow in layers around grains of sand or sharks' teeth.

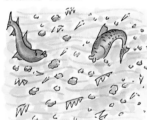

Taming the tides

Scientists are now looking to the sea as a source of energy. The world's first large tidal power station was built on the River Rance in France. A dam with 24 tunnels in it runs across the river mouth. As the tides rush in and out, they turn generators in the tunnels to produce electricity. Each generator makes enough power to light a medium-sized town.

Oceans in danger

Dirty water

Over 80 per cent of the waste which pollutes the oceans comes from the land. Here are some of the main causes of ocean pollution:

1 Sewage pumped straight into the sea.
2 Poisonous metals, such as mercury, tin and lead which come from factories, mines and boats.
3 Nuclear waste from power stations.
4 Chemical fertilizers and pesticides, washed off farmland and carried by rivers into the sea.
5 Oil and petrol are washed off the land into the sea. Oil also comes from oil tanker accidents and oil rigs.

Suffocated sea

In summer, parts of the Adriatic Sea are covered in a thick, green slime of plant plankton. The plankton uses sewage and fertilizers washed into the sea to grow. It blocks out sunlight which other sea plants need to make food. As it decays, it uses so much oxygen that fish and shellfish suffocate.

Oil slick

In March 1989 the huge oil tanker, *Exxon Valdez*, ran aground in Prince William Sound, Alaska. The ship poured some 45 million litres of oil into the sea in one of the worst oil spills ever known. Some 100,000 sea birds died as their feathers became clogged with oil and lost their warmth. They included 150 rare bald eagles. About 1,000 sea otters and hundreds of thousands of fish, seals and shellfish also died.

Overfishing

As the number of people in the world grows, so does the need for more food. Fish are being taken from the sea faster than they can grow and restock. In 1965 about 250,000 haddock were caught in the North Atlantic. By 1974 this had dropped to 20,000. Some countries now have limits on how many fish can be caught each year. Others use nets with a large mesh to let young fish escape.

Amazing But True

Each year thousands of sea birds and mammals die when they become entangled in drift nets, used for catching squid. These plastic nets are trailed across the ocean like giant walls. Each net may be 20km (12 miles) long. Over 48,000km (30,000 miles) of net may be used by just one fleet of boats.

Rubbish tip

The oceans are the biggest rubbish tip on Earth. Ships dump about 6 million tonnes of rubbish into the sea every year. It includes glass bottles, tins, plastic containers, wire, wood and food.

Sea animals in danger

Blue whale	Originally some 250,000 in the Southern Ocean. Today as few as 11,000 are left.
Fin whale	Numbers have dropped from 500,000 to 120,000.
Kemps Ridley turtle	Once common in the Gulf of Mexico but killed for meat, shells and eggs.
Florida manatee	Killed for meat. Fewer than 1,000 are left.
Juan Fernandez fur seal	One of the rarest seals. Only about 705 are left.
Sea otter	Hunted for fur. Now protected and numbers have risen steadily.

Marine park

The Great Barrier Reef is home to 400 species of coral and 1,500 species of fish. But coral reefs all over the world are in danger from tourists, pollution and overfishing. In 1980 the Barrier Reef Marine Park was set up to protect the reef. There are now special areas set aside for nesting sites, research zones, fishing zones and for tourists.

Keep Out

DID YOU KNOW?

Many sea animals have already died out (become extinct). The great auk used to live in the North Atlantic Ocean. It could not fly and was easy to catch for its fat, meat and feathers. People were also afraid of it. In 1834 a great auk was killed in Ireland because it was thought to be a witch. The last great auk ever was killed in 1844.

Fight for survival

The Mediterranean monk seal is Europe's most endangered mammal. So many seals have been killed for their meat and skins and by fishermen who consider them a pest that there are fewer than 500 now left.

Law of the Sea

The Law of the Sea aims to protect the sea and control how it is used. It was drawn up by the United Nations in 1982. It divides the sea up into areas for different countries leaving about two thirds of the open ocean free for all.

Sea myths and legends

Abandoned ship

On 3 December 1872, a ship called the *Marie Celeste* was found drifting in the Atlantic Ocean. The whole crew had completely vanished, leaving their breakfasts half eaten on the table. No clues to the crew's whereabouts have ever been found.

Sunk without trace

The legendary island of Atlantis flourished in about 10,000 BC. Then the island was destroyed by a volcanic eruption and sank without trace. No one really knows if Atlantis ever existed but there are many suggestions of where it might have been. These include the Greek island, Santorini and the Canary Islands.

Amazing But True

The Bermuda Triangle is a large stretch of the Atlantic Ocean between Bermuda, Miami and Puerto Rico. Many ships and even aircraft have disappeared here without trace. Some people believe that the vanishing ships and aircraft are hijacked by UFOs and their crews kidnapped by aliens.

Ghost ship

The *Flying Dutchman* is said to bring bad luck to anyone who sees her. The ship left Amsterdam for the East Indies in the 17th century. On the way she was hit by fierce winds but the captain refused to change course. A ghostly devil dared the captain to sail straight into the storm. The captain did so and the ship was doomed to haunt the seas for ever.

Sea monsters

There have been hundreds of reports of terrifying sea monsters. Norse legends tell of the huge "kraken" which could easily overturn a ship. The kraken was a cross between a squid and an octopus. It had suckers and claws, and a beaky mouth strong enough to bore through a ship. The legend is probably based on the giant squid.

Sea dragons

In Chinese mythology, the seas were ruled over by four great dragon kings. Each lived in a crystal palace and commanded a huge army. The army included fish, crayfish, crabs and watchmen who patrolled the bottom of the sea.

Finger seals

Sedna is the Eskimo goddess of the sea. She was taken from home by a sea bird disguised as a handsome man. Her father rescued her but a fierce storm hit their boat. To calm the storm gods, her father threw Sedna into the sea. As she gripped the boat, he cut off her fingers which turned into seals, whales and walruses.

Gift of the tides

A Japanese legend tells how the sea god gave the tides to another god, Hikohohodemi, as a gift. Hikohohodemi went to the bottom of the sea to find a lost fish hook. While he was there, the sea god gave him two jewels. One made the tide rise and the other made it fall. By throwing the jewels in the sea, Hikohohodemi could control the water.

Ocean gods

For thousands of years, people who rely on the sea for their living and safety have worshipped sea gods and goddesses.

People	Sea god
Ancient Greeks	Poseidon
Romans	Neptune
Ancient Egyptians	Nun
Chinese	T'ien Hou (the goddess of sailors)
Japanese	O-Wata-Tsu-Mi
Tahitians	Ruahatu
Eskimos	Sedna
Celts	Manannan

DID YOU KNOW?

A Polynesian legend tells how the world was created in a giant clam. At first there was only a sea and a goddess, Old Spider. She picked up a giant clam and squeezed inside it. There she found two snails and a worm. She made the smaller snail the Moon and the larger snail the Sun. Half the clam shell became the Earth, the other half the sky and the worm's salty sweat the sea.

Dolphin rescue

A Greek legend tells how dolpins saved the life of the musician, Arion. He was sailing back to Greece after winning a music competition in Italy. The ship's crew wanted the prizes he had won and attacked him. They allowed him to play one last tune which attracted a school of dolphins to the ship. Arion quickly leapt overboard and was carried safely home on a dolphin's back.

Ocean record breakers

Arctic Ocean

● 11

3

USSR

10

Europe

8

4

China

9

India

Africa

8

5

2

3

Indian Ocean

Key to boxes
○ Pacific Ocean
● Atlantic Ocean
● Indian Ocean
○ Arctic Ocean
○ Southern Ocean

4

10

Australia

12

Southern Ocean

● **1** Largest ocean –
Pacific Ocean
(166,241,000 sq km)

● **2** Highest mountain
on Earth – Mauna Kea,
Hawaii (10,203m)

● **4** Longest coral reef –
Great Barrier Reef
(2,028km)

● **6** Largest mountain
range in the world –
Mid-Atlantic Ridge
(over 11,265km long)

● **3** Deepest point on
Earth – Marianas
Trench (11,034m)

● **5** Greatest tides – Bay
of Fundy, Canada
(rise over 15m)

● **7** Largest bay –
Hudson Bay (shoreline
12,268km)

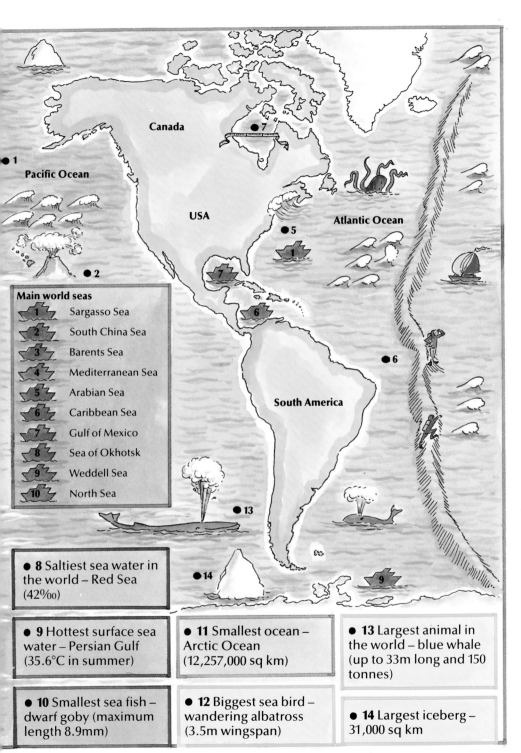

Canada

Pacific Ocean

● 1

● 2

● 7

USA

● 5

Atlantic Ocean

● 1

● 7

● 6

● 6

South America

● 13

● 14

● 9

Main world seas

1	Sargasso Sea
2	South China Sea
3	Barents Sea
4	Mediterranean Sea
5	Arabian Sea
6	Caribbean Sea
7	Gulf of Mexico
8	Sea of Okhotsk
9	Weddell Sea
10	North Sea

● **8** Saltiest sea water in the world – Red Sea (42‰)

● **9** Hottest surface sea water – Persian Gulf (35.6°C in summer)

● **10** Smallest sea fish – dwarf goby (maximum length 8.9mm)

● **11** Smallest ocean – Arctic Ocean (12,257,000 sq km)

● **12** Biggest sea bird – wandering albatross (3.5m wingspan)

● **13** Largest animal in the world – blue whale (up to 33m long and 150 tonnes)

● **14** Largest iceberg – 31,000 sq km

Glossary

Abyssal plain A vast, flat area of the ocean floor, below 4km (2.5 miles).

Algae A group of simple plants ranging from tiny one-celled plants to giant seaweeds.

Atoll A horseshoe-shaped or circular coral island around a deep lagoon.

Continental shelf The shallow sea bed around the continents, not deeper than 200m (656ft) below sea level.

Continental slope The sloping area leading from the continental shelf to the abyssal plain.

Crustaceans A group of sea animals with hard shells. Lobsters, crabs and shrimps are all types of crustaceans.

Current A huge river of water running through the sea.

Dinoflagellates Tiny one-celled sea plants. Some are poisonous; others can produce their own light.

Invertebrate An animal without a backbone.

Knot A measurement of speed at sea. One knot equals 1.85kph (1.15mph).

Mammal A warm-blooded animal with a backbone. Mammals feed their young on milk.

Molluscs A large invertebrate group, often with shells. They range from giant squid to limpets and scallops.

Oceanography The scientific study of the oceans and seas.

Ooze A fine, smooth mud covering the sea floor. Made of the bodies of countless sea plants and animals.

Phytoplankton Tiny sea plants.

Pinnipedes A group of sea mammals which includes seals, sea-lions and walruses.

Plankton Tiny plants and animals which drift on the surface of the sea.

Plate A piece of the Earth's hard crust.

Polyp A tiny sea animal about 5mm (0.2in) long. Coral is made up of the hard skeletons of millions of polyps.

Salinity The saltiness of sea water.

Seamount An underwater volcano which never grows above sea level.

Seaquake An underwater earthquake.

Sediment Pieces of mud, sand and rock which settle on the sea bed.

Siphonophore A sea animal, such as a Portuguese man-of-war, which is made up of a colony of tiny animals.

Spreading ridge An underwater mountain range, formed when liquid rock rises to fill cracks in the sea floor.

Subduction zone The place where two underwater plates collide. One plate is pushed underneath the other.

Submersible A free-moving submarine vehicle for carrying ocean scientists.

Trench A deep, V-shaped dip in the sea floor, formed at a subduction zone.

Turbidity current An avalanche of mud and sand which may be caused by an earthquake.

Water pressure The weight of water pressing down on things in the sea.

Index